ANTIQUE COLLECTING FOR PLEASURE

Edited by David Coombs

EBURY PRESS
LONDON

Front cover illustrations

Collection of sweetmeat glasses, dating from 1725 to 1765.
PRIVATE COLLECTION

Hicks & Mead stoneware tureen and stand of about 1820.
GRAHAM & OXLEY ANTIQUES

Mid 18th century spray of emeralds and rose diamonds.
CAMEO CORNER

Detail of 'Royal William under way in the Thames Estuary' by Richard Paton.
DAVID MESSUM, BEACONSFIELD

Mid 19th century walnut gaming table with chess board.
D & H LEWELLEN

First published 1978 by Ebury Press
Chestergate House Vauxhall Bridge Road
London SW1V 1HF

ISBN 0 85223 136 9 (hard cover)
ISBN 0 85223 131 8 (paperback)

Filmset by
Surrey Fine Art Press Ltd and
printed in Great Britain by
BAS Printers Ltd, Over Wallop, Hants,
and bound by
Webb Son and Co. Ltd.,
Ferndale, Glamorgan.

The articles in this book are adapted from those that have been
previously published monthly in *Antique Collector* magazine.
Where prices in US dollars have been quoted, these have been
converted from the pound Sterling at a rate of £1 = $1.80, the
approximate rate at the time of going to press.

Contents

A Note on the Contributors

The articles on furniture of the Queen Anne period and on Chippendale and his peers are by *Graham Shearing*; those on papier mâché and screens by *Sarah Seymour*, bamboo by *Gillian Walkling* and stripped pine by *James Knox; Sally Budgett* contributes the article on games and card tables.

The articles on silver are by *Judith Banister. James Knox* is the author of the article on London in watercolours, drawings and prints, and Dutch drawings of the 17th Century; *Felice Mehlman* writes on British marine painting. *Fiona Peake* is the writer of the article on the 'Ruined Abbey', *Jane Kentish* that on the icon, and *Thalia Booth-Jones* contributes the article on the 'unassuming' watercolour.

The writer on Chinese export porcelain is *Oliver Mathews*; and *Fiona Peake* writes on Parian Ware; *Sarah Seymour* on miniature porcelain and also on Victorian majolica; the article on tureens is by *Sally Budgett* and that on English pottery tiles is by *James Knox*.

Two articles are contributed by *Philip Trubridge* on pressed glass and English ale glasses; *Felice Mehlman* writes on cranberry and Roman glass; *Nolly Mathew* on decanters, and *Roger Ashford* on Slagware.

In the final chapter *Sarah Seymour* writes on patchwork quilts; the article on playing cards is by *Colin Croft*; that on Himalayan bronzes is by *J. B. Donne; Vivienne Becker* contributes those on scissors and rings; *Graham Shearing* writes about money boxes and also on early brass and copper; *Georgina Fuller* about carriage clocks; *Oliver Mathews* on early photographic postcards; and *Felice Mehlman* on Art Deco cigarette cases.

Editor's Introduction

You should know from the beginning that this is not a book that will tell you all about antiques. No book ever could. Nor will we tell you how to invest in antiques – for nowadays this implies that it is always possible to make money from antiques and not even the professionals (the dealers or auctioneers) can do this every time.

The basic idea of this book is to show you how to look at antiques and it is surprising how few people really know how to do this. The more you learn about antiques the more you will enjoy them; and the greater the knowledge and appreciation that you have then the better the chance that you may one day spot a bargain.

A word about the illustrations: in nearly every case the objects shown in this book have been specially photographed and chosen from objects recently for sale. There are few if any museum pieces here, though many may be good enough for inclusion in a public museum or art gallery; the point is that the illustrations show what it has been possible to buy more or less easily over the last two or three years.

The various chapters have been chosen from those published month by month in the magazine *Antique Collector*. The specialist collector may not be able to find his own particular interest, but people who buy antiques or pictures primarily to enhance their own homes, be it room, flat or house, should find something to stimulate new thoughts or ideas. In the magazine we are able to give a price or value for everything we show; but a book takes much longer to produce and each section has its own introduction including as much specific information about prices as it is possible in the circumstances to give. Certainly we aim to give enough to show you where you stand, so that you will know quickly whether or not a particular kind of object is within or outside your own particular price range.

A few dedicated even passionate collectors remain, mainly of the smaller more portable objects, but for most of the rest of us our ambition lies merely in the wish to have a few nice things. This is an old and honourable tradition and few, even of the grandest houses, were furnished completely at once. There is much pleasure to be had from buying quietly and occasionally, when you can really afford it and are certain that you like the piece and have a place for it. Whilst it is always a good idea to seek advice, you will find it better in the long run to make sure that the final decision is made by you – to your own full satisfaction. After all, it is your money that you are spending.

If you have never bought any kind of antique before or have just started to do so and still feel anxious about whether or not you are doing the right thing, then it might help if you were to understand some of the basic simplicities, as well as the basic complexities, of the world of art and antiques. Whatever happens though, you should never forget that the whole system essentially depends on human interaction and thus on human frailties as well as human enthusiasms.

Some factors affecting price

So how does a dealer set his or her price? The first thing they take account of is how much they had to pay – and this will include such things as any cleaning or restoration as well as the usual overheads. Then they consider how much they can expect to receive for the item, and this in turn can depend on the nature of their clientele; the effect of this is to create the situation where the price for a similar kind of object can vary quite widely from one area to another, or even, at extremes, from one end of the street to the other. It all depends on who the customers are. The other thing to remember about price is that just because something is old or fine or beautiful, it will have no value in money terms unless someone wants to buy it – whether a dealer or a private collector.

You will often hear people talking about quality – this piece is much better quality than that one, for instance. It is impossible to define exactly what they mean, but it will be a combination of comparative craftsmanship and condition; everything else being equal the better something is, the higher the price it will command. In Britain we are very lucky in that we have many public museums and galleries and many historic houses, which we can all visit and see with relative ease the best kinds of paintings and antiques. That is the way to learn how to judge quality.

It is fairly obvious that the general condition of a piece will markedly affect its price; but for very rare items very high prices may still be asked even if the condition is obviously bad. There is a very simple reason in that there are no perfect, or near perfect, examples to be had for any kind of money; and in the past, people did not look after their antiques as we all try and look after them now.

Restoration may be a problem for some people. The first

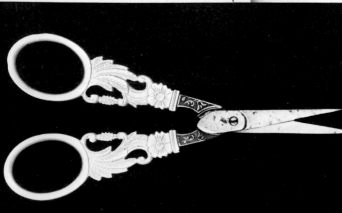

thing to remember is that an antique is, by definition, old. Most have been in more or less continual use and most will have suffered some sort of damage which has needed or will need repair. Even the lovely colour of old furniture is the result of fading and dirt! So do not be surprised to learn that the piece you are interested in has been restored – in fact the more open the dealer is about it, the more happy you can feel. It is those who try to hide things that you most need to worry about.

Many people when they first set out to buy an antique or work of art are consoled and impressed when a signature or maker's mark is produced. There is no doubt that such can vary the price upwards. On the other hand, by themselves they are no guarantee of authenticity, merely a kind of supporting evidence. It is here that experience comes in, for many different things suggest to an expert who the maker or artist might have been; these include the obvious ones like style and quality as well as rather more complicated ones like type or method of manufacture.

Knowledge is the best defence

Despite all the precautions everyone, sooner or later, will buy a fake or a forgery – which is not the same thing as a reproduction. Fakes or forgeries abound where more people want something than the natural supply can satisfy. When that happens those who keenly want to buy a particular kind of thing will tend to overlook the tiny inconsistencies or inaccuracies that in calmer times would have given the forger away. It is nobody's fault, merely a very powerful reason for not rushing the purchase of anything; as well as of being absolutely certain that you want the item whatever it may eventually turn out to be. The better the dealer the more likely he will be to admit that he can make a mistake; but it is not fair to expect them to give an absolute guarantee when such a thing is impossible. In the end it is you that must decide, and the better informed you are the better chance you will have of making the right decision – for you.

Sometimes you may call on a dealer and find that all the prices are written in code. The most likely reason for this is that his trade is mostly with other dealers who will have a very fair idea of what the object is worth anyhow, so that the figures in code may simply represent the basic cost before a profit. Whether or not this type of dealer may be prepared to sell privately to you must be an individual decision; all you can do is ask. Similarly some dealers may be prepared to bargain over the price when it has been shown in plain figures, and you can find this out quite simply by making an offer and seeing where it gets you.

Some of you may like to buy at auction. It is largely a matter of temperament. If you enjoy the competitive situation and know when to stop, then buying at auction can be very rewarding. But you should never forget two things. First that the catalogue description may not be accurate, with a fair chance in certain circumstance that it may be wildly wrong – through ignorance, not malice. Second, remember that for many dealers buying at auction is essential for their livelihood, so you cannot expect to be helped or protected from your own folly. Again it all comes down to your own knowledge and experience; in time there is every chance that you will come to know more than the average dealer about a certain category of object, and may therefore expect to bid for and buy it at something below its real worth to you.

Which brings me to the question of every collector's dream –
the big bargain. There is not one of us that doesn't hope to discover for very little money something that is worth very considerably more. In that sense at least, inside every collector lurks a profit-hungry dealer. There is another side to all this though. It rarely occurs to any of us when hot on the scent of a bargain that the so-called bargain represents in reality someone else's considerable loss. That's their lookout you may say; but tomorrow it may be you. Who was it that claimed that antiques were an investment? Obviously a speculator – which is a much more healthy way of looking at it, if you must take this view.

What is an antique?

Finally a word about the definition of an antique. There is no universally accepted definition. For many there is some magic about the year 1830; true as far as it goes but based in fact upon an outdated and arbitrary customs definition, which now applies the term to everything over one hundred years old. This is more satisfactory but causes just as many complications in the way, for instance, it cuts across the Victorian period. Nonetheless it must mean something for an object to have survived 100 years and this will probably remain the best working definition.

A further complication arises now that the word antique has come to mean virtually the same as collectable; and many people happily buy objects made for instance in the 1900s or the 1930s (or even later) from stalls in antique markets or even from antique shops. Which all goes to show once more, that you should be certain that you are buying any item because you like it first. Its actual or assumed date and maker is something else.

Just to make it more complicated still, it is always worth remembering that all those things that we lump together for convenience as antiques were once themselves new, fashionable and the subject of much comment and debate. Yet each in their turn was inevitably put aside in favour of something else – even more new, even more fashionable, even more attractive to argument and gossip. It is very hard for us to realise this; yet this is the very reason for the existence of so many kinds of antiques, so many varieties of picture, all made over so many years.

Putting all that aside – there is still a great deal of pleasure to be had from buying antiques at all levels of prices. All of us who have made this book hope that it will help you and encourage you, amuse you and inform you.

Good hunting.

DAVID COOMBS
Editor, <i>Antique Collector</i>

FURNITURE

When it comes to furnishing a house, everyone should stop and think first whether to opt for antique or modern furniture, rather than assume that the three piece suite in the High Street is the obvious choice. A decision in favour of antique furniture can make the decoration of a house something totally individual and an expression of the tastes (and prejudices) of the owner. Antiques can be cheap (or very expensive) but once you are bitten by the collecting 'bug' – whether you are wealthy or hard-up – to pass by an antique shop and see precisely that little seat to go between the windows in the study, or, quite by chance a Sheraton writing table of the type known as a 'bonheur du jour', is to experience a thrill of excitement that you may have to struggle to control. I started to collect quite fortuitously in a saleroom, an unexpected bid – was it a nervous twitch of the arm? – and I was the bemused owner of a Georgian lacemaker's table for £5 (around $9).

In this chapter you will see illustrated objects which, although in some cases esoteric, yet have a single characteristic – utility – they can all be sat upon, eaten off or whatever. I do not think that there can be a better reason for possessing a table than to write a letter on it, keep papers inside it and get pleasure additionally from careful construction, design and its historical associations. What is more, if used with regard to their age, antiques can actually improve through continued polishing and general care.

Beyond the area of utility it is extremely difficult to decide what makes collecting furniture 'pleasant' (it would be idle to pretend that most collectors have not at times found it distinctly unpleasant when, for instance, a desired object turns out to be far beyond one's means). There surely can be only one answer; the pleasure is in pursuing some private taste or pure whim; I once knew a devoted collector who sought to reproduce from a photograph the drawing room of his grandparents, and very fine it looked too. Personal associations are as creditable motives as say, the desire to have a typical Queen Anne room. The interest may be more academic – collecting a representative group of oak joint stools, or English furniture in the Egyptian taste.

A collector's cross-section

Consider the subjects grouped together in this chapter. They are not representative of the whole range of furniture, but they are a fair cross-section of what you can and perhaps will collect for many diverse or perverse reasons. Papier mâché

(page 19) provides a most interesting insight into the competition between the manufacturers of japanned tinwares and of papier mâché in the early years of the 19th century. Bamboo (page 22) records the English fascination with the Orient for some 150 years. Screens and gaming tables (pages 30 and 37) are explorations of single subjects to show what a collector can expect to find on the market at a given point of time. The article on pine furniture (page 24) studies the uses to which this attractive and underestimated wood has been put and the indignities it has suffered in response to slightly unsympathetic public demand. Queen Anne and Chippendale furniture (pages 12 and 40) show perhaps the two high watermarks of English furniture. Beyond those included here, remember there are collecting fields as diverse as can be imagined.

To those that ask whether there are any pitfalls that impair the pleasure of collecting the answer is necessarily 'yes', but even so they should deter no one. All collecting requires some degree of familiarity which can only come *with* collecting, and the first faltering mistakes made will become the half-pleasurable recollection of the experienced. The eye is easily trained to spot the virtues and defects in furniture.

PRICES

The best way of approaching the question of prices is not to ask how much any individual piece will cost, but what one can get for a given amount of money. Most collectors are constrained by the depth of their pockets and inevitably a collection will reflect that as much as the particular taste of the collector. Further more, the price of, say, a Queen Anne wall chair in different shops can vary by over a hundred pounds ($180) – a difference that can only be explained by reasons which have nothing to do with the 'value' of the chair.

The lower price range

Suppose that one had only £150 ($270) to spend on a piece of furniture. For this sum you would not expect to buy first rate examples of period furniture – but you would be wrong: by diligent searching examples of 20th century furniture of the Art Deco period are quite frequently found. Similarly, Victorian examples of widely varying quality come within this range, a pair of balloon back chairs, a mahogany chiffonier, a small table, can cost even in specialist shops under this limit. Admittedly pre-1837 furniture (the year Queen Victoria came to the throne) tends to be expensive – but not necessarily so.

An excellent area is painted pine, where a table, suitable for use as a desk, costs less than £50 ($90). Screens or papier mâché (both unusual subjects for collecting) can be of good design, and still within the £150 ($270) range. But the better pieces are usually priced above this arbitrary figure. Two groups then appear, London or London-inspired and country furniture, of which the latter is in oak, ash, yew, beech, elm or pine make a distinctive and inexpensive field; again good examples can be found within this range.

The middle price range

The next price range is that of £150-750 ($270-$1350), wide, but before you say 'Too much' take a walk through your local furniture store on the High Street, or even the local bargain basement. Antique furniture is and always has been very competitive with modern. In this range you will find what you need most in a house or a flat, the set of dining room chairs, the dining room table, the bookcase, the sofas and armchairs, all of good (not museum) quality. In this range also can be included furniture the object of which is not purely utilitarian – a papier mâché spoon-backed chair for under £300 ($540), or, luxury of luxuries, a gaming table for under £600 ($1080). The best examples obtainable of bamboo furniture usually come in this range, being priced in the area of £300-400 ($540-720) although run-of-the-mill pieces generally cost less than £50 ($90) Here one will expect to find simpler, countrified examples of Queen Anne walnut furniture and similar Chippendale period chairs and chests. Good sets of chairs are very expensive.

The upper price range

The final price range is over £750 ($1350). Most people will buy only a few objects in their lifetime over this level, usually something with which they 'have fallen in love', which will give them abiding pleasure. Such an example is the 'Welsh' dresser, now, even in pine, costing over £750 ($1350). This price is explained by pure demand, but it has the advantage of leaving other objects of comparatively better value (for example, mahogany Georgian wardrobes). A good oak dresser of the 18th century will cost £1250 ($2250) and more. A Queen Anne armchair, a chest-on-a-stand in walnut, a set of Chippendale period dining chairs, because of the demand of discerning collectors and other causes that have led to an inflated price, will all cost a great deal of money; good examples will

rarely cost less than £1750 ($3150) and often much more. Yet another, and perhaps the best reason for this high price level is the excellence of them all: the Chippendale pieces illustrated here are extremely expensive because they are the very best quality outside museums and famous collections. Some are well into five figures. Nothing here costs over £100,000 ($180 000))! But there are people (collectors, like ourselves) who are prepared to pay just that.

These prices assume that the pieces are genuine and in a nearly unrestored state. Restored pieces when heavily repaired *should* cost less.

Does furniture ever drop in price? So far, I think the answer in general, is 'No', although there are instances of prices being reached in certain fashionable sales that are unlikely to be reached on resale in the near future. This should not deter the collector who has motives which include investment; it *may* be safer than the Stock Market. But as a guiding principle, do always buy furniture to sit on, not to retire on . . .

GRAHAM SHEARING

Furniture of the Queen Anne Period

It is one of the saddest things in the history of English furniture that the victory of mahogany over walnut was so complete. But it was not just walnut that was forgotten in the rush and tumble for the Spanish and Honduran mahogany. Walnut was the cabinetmakers' first choice, because it was a wood that they were taught to use by the Dutch. But no cabinetmaker trained to seek out good figuring would ignore the claims of burr elm, yew, maple or laburnum wood. In the years following 1720, when mahogany appeared in the holds of ships from the West Indies, even the burr woods were relegated to subordinate pieces of good furniture and country examples.

The natural wood of England is oak. Its durability and resilience made it the essential wood for the 16th and 17th centuries, a time when ideas of comfort were generally developed only to a rudimentary degree. Charles II when he returned from his 'travels' came home to a country where discomfort was associated with a sense of virtue. A court in exile will invariably surround itself with anodyne comforts and can hardly be expected to return to power without the pleasures it has become used to. And with that monarch came Dutch cabinetmakers using either solid walnut or walnut veneered on oak or pine carcases, making furniture which was at first indistinguishable from Dutch prototypes. The Dutch pieces themselves took their inspiration from (primarily) French and Italian models. It was therefore about 1660 when the reception of this foreign style in furniture became possible.

Walnut is a luxury wood. It is not a strong wood and is easily given to splitting. It does not grow quickly nor were there any great stocks in England, as John Evelyn noted in his book, *Silva* in 1664. So from the first the wood was usually imported. It is also useful to note that English soil produces good speciments of mature walnut trees. The best figures in wood, however, are produced from wood that if not stunted has had uneven growth. One hopes it is not too xenophobic to suggest that walnut grows best in England but tradition has it that the best veneering walnut comes from Grenoble in south east France.

The most sought after characteristic of good walnut is the patina. This is a surface condition difficult to reproduce and is the simple result of care and ageing. By exposure to the air, by rubbing with wax polish, by handling, the piece will take a soft mellow tone and deep polish. It is fatal to remove this patina, as sometimes happens, and replace it with the ghastly glistening treacle called 'French Polish'. Equally to be sought is good design. The purity of style and the simplicity of even the grandest furniture after 1700 (when it was wholly assimilated as an English style) has an eloquence that immediately identifies it. Before 1700 the furniture owes a great deal to Dutch and French models which are heavier in outline and the marquetry decoration is extensive and frequently complicated. But it would be wrong to suggest that the decoration becomes overloaded; it balances the more expansive proportion of the pieces. In this complicated art, different woods were used to produce 'flower', 'seaweed' or 'endive', or 'arabesque' marquetry. The list of woods, plain and dyed, would sound tedious but for the exotic profusion: coromandel, lignum vitae, holly, apple, pear, sycamore, yew, bog oak, orange, citron and sandalwood. Ivory and bone augment the inlay. The use of inlay is frequently as characteristic as a signature, although few pieces can be safely attributed.

Cabinetmakers

The magnificent oak book presses in the Pepys Library at Magdalene College,

Below
Late Queen Anne armchair upholstered in silk damask. The stretchers typical of some years earlier have been discarded in this admirable example.
H 113 cm (44½ in).
PHILLIPS OF HITCHIN

Below
Queen Anne tallboy on bracket feet, the corners of the upper part with simple fluting. The handles are original and the figuring has been well chosen by the cabinetmaker. About 1714.
VICTOR MAHY

Cambridge were made, as Samuel Pepys records in his Diary, by 'Sympson the joyner' in the 1660s. During the reign of Charles II the social position of joiners was improved and they became known as 'cabinetmakers'. The Dutch were essentially a middle class nation, and tended not to belittle craftsmen, unlike those English noblemen who commissioned grand furniture and called the manufacturer a 'joiner'. We know little of cabinetmakers except by preserved receipts and by makers' labels. The best, such as Gerritt Jensen, cabinetmaker to Queen Mary, appear to have used no labels, but in and around St. Paul's Churchyard the cabinetmakers (not inferior to the others) used labels, which are of invaluable use in dating their distinctive furniture. Most famous of these labels advertise John Coxed (fl 1700) and G. Coxed and Thomas Woster (fl 1710-1730). Philip Hunt from 1680 to 1720 advertised thus: 'cabenetts, looking glasses, tables and stanns (sic), scretor chests of drawers and curious inlaid figures for any worke'.

OTHER ASPECTS OF FURNITURE: 1660-1730

Lacquer

Pepys and Evelyn refer to 'Indian pieces' in the collection of the Duke of York. These pieces would be of oriental lacquer, made up by a laborious process of building up layer upon layer of resinous matter and incising it to produce a hard, lustrous and brilliantly decorative design. Attempt at imitation was inevitable and the English equivalent was called 'japanning'. In 1693 a company was formed 'The Patentees for Lacquering after the manner of Japan'. Less actual skill was involved than with the oriental models, but nonetheless the decorative talents of the japanners was seldom deficient, even in the hands of an amateur. The Yorkshire antiquary, Ralph Thoresby, wrote of 'the ingeniose Mr Lumley, an excellent artist in many respects, (who) paints excellently, japans incomparably. . .' The much travelled Celia Fiennes wrote at Burghley, 'my ladyes closet is very ffine the wanscoate of the best Jappan, the cushons very riche worke' and in her will disposed of 'Japan cabinets'. English japanning comes principally in the colours of red and gold, green and blue and black and gold. Often the condition is unhappy as many pieces have been repaired with mastic varnish.

Black Painted Beech

Many dealers think black painted beech unsaleable, and it has to be agreed that it does not have the immediate attractive qualities of lacquer or walnut. But it has a beautiful line and yet is almost ignored by many except the real experts. This is therefore a good branch of collecting on a limited budget in a field which cannot pretend to be inexpensive.

Upholstered Furniture

The English have until now been very careful in the way they keep their furniture. Beautiful cases (often of leather) were made to preserve the expensive upholstery which would otherwise have rotted. Equally the best furniture tended to be used less. This helps to explain why so many pieces of upholstered furniture have survived. It is often difficult for the collector to determine whether the tapestry is in fact original to the chair or merely of the period. The truth comes to light when repairs are necessary. Tapestry may be of gros-point or petit-point, or a combination of these two. Luxurious chairs were also covered in damask of the silk or wool varieties which are almost too good to be used. However, a Queen Anne armchair is about the most comfortable chair ever designed, though not so soporific as to make conversation a burden.

G.S.

Where to buy

Many of the best pieces gravitate towards London, but the process is not ineluctable and there are dealers of the highest standing in the provinces. This list is not completely representative, but it does show that the furniture of this period can be found broadly throughout the country. There are many fraudulent examples of period furniture, and walnut is skilfully forged, so beware.

ASPREY AND COMPANY, 165-9 New Bond St, London W1. (01-493 6767)

T. G. BAYNE LTD, 98 Crawford St, London W1 (01-723 6466)

WILLIAM BEDFORD ANTIQUES, 327 Upper St, London N1 (01-226 9648)

JOHN BLY, 50 High St, Tring, Herts (044282-3030)

ARTHUR BRETT AND SONS, LTD, 42 St Giles' St, Norwich (0603-28171)

DAVID GIBBINS ANTIQUES, 21 Market Hill, Woodbridge, Suffolk (03943-3531)

JOHN KEIL LTD, 154 Brompton Rd, London SW3 (01-589 6454)

MALLETT AND SON (ANTIQUES) LTD, 40 New Bond St, London W1 (01-499 7411)

VICTOR MAHY, 19 Little Minster St, Winchester, Hants (0962-64763)

GERALD E. MARSH, 32a The Square, Winchester, Hants (0962-4505)

PARTRIDGE (FINE ARTS) LTD, 144-146 New Bond St, London W1 (01-629 0834/5)

PHILLIPS OF HITCHIN (ANTIQUES) LTD, The Manor House, Hitchin, Herts (0462-2067)

SPINK AND SONS, LTD, 5-7 King St, London SW1 (01-930 7880)

STAIR AND COMPANY, 120 Mount St, London W1 (01-499 1784/5)

Left

Queen Anne gateleg table of good colour and patina. The top is crossbanded. The square cabriole legs terminate in hoof feet.
H 73 cm (29 in).
VICTOR MAHY

Below

This detail of the inside of a desk shows the close association between the styles of the engraver and cabinetmaker. From an important piece by Gerritt Jensen.
Courtesy of ASPREY AND COMPANY

Left

Early Queen Anne burr walnut cabinet on stand containing drawers within. The handles and fittings have their original gilding. The legs are developing toward square cabriole legs and the feet are hoofed.
H 183 cm (70 in).
VICTOR MAHY

Above

Rare Queen Anne bureau cabinet decorated with flowers on a black ground. This was probably painted by a Dutchman working in London. Dated about 1714.
W 79 cm (31 in) D 48 cm (19 in) H 196 cm (77 in).
SPINK AND SON

Left and detail below

Late Queen Anne secretary cabinet in burr walnut. The secretary part is concealed in a drawer which pulls out to reveal a well fitted interior. The shilling keyplate and ring handles are especially characteristic. Note the slides for candles which are reflected in this original bevelled glass plate.
H 244 cm (96 in).
SPINK AND SON

Below

This is a very small William and Mary miniature chest of about 1790. An attractive example of oyster veneering. The top has box stringing in a concentric and overlapping ring design.
W 30.5 cm (15 in) D 25.4 cm (10½ in) H 33 cm (13 in).
STAIR AND COMPANY

Left

*One of a pair of laburnum card tables of good colour.
The table opens by a concertina action. Notice the skill
of the maker in using and matching laburnum, a
wood that only comes in small logs.*
H 72 cm (28½ in) W 86 cm (34 in).
PHILLIPS OF HITCHIN

Right

*Bureau veneered in burr elm, crossbanded in walnut
and with black and white inlay. Both the handles and
the bracket feet are original. On the bottom drawer is
an attractive sunburst inlay set back in a hemisphere
into the drawer. Elm is a most unusual wood to be used
in veneering pieces of this quality, but as may be seen,
the figuring is so marked, that no cabinetmaker would
readily discard it.*
H 99.cm (39 in) W 76 cm (30 in) D 50 cm (20 in).
ARTHUR BRETT AND SONS LTD

Left

*Solid walnut bachelor chest dated about 1715, which
has faded most attractively. The handles and key
plates are original. Walnut was always a scarce wood
in England and it is somewhat surprising to find even
a small chest of drawers made completely of walnut.
This wood is cut along the grain and does not have the
elaborate figuring that the veneered walnut chests
have; nonetheless it is of pleasing restraint and is very
small.*
VICTOR MAHY

Below

*Small Queen Anne
mirror of about 1710.
This example has two
candle brackets and its
original bevelled glass.
The effect is heightened
by the judicious use of
gilding.*
VICTOR MAHY

Left and details below

*This Queen Anne armchair has a most beautiful line,
but has had some very skilful repairs. One back leg has
been replaced and the details show how the left leg has
lathe turning marks just apparent (the right is
original). The central cross stretcher is a replacement
and the bruises and distressing are too regular to be
genuine.*
Courtesy of JOHN BLY
The author is extremely grateful to Mr Bly for
these candid photographs.

Right

*Walnut veneered longcase clock of about 1705. The
case, of simple design, is unfaded, and has good
figuring. The movement was made by Brouncker
Watts of Fleet Street who was admitted to the
Clockmakers' Company in 1693 and who died in
1719. A 30-day striking movement.*
GERALD C. MARSH (CLOCKS)

An important 'mulberrywood' cabinet on stand; the stained burr maple cabinet with fine gilt metal mounts, the doors enclosing ten drawers. It has an elaborate gilt stand. About 1690.
W 104 cm (41 in) D 53 cm (21 in) H 170 cm (67 in).
ASPREY

Far right
Secretary bookcase cabinet of fine colour on bracket and bun feet. The interior fittings are veneered with carefully chosen walnut. About 1690-95.
H 249 cm (98 in).
W. R. HARVEY

Below
This is the Queen Anne wing armchair illustrated in colour on the opposite page with the original tapestry removed during restoration. It is important to note that the stuffing is not too proud and complements the flowing line of the chair.
Courtesy of VICTOR MAHY

Above
Important and rare early 18th century George I double sided pedestal desk veneered throughout in richly coloured burr yew wood. There are stylistic affinities with the firm of Coxed and Woster. About 1730. The waist moulding is of black painted beech.
JOHN KEIL

Below left
Lowboy of about 1720. The walnut veneers have feather crossbanding. The top has quarter veneering, that is, four pieces of veneer from the same plank have been used to improve the figuring on a plain surface.
H 74 cm (29 in).
W. R. HARVEY

Above
This mellowed Queen Anne box mirror, is simply designed with carefully chosen veneers, and may well be the collector's first acquisition. On a small scale all the characteristics of the good pieces are present.
THORPE AND FOSTER, DORKING

Left
This walnut veneered chest of drawers is of good colour and patina and stands on bracket feet. About 1715.
H 137 cm (54 in).
W. R. HARVEY

Right
This red and gold lacquer bureau cabinet is of the greatest rarity. It is believed to have been made by Giles Grendy, an Englishman who had connections with Spain. This cabinet, one of a pair, was perhaps made in Spain for the Royal family and subsequently found its way to the Palazzo Quirinale in Rome. It is in superb condition. About 1700.
W 140 cm (55 in) D 74 cm (29 in) H 254 cm (100 in).
MALLETT AND SON

Far right
Late William and Mary chest of drawers inlaid with endive or seaweed marquetry. The original petal-like handles are very characteristic.
H 86 cm (34 in).
W. R. HARVEY

Below

This cabinet on stand is an exceptional piece of William and Mary cabinetmaking. Olivewood has been veneered on a pine carcase in an oystershell pattern and the crossbanding is in kingwood. The colour of this veneering suggests that this has rarely been exposed to strong light. Inside is the rare feature of inlaid panels of pietra dura, (briefly, marquetry using marble), sunk into drawers of veneered olive and kingwood on oak. The insides of the drawers are lignum wood, a hard oriental wood that by reason of its strength has been used with the marble panels, which are possibly of a slightly earlier date. John Evelyn had a similar cabinet.
JOHN KEIL

Right

Queen Anne wing armchair of about 1710. The cabriole legs are carved with acanthus leaves on the knees. The original tapestry has been removed for repair and replaced on the original stuffing. The design is typical for the period and the colour has lost little of its brilliance.
VICTOR MAHY

Below

One of a pair of fine Queen Anne stools upholstered in a subtly coloured contemporary tapestry. Pairs of stools are of considerable rarity. The legs are supported with elegant stretchers.
H 44 cm (17½ in). PHILLIPS OF HITCHIN

Above

Armchair with drop-in cane seat, and painted decoration. Unsigned, about 1850. Delicate furniture was not suitable for use by heavily crinolined ladies of the 1860s and this contributed to the fading popularity of papier mâché.
JUBILEE ANTIQUES

Above

A perfect example of the work of Jennens & Bettridge at its finest, this tray is particularly unusual for its green background colour. The central floral design and gilt garlanded surround is delicately painted. Signed.
DELOMOSNE

Top

Tray with a central naïve painting which makes this example more original than the usual type which would be decorated with some kind of floral painting or mother of pearl. In the 1790s these paintings were often copies of pictures by Guido Reni and they demonstrated the fine qualities of this surface.
SUSAN BECKER ANTIQUES

Colour far left
Letter rack delicately painted with gilded chinoiserie scenes. The simplicity of the gilding alone is unusual and elegant against the background.
R. A. BARNES

Papier Mâché

It was the competition with the popularity of the 'Pontypool' japanned tinware that sowed the seeds of English papier mâché production in the middle of the 18th century. After much experiment, a rival factory in Birmingham achieved a paper substance which provided an alternative to tin for lacquer decoration. As the Birmingham based industry was getting under way, Henry Clay's invention of heat-resistant paperware in 1772 firmly established the future prosperity of the papier mâché trade in the Midlands. Continual experiment with new and improved methods and decorative techniques by highly skilled designers, artists and gilders resulted in the enormous range of items, all superbly executed and beautifully embellished, that became the height of fashion in the 1840s and '50s. The quality of work done in Birmingham and Wolverhampton was unrivalled. Trays were the first items to be made by Henry Clay, following on from the manufacture of Pontypool tin trays. Decoration is often so fine that they can be used in the same way as pictures on walls. The various shapes, such as the parlour-maid's tray shaped for carrying-comfort, and the decorative styles often perfected on these articles could make a detailed study in themselves. Apart from the more familiar snuff-boxes, tea caddies and desk accessories, the factories produced pretty and elegant chairs, tables, cabinets, work tables and even beds, many of which have been kept for today's collector in excellent condition.

But the novelty value was soon swamped by the quantities demanded by customers, and enthusiasm for papier mâché was fading in the 1860s. The industry, too, had gone too far, and in satisfying an increasing foreign market it had sacrificed its standards of decoration until it became overworked and vulgar. At this stage papier mâché was being used for pieces of furniture entirely unsuited to the material. The major firm of Jennens and Bettridge closed down in 1864 and although the trade continued, it catered for a different market by turning out cheap, poor quality pieces.   s.s.

Above
One of a pair of paper racks of about 1860 with mother-of-pearl decoration. The quality of inlay and painting varies considerably and is something which should be taken into account. After this time cheaper methods produced badly designed and decorated pieces.
JUBILEE ANTIQUES

Above
Tea caddy painted and inlaid with mother-of-pearl. Dated about 1860. Tea caddies were made in large quantities particularly in Birmingham and exported all over the world.
R. A. BARNES

Right
Circular, lobed tray, painted with a view of Mont St Michel.
HENNING

Right
Unusual work table. The circular box lined with satin is supported on a central baluster mounted on lacquered wooden tripod base. About 1870.
SUSAN BECKER ANTIQUES

Above
One of a pair of Regency face screens to hang at either end of the chimney piece, with delicate mother-of-pearl inlay and turned and gilded wooden handles. Dated about 1830.
CHEPSTOW ANTIQUES

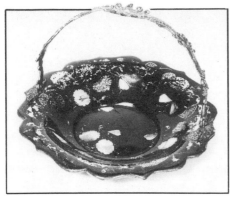

Above
Card tray with typical gilt metal handles. This was another favourite item, here patterned with mother-of-pearl and painting, which was protected from rubbing by varnish.
JUBILEE ANTIQUES

Below
Cabinets are relatively rare: this one is mounted on a wooden base and decorated with a 'Persian style' border pattern in red and green. This type of decoration became popular about 1850, and usually indicates later work. Although on the surface this piece looks deceptively like lacquer, papier mâché is lighter to feel and will craze more easily.
H 116 cm (46 in)
CHEPSTOW ANTIQUES

Left
Small counter tray signed by Clay and painted with gilt 'chinoiserie' butterflies and leaves, a decoration typical of this factory. In 1816 Jennens and Bettridge took over the business started by Henry Clay in the 1770s, when he invented heat resistant paper ware. Previously trays had been japanned on tin.
MRS GRACE

Left
Blotter with a black background and central pattern of mother-of-pearl. One of the many small objects usually associated with papier mâché: letter racks, pen trays, tea caddies and all kinds of boxes are popular examples. This stunning black ground was an unrivalled feature of the Midlands skill.
JUBILEE ANTIQUES

Below
Regency Easter egg, coloured in green heightened with gilding. Green and red coloured papier mâché is substantially more rare than its black counterpart and consequently more desirable. This kind of objet d'art was much favoured by the rich and is in a very different category to the more utilitarian ware.
H 38 cm (15 in)
PHILLIPS & HARRIS

Left
Pedestal table on unusual pumpkin shaped base, the centre of the table well painted with a chinoiserie scene. Papier mâché tables followed designs of their wooden counterparts.
H 44.5 cm (17½ in)
LENNOX MONEY ANTIQUES

Above
Oval tray, stamped Jennens & Bettridge, with black background and delicate gilt floral decoration. Gilding was done with gold powder and a very fine brush.
HENNING

Above
Unusual box, signed by Clay and surmounted with a decorated glass lid. Early 19th century.
LENNOX MONEY

Left
Inkstand painted with a floral pattern. Most of the many inkstands produced have lost their original inkwells and have been replaced with later examples.
A. J. REFFOLD

Below
Shaped tray signed 'S Walton & Co. Warranted' and painted with a Crusader Castle, Syria. The reverse is inscribed J Williams, Barnstaple. Less well known than Jennens & Bettridge, Walton was another foremost papier mâché manufacturer.
HENNING

Right
Early 19th century tripod table of about 1825, still using the graceful form of the 18th century but decorated with typical mother-of-pearl inlay and gilt. The quality of the painting and pearl shell ornament in early pieces tends to be of a higher quality as it was made for a prosperous clientèle, eager for novelty, unlike the cheaper commercial products made later to satisfy popular demand and a foreign market attracted by over elaborate decoration. H 106.5 cm (42 in)
CHEPSTOW ANTIQUES

Above
Black spoon-backed armchair elaborately painted, gilded and inlaid with mother-of-pearl. Signed Jennens and Bettridge, and dated 10 August 1844. The name of the individual artist never seems to appear in signatures. The best known of all papier mâché manufacturers, they made especially fine trays but by 1851 were making various articles of furniture which are mentioned in the catalogue of The Great Exhibition — chairs, tables and casings for pianofortes being especially popular.
H 94 cm (37 in)
W 58.4 cm (23 in)
A. J. REFFOLD

WHERE TO BUY

Bamboo Furniture

Bamboo furniture first came to light in Europe with the publication of William Chambers' *Chinese Designs* in 1757. Surprisingly enough, despite the fashion for Chinoiserie which had been raging for over a century, there is no evidence that any was imported from China until after 1802 when the Prince of Wales, later George IV, commenced the building of the Brighton Pavilion. Through an agent he purchased bamboo furniture direct from Canton to add authenticity to his Chinese interiors. He later supplemented these with carefully imitated pieces made in beechwood by the London firm of Elward, Marsh & Tatham. The idea soon caught on and other houses, such as Hinton House in Somerset and Claydon House in Buckinghamshire, added bamboo to their collections. Although it was imported throughout the 19th century, the popularity of Chinese bamboo was relatively short-lived and the majority of pieces can be attributed to the period 1800-1830. Chinese bamboo is difficult to date as traditional methods of construction and designs are still being used today. However, it is easily identifiable – points to look for are tightly packed latticework, plain lacquer or canework surfaces, bandings and stretchers continuing around the outside of uprights, and wooden pegs holding all joints.

English bamboo
Ninety per cent of bamboo furniture available today, although often described as Oriental, is quite definitely English. During the years 1870-1930 there were well over 150 registered producers, the majority in London's East End, but other important firms in Birmingham, Leicester and Nottingham. This new craze for bamboo stemmed from the general passion for Japanese art in the 1860s, a strange phenomenon, as Japan did not make bamboo furniture itself. Nevertheless, lacquer panels, rolls of matting and bamboo poles were imported from Japan by the thousand and made up into an astonishing variety of 'Japanese' articles – what-nots, jardinieres, bedroom suites, standard lamps, pen holders etc. – few of them displaying much resemblance to Japanese furniture, but charming enough in themselves. The export business thrived, too, cargoes going as far afield as South America and Australia. The largest producers were W. F. Needham in Birmingham, W. T. Ellmore in Leicester and Matthews & Clark and Model & Co. in London. In 1896 Needham's claimed to be producing the almost incomprehensible figure of 4,000 pieces per week. With such a high rate of production it is not really surprising that so much bamboo has survived until today, despite 50 years of positive derision.

Cheap to buy, expensive to repair
At last bamboo has come in to its own again and a new craze is in full swing. A discerning buyer can still find well made and attractive pieces at modest prices. Some words of advice though – bamboo is more difficult and expensive to repair than it looks, so if it wobbles badly, don't be tempted by lower prices. Damaged lacquer touched up with paint doesn't really give the same effect, but on the other hand Japanese matting is available, cheap and easily glued.   G.W.

Above
Cake stand, about 1900. The shelves are of random geometric inlay of various woods, rare in bamboo furniture, but commonly seen on small boxes and trays made in Japan for export to Europe at the end of the 19th century.
H 69 cms. W 25 cms. D 25 cms
(27 × 11 × 10 in.).
RODD MCLENNAN

Where to buy
Most junk shops have the occasional piece of bamboo, but the following dealers usually have a good selection. Rare early examples of the Regency period can be found in the better shops. Modern production, made to traditional designs, is often very expensive.
BAMBOO PROSPERITY, 91 Lots Road, London SW10 (01-352 0763)
LIBERTY & CO., Antiques Department, Regent Street, London W1 (01-734 1234)
RODD MCLENNAN, 24 Holbein Place, London SW1W 8NL (01-730 6330)
MALLETT AT BOURDON HOUSE LTD. (for Chinese bamboo), 2 Davies Street, London W1 (01-629 2444/5)
MYRIAD ANTIQUES, 133 Portland Road, London W11 (01-229 1709)

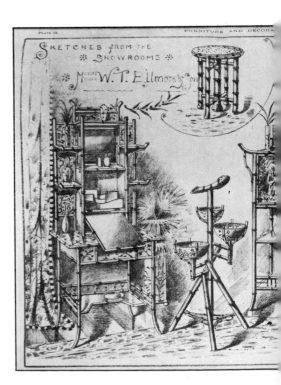

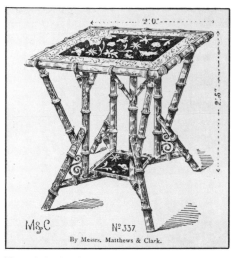

Below
Revolving bookcase with lacquer top and embossed paper shelves, about 1890. These bookcases are quite rare in bamboo and this one, being small, is particularly attractive. Embossed paper was originally imported from Japan but later copied by English manufacturers. Top 47 cms square. H 67 cms (18.5 sq × 26 in.).
Rodd McLennan

Top right & above
Tea table (top right) of 'tortoiseshell' bamboo with lacquered top and lower shelf. This table was made by the firm of Matthews & Clark, London, as can be seen from the accompanying advertisement (above) from the Cabinet Maker, *November 1897. The 'tortoiseshell' appearance is given by the use of a particular type of bamboo, but sometimes a varnish was applied to plain bamboo to simulate the effect. Top 61 cms square. H 74 cms (24 sq × 29 in.).*
Myriad Antiques

Right
China cabinet and a pair of chairs, about 1900, of 'tortoiseshell' bamboo. Chairs were generally made as part of a bedroom suite rather than as dining chairs. Cabinet W 75 cms. D 34 cms. H 194 cms (29.5 × 13 × 76 in.). Chairs W 43 cms. D 37 cms. H 95 cms. (17 × 14.5 × 37 in.).
Rodd McLennan

Below
Chinese child's chair, about 1880. This chair is typical of the simpler type of Chinese bamboo furniture. The seat is of small squares of split bamboo and the ends of the bamboo are left uncovered. The joints are held together by small wooden pins. W 35 cms. D 25 cms. H 67 cms (14 × 10 × 26 in.).
Liberty & Co., Antiques Department

Right and detail
Piano stool, dated about 1890 but re-upholstered in 1920s original fabric. The sides are of embossed paper. Piano stools in bamboo are extremely rare. L 51 cms. W 40 cms. H 51 cms (20 × 16 × 20 in.).
Bamboo Prosperity

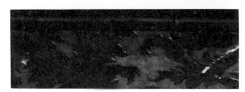

Left
Advertisement for W. T. Ellmore & Son from Furniture and Decoration, *November 1891 showing an extraordinary variety of bamboo designs.*

Stripped Pine Furniture

Pine is the common name for over 100 species of tree. It is a soft wood which is fast-growing and harvested in large quantities. The most common use of pine in the 18th century was for panelling and as a carcase wood for veneer. In the 19th century it was used in the manufacture of cheap, mass-produced furniture and its coarseness was disguised in a number of different ways. The most popular way was to stain it in imitation of more beautiful and more fashionable woods such as mahogany or satinwood. The results are always attractive and often quite startling. At the beginning of the 19th century it became popular to paint pine. A number of Adam colours were used, one of the most beautiful being a rich matt blue, and often classical or floral motifs were added as detail. The third way was to leave the pine unstained or painted. This is most commonly found in country pieces such as dressers or dole cupboards, which imitated more expensive oak pieces.

Dating pine furniture is extremely difficult as certain styles were continually produced over a number of decades. Thus a chest-on-stand or kneehole desk, which was first made in walnut in 1710 would still be made in pine as late as 1800. Similarly styles in country pine remained the same decade after decade. Dating the painted furniture is easier as the colour and detail are indicative of the period.

In the 20th century the demand for pine has continued because it is still one of the cheapest forms of old furniture, but the desire to have it disguised in a more elegant manner has been discarded. This is partly the result of the belief (stemming from the Arts and Crafts movement) that in furniture, wood should be allowed to express its natural function. The fallacy of this notion is self-evident: the only natural function of wood is to grow into a tree, this cannot possibly be continued after it has been cut down and made into a piece of furniture. Therefore before people decry veneer and staining as somehow immoral

and strip a piece of furniture bare they should pause to consider the quality of the work and the fact that the furniture maker originally intended it to be there. The second reason for stripping pine is practical. The wear and tear of past years has meant that much of the original stain and paint work has been either completely repainted or else it has become so badly scuffed as to be unrecognisable. Often the only answer is to strip the piece, which immediately becomes more attractive as a result.

The golden rule for pine, to be obeyed by all who love antique furniture, is to preserve the original painting or staining wherever possible. But if not, to buy pieces which have been properly stripped and restored by respectable dealers.

Stripping Pine, the dangers and difficulties

The most common method of stripping pine is by dipping it in a bath of caustic acid. Caustic is an ICI product and it is more commonly used for burning off warts. The danger of the method lies in the furniture being left too long in the tank. One experienced furniture restorer described this method as 'pickling' and it results in the glue rotting away at the joints and the piece of furniture invariably falling apart. The surface of the wood also goes furry and comes out in white patches. Watch out for all these points. Responsible pine dealers take great care in their use of caustic, they either dip it for a short time or else 'bucket strip' the piece, that is do it by hand. They also take great care to see that every inch of the piece is stripped. This is most important with drawers, 'backyard' strippers often just place the front end in the dip. A second method of stripping, which is much softer on the wood is to use a recommended paint stripper, which is rubbed on and scraped off by hand. After each process the piece of furniture should be hosed down with water, either sanded or finished with wire wool and finally waxed. It is worth mentioning that under new EEC regulations the majority of 'backyard' strippers are now illegal in that they discharge unneutralised acid down the drain.

Two specialist strippers, who work on a large scale and quite legally, are:

KEMSTRIP, 112 Greyhound Road, London NW17

(01-381 2155/4) and STRIPPED PINE (SUSSEX) LTD, Unit 1, Newcroft, Tangmere, Chichester, Sussex (Halnaker 707). Michael McGrath, the director of Stripped Pine, was an industrial chemist by profession. He used his experience to develop a new chemical for stripping pine, which was not caustic. It only takes 15 minutes to work and the results so far are excellent. He will undertake both large orders from the trade (with delivery) as well as individual items from private customers. Prices, like those of Kem-strip, are charged on a sliding scale according to the size of the object.

Left

The process of stripping the base of a tall boy as carried out by STRIPPED PINE (SUSSEX) LTD. *The condition of the original staining was very bad (see detail) with the very heavy lead content staining the wood red. The piece was lowered into the tank of chemical (covered with poly bubbles to prevent splashing and evaporation), 15 minutes later it emerged and was thoroughly hosed down. The result even when still wet reveals that all the paint was removed and the pine revealed.*

Where and what to buy

The main reason for buying pine furniture is that it is practical and cheap. It is important therefore that readers should buy pieces such as chests of drawers that actually work and also that they are not asked to pay too much. Research for this article has revealed the enormous number of down market pine dealers, who have cropped up in every conceivable area of the country. They are to be avoided for the following reasons. First they tend to be expensive for what they offer. Often they will sell, say, an ordinary chest at an inflated price that they have bought painted for a pittance and had stripped. Secondly they will often not state that pieces such as bureaux are sometimes made up from chests of drawers and that the backs of some dressers are modern. It is worth remembering that most pieces of pine have had to have new handles and that bun feet are invariably replaced by bracket legs. All good dealers will point this out; it is one reason why pine is so cheap. Therefore do not be taken in by attributions of authenticity as excuses for high prices. For reasons of libel I list no dealers from the bottom end of the market. But they are easy to find: cleverly named shops stacked from ceiling to floor with junk.

The most recommended dealers are those who are well-established and who deal in sensible, well-finished furniture. They will always make sure that the pieces are in good working order: completely restoring badly stripped pieces; making practical alterations such as lining all draw runners (which are cross-grained) with formica; and de-worming each piece properly, for, contrary to popular belief caustic does not necessarily kill worm. The dealers listed below all stock a wide range of good quality furniture that is attractive as well as useful and cheap. A number are referred to in the text.

DAVID CLARK, The Plestor, Selbourne, Hampshire (042050 274)
THE CRAFTSMAN, 16 Bridge Street, Hungerford, Berkshire (048 86 2262)
HATHAWAY PINE FURNITURE LTD, The Web, Shottery, Stratford-upon-Avon, Warwickshire (0789 5517)
KINGSHEAD ANTIQUES, Birdlip, Gloucestershire (045282 2299)
BRYAN MANN ANTIQUES, The Square, Ramsbury, Wiltshire (06722 552)
NIMBLE FURNISHINGS LTD, Staple Ash Lane, Froxfield, Petersfield, Hampshire (0730 3640)
OLD PINE, 545 Kings Road, London SW6 (01-736 5999)
THE PINE SHOP, 12b Camden Passage, London N1 (01-226 2444)
SAVILE ANTIQUES, 560 Kings Road, London SW6 (01-736 3625)
YESTERDAY'S PINE, 13 Dunstable Street, Ampthill, Bedford (0525 402260)

There are regrettably few pine dealers who have the original painted or stained pine. This is purely because of a lack of popular demand. It is just as cheap if not cheaper than stripped pine, and in the author's opinion infinitely more attractive. So if you are thinking of buying pine, why not consider some which bears the original decoration? The following dealers should always have some in stock.
ALISTAIR COLVIN LTD, 116 Fulham Road, London SW3 (01-370 4101)
GORE & PLAYER, 49 Church Road, London SW13 (01-748 8850)
BRYAN MANN (see above)
PETER NELSON, Fosse Way, Stow-on-the-Wold, Gloucestershire (0451 30771)
WADE GALLERIES, 19 Camden Passage, London N1 (01-226 3803)

Finally there is the top end of the market, who specialise in 18th century pine. This is extremely rare. Prices are high: as expensive as an equivalent piece in mahogany. Some of the most satisfactory 18th century pine comes from Scandinavia and a number of British dealers are beginning to import this to Britain. There is only one dealer who specialises in 18th century pine.
JOSÉ HORNSEY, 48 New Park Street, Devizes, Wiltshire (0380 2080)   J.K.

Right

Bureaux are some of the easiest pieces of furniture to fake. Often the base of a chest of drawers has a writing slope added to it. However as long as the bureau works and as long as the dealer tells you it is a marriage, this does not really matter. It is highly likely that this example was constructed in such a way: the proportion and the number of drawers are unusual for a bureau. The bracket feet are not original: as pine is such a soft wood, feet of furniture made from it are especially prone to decay, thus in many cases the original bun feet are replaced by more elegant brackets. The handles are not original. H86 W91 D43 cm (34 × 36 × 17 in)
THE PINE SHOP

Above
Small, cheap corner cupboard. H63 D29 cm (24 × 11.5 in)
DAVID CLARK

Above
This pale green wash stand with olive-green decoration is typical of the Adam colours used on pine furniture at the end of the 18th century. It is reputed to have come from Painswick House in Gloucestershire. H91 × W124 × D62 cm (36 × 49 × 24.5 in)
GORE & PLAYER

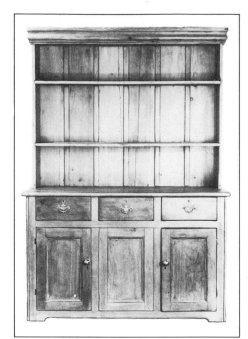

Left
It is fairly difficult to find 18th century pine dressers. This is a good example, it is bowed and has reeded decoration. The handles, as is the case with nearly all pine furniture, are not original. H 210 W 210 D 48 cm (80 × 80 × 19 in)
DAVID CLARK

Right
There is a considerable difference in price between this mid-19th century dresser and the more sophisticated 18th century example. H 210 W 138 D 51 (80 × 50 × 20 in)
THE CRAFTSMAN

Right
Milk yoke. L 91 cm (36 in)
KINGSHEAD ANTIQUES

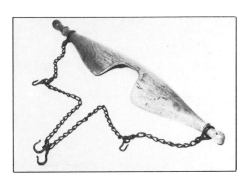

Left
19th century French provincial buffet made in imitation of the Louis XV style. Such details at the tentative cabriole legs reveal that this was made by a provincial craftsman. Pine was a fairly common wood for French furniture of this sort, although they also used oak, chestnut and beechwood. H 250 × W 132 × D 51 cm (100 × 52 × 20 in)
BRYAN MANN

Above and detail
The fine proportions of this corner cupboard, particularly in the cornice, date it to the late-18th century. H 97 × W 74 × D 63 cm (38 × 28.5 × 18 in)
THE CRAFTSMAN

Above
Dole cupboards were originally used to store bread for the poor. The grill was used for ventilation, later they were used in country households where they would be hung on the wall. This is a fairly late example.
H *53* × B *51* × D *24 cm (21 × 20 × 9.5 in)*
JOSÉ HORNSEY

Left
Chiffoniers were introduced in the late 18th century, and consist of an open shelf on top for books with a cupboard below. The detail of this Regency example is painted in imitation of lacquer. Chinese scenes are depicted in black, brown, gold and yellow colours.
H *121* × W *85* × D *34 cm (47.5 × 33.5 × 13.75 in)*
GORE & PLAYER

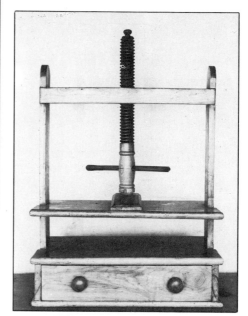

Right
Early 19th century letter press. These attractive objects were used a lot in banks for pressing letters before they were filed, as well as pressing bank notes.
H *83* W *63* D *37 (32 × 160 × 94 in)*
THE CRAFTSMAN

Left
This corner wardrobe is ideal for a bedroom with little space. It is probably Edwardian. H *180* × W *74* × D *63 cm (71 × 29 × 24 in)*
THE CRAFTSMAN

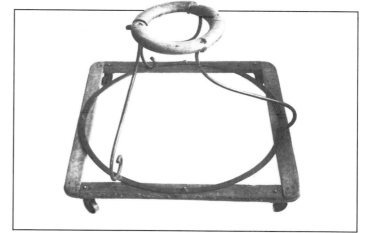

Right
Baby Walker.
H *44 Diam of base 69 cm (17.5, 27 in)*
JOSÉ HORNSEY

Left
Carved sideboard, about 1860.
H *145* W *53* D *57 cm (57 × 22 × 23 in)*
DAVID CLARK

Right
Notice the elegant turning on the top of this bird cage. H *112 cm (44 in)*
BRYAN MANN

Left

Although the style of this desk is mid-18th century, this particular example was not made until the early 1800s. It is rare to find such high quality craftsmanship in pine, note the cockbeading round the drawers.
53 × 51 × 24 cm (21 × 20 × 19.5 in).
JOSÉ HORNSEY

Above

This set of shelves is only about 30-40 years old, but it is an attractive example of the type of cheap well-finished furniture which can be found in pine.
H *124* W *90* D *17 cm (49 × 35.5 × 6.5 in)*
DAVID CLARK

Right

This Regency chiffonier still bears its original staining, which was put on in imitation of rosewood with gilt borders.
H *112* × W *76* × D *33 cm (44 × 30 × 13 in)*
BRYAN MANN

Above

This cricket table is held together with wooden pegs driven into mortices. It could have been produced at any time between 1780 and 1850. The style is based upon oak models and it is unlikely that it was ever painted or stained. H *73* D *70 cm (29 × 27 in)*
KINGSHEAD ANTIQUES

Above

This Regency cradle was originally painted blue with an elegant stencil round the edges.
H *64* × W *90* × D *37 (25 × 35 × 14.5 in)*
KINGSHEAD ANTIQUES

Right

This detail from a late-19th century dresser illustrates how pine was disguised as mahogany with satinwood banding. The overall effect was much grander than the detail implies, unfortunately this too was sent to the stripper soon after the photograph was taken. The measurements of the whole are
H *105* × W *160* × D *51 cm (79 × 63 × 20 in)*
PETER NELSON

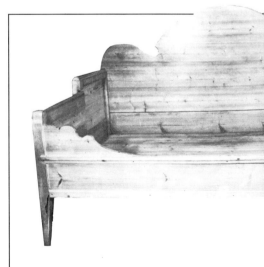

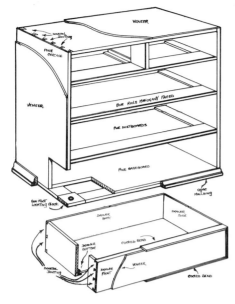

Left

This elegant 18th century Dutch sleigh was designed for aristocratic children. The family coat of arms would probably have been mounted on the prow. H170 × W130 × D55 cm (67 × 51 × 21.5 in) JOSÉ HORNSEY

Below and detail

This small Irish dresser dates from around 1860. Irish pine is always much cruder than English; it also adapts any number of stylistic motifs such as reeding and gadrooning in one piece. Some of the most typical pieces, but also some of the most rare are those which contain a hen coop in the base, where the fowl were kept at night. H205 × W98 × D38 cm (79 × 38.5 × 15 in) KINGSHEAD ANTIQUES

Left

This detailed drawing by a skilled restorer and cabinet maker shows how to recognize furniture that is veneered (e.g. the cockbeading round the drawers would be in a different wood). Such furniture should not be stripped if the veneer can be restored.

Left and detail below

Again this handsome chest-on-stand is deceptively late dating around 1800. It would probably have been stained in imitation of walnut veneer. The original handles would probably have been drop. H150 × W80 × D50 cm (59 × 31.5 × 19.5 in). JOSÉ HORNSEY

Right

The popular Victorian name for items such as this was a monk's bench. The proper name is a table settle. The top folds back to make a seat. This is a 19th century example. H74 × W150 × D83 (29 × 59 × 32 in) KINGSHEAD ANTIQUES

Left

Some of the most unusual pieces of antique pine come from Scandinavia. This is a cabin bed from Norway, which is seen here fully extended, during the day it telescopes into a day bed. H77 × L170 × D106 (ext) 55 cm (30.5 × 67 × 42 (ext) 21.5 in) KINGSHEAD ANTIQUES

Screens

Below
18th century Japanese 6-fold table screen with an attractive stylised design of birds in their birdcages. Japanese screens tend usually to have either two or six panels and other examples could have originally been wall panels which later have been made up into screens.
H 61 cm (24 in)
JOHN SPARKS

In the same way that successive generations can have completely opposing views about an established picture, so also can they have differing views about furniture. Screens have rather fallen into this category (with the exception of Chinese and Japanese examples) and whereas they were dearly loved in the 18th and 19th centuries for their decorative qualities – they are now considered by most to be large, cumbersome and fairly useless objects, best stored away in a convenient attic or sold to the local junk shop. This is not an imaginative solution and although they no longer serve as protection from heat and cold – in an open plan area, both their 'practical' and 'decorative' qualities can be adapted to shield off an unsightly kitchen, front door or even play their original role as a movable wall between a sitting cum dining room.

Brief History

Although screens have always been an integral part of a Chinese and more especially a Japanese household – we did not, as is commonly assumed borrow the idea direct. Architecturally, screens had been used in churches and houses since medieval times and the inventories of Henry VIII mention movable screens with fixed or folding framework inset with costly materials. However, it is undoubtedly true to say that the great vogue for screens grew with the importation of lacquer to Europe by the East India Company during the latter part of the 17th century. People were fascinated by this exotic oriental technique – a totally new innovation to the European eye – and as well as commissioning designs (see the screen made for the Burghers of Amsterdam, page 34) which was a very costly pursuit, they rapidly devised their own form of imitation lacquer called 'japanning'. This substitute was made up of layers of varnish composed of shellac dissolved in spirit but nothing like as resilient as the many layers of true lacquer, although to the unpractised eye the two techniques can look very similar. By the mid 18th century every great house boasted some oriental screens and like everything rare, a status was definitely attached. These screens are now commonly referred to as 'coromandel' which is a misconception on two counts: firstly 'coromandel' applies only to screens where the design is cut out in intaglio and secondly they were called 'coromandel' because they were exported to Europe by way of the Coromandel coast of India. The taste for lacquer and chinoiserie continued intermittently in Europe throughout the 18th century as it appealed greatly to Rococo taste and in addition to the techniques already mentioned, other materials and forms of decoration began to be used for making screens: painted canvas with fêtes champêtres, oils on leather, painted wallpaper and tapestry. In France these needlework screens were particularly popular and generally upholstered en suite with the Louis XV or Louis XVI furniture, whereas in England it gave the lady of the houses the chance to show off her dexterity with the needle. Fire screens had become enormously popular and developed into a variety of different forms: the pole screen which consisted of a wood or metal pole supported on a tripod with a sliding panel of framed needlework or painted wood; the cheval screen supported on feet with a swinging panel, varying types of hand screens to protect the complexion from the heat and even a type of screen that you could fix on your chair. The Victorians, with their unabashed and as some would say undiscriminating love of decoration, were perhaps the biggest devotees of screens and adorned them in an incredible number of different ways – embroidered, painted, papier mâché, embossed and finally and possibly the most charming of all – their efforts at collage. These colourful screens were made up of scraps cut from old newspapers or magazines and stuck on to a wood or canvas background, then heavily varnished.

S.S.

Above
Scottish carved mahogany fire screen with reading shelf above. Dated around 1790. Fire screens became very popular during the latter part of the 18th century and are generally inset as is this example with a tapestry panel, although embossed leather was also popular.
H 91 cm (36 in)
PAUL COUTS OF EDINBURGH

The cost of collecting

Prices vary enormously. Japanese screens, apart from the ones made at the end of the 19th century for export are a specialised subject and fetch high prices. The best selection can be found at John Milne Henderson. 18th century Chinese lacquer screens made for the European market also fetch high prices, depending on quality and historical value but the biggest and most varied range is undoubtedly in the 19th century where prices are still reasonably low, and there are many different styles to choose from. For an 18th century screen in good condition you must expect to pay several times as much as for a Victorian screen.

Where to buy

JOHN BLY, 50 High Street, Tring, Hertfordshire (044-282 3030)

CARSON BOOTH ANTIQUES, 45 and 80-28 Pimlico Road, London sw1 (01-730 7004)

CHRISTIE'S SOUTH KENSINGTON, 85 Old Brompton Road, London sw7 (01-581 2231)

PAUL COUTS LTD, 101-107 West Row (Victoria Street), Edinburgh (Edinburgh 3238)

ROBIN GAGE, 50 Pimlico Road, London sw1 (01-730 2878)

BIBI HARRIS ANTIQUES, 556 Kings Road, London sw6 (01-731 2016)

LENNOX MONEY (ANTIQUES) LTD, 99 & 68 Pimlico Road, London sw1 (01-730 3070)

LOOT, 76 & 78 Pimlico Road, London sw1 (01-730 8097)

MALLETT & SON (ANTIQUES) LTD, 40 New Bond Street, London (01-499 7411)

DAVID MARTIN TAYLOR ANTIQUES, 592 Kings Road, London sw6 (01-731 5054)

RODD MCLENNAN, 24 Holbein Place, London sw1 (01-730 6330)

MILNE HENDERSON, 99 Mount Street, London w1 (01-499 2507)

PORTMEIRION ANTIQUES, 5 Pont Street, London sw1 (01-235 7601)

RENDLESHAM & DARK LTD, 498 King's Road, London sw10 (01-351 1442)

JOHN SPARKS LTD, 128 Mount Street, London w1 (01-499 2265)

ROWLAND SPILLANE, The Kent Gallery Ltd, 15 Pont Street, London sw1 (01-235 3851)

SPINK & SON LTD, 5-7 King Street, London sw1 (01-930 7888)

TROVE, 71 Pimlico Road, London sw1 (01-730 6514)

WISHART GALLERY, 130 Ebury Street, London sw1 (01-730 1662)

Above

Magnificent carved 4-fold Chinese screen made for the export market and inset with four embroidered panels of cream coloured flowers on a black silk background. Late 19th century but with modern castors.

H 178 cm (5 ft 10 in)

BIBI HARRIS

Below right and detail

Chinese 17th century table screen of dark green jade, carved in unusual depth with a rocky landscape with sages among pine, fir and prunus trees: the reverse entirely plain. Jade had magic propensities for the Chinese rather like the European reverence for gold. Prices vary according to quality but are generally high.

H 25.5 cm (10 in) W 17 cm (6¾ in)

SPINKS

Right and detail left

French Art Deco screen in grey and silver tones depicting stylised heads of fawns and a forest like effect. Dated 1925 and signed by Lattry, a comparatively well-known designer and illustrator.

H 188 cm (6ft 2 ins)

CARSON BOOTH ANTIQUES

Left

Early 19th century embossed leather screen in blue and gold colouring. Unlike so many screen this example has not been restored and revarnished and the colours have faded into subtle tones.
H 183 cm (6 ft)
BIBI HARRIS

Below and detail

English late 19th century 4-fold painted leather screen with four marine prints.
H 183 cm (6 ft)
TROVE

Above

Oriental three fold screen painted with floral scenes on a carved wood support, the top surmounted at each end by a carved wood dragon. Many screens were made both in China and Japan during the 19th century for export to Europe.
H 155 cm (5 ft 1 in)
CARSON BOOTH

Left and detail below

One of a pair of late 19th century Chinese hardwood and lacquer screens made for the European market and inlaid with a design of birds in ivory and bone. Mounted on modern castors. Although these screens are extremely decorative, they were produced in large quantities because of the cheap labour available at the time and the standardisation of design has tended to keep prices quite low.
BIBI HARRIS

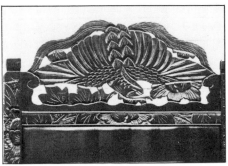

Above

Hand painted 3-panel screen on a laminated wood surface, shaped in the gothic style and decorated with an attractive pattern of trailing poppies, butterflies and insects on a blue drag painted background. These new screens are the imaginative work of Mrs McKelvie and can be ordered in three sizes (4 ft 4 in, 5 ft and 6 ft). The choice of designs will range from naturalistic, modern, 'antiqued' and nursery.
H 132 cm (4 ft 4 in)
WISHART GALLERY

Left

Early 18th century English japanned 6-fold screen decorated with birds and flowers enriched with gilding on a dark background. The popularity of lacquer grew after the Restoration and the East India Company, quick to realise the European demand, imported many screens, some of which were cut up and made into cabinets, chests, chairs etc.
H 236 cm (7 ft 11 in)
MALLETT & SON

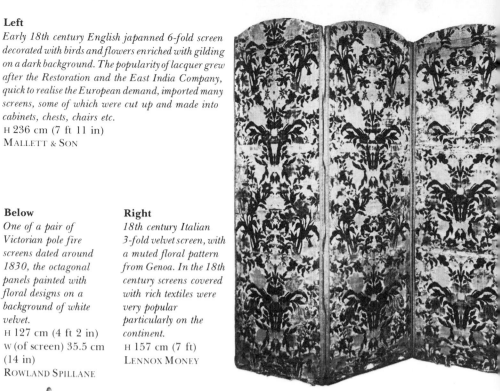

Below

One of a pair of Victorian pole fire screens dated around 1830, the octagonal panels painted with floral designs on a background of white velvet.
H 127 cm (4 ft 2 in)
W (of screen) 35.5 cm (14 in)
ROWLAND SPILLANE

Right

18th century Italian 3-fold velvet screen, with a muted floral pattern from Genoa. In the 18th century screens covered with rich textiles were very popular particularly on the continent.
H 157 cm (7 ft)
LENNOX MONEY

Below

Late Victorian screen sentimentally decorated with classical scenes and baskets of flowers, on a leather background. Because leather tends to decay quickly these screens are usually restored and revarnished.
H 183 cm (6 ft)
BIBI HARRIS

Left

One of a pair of English Regency shield shaped hand screens used for protection from the fire. Decorated in silver – one with groups of figures dancing and making music and the other with figures talking and playing cards. On turned ebonised handles the backs are inscribed 'Lady Carhampton at Home'.
W 26 cm (10¼ in)
CHRISTIE'S SOUTH KENSINGTON (collection Countess of Portarlington)

Above

Late 19th century coromandel Chinese screen unusual for its background of white lacquer, attractively decorated with birds and flowers in shades of browns and pastels. Although most people refer to all lacquer screens as coromandel, there is a difference in that coromandel is a form of incised lacquer work.
H 188 cm (6 ft 2 in)
RODD MCLENNAN

Right
Mahogany cheval fire screen of Hepplewhite period and design with a pierced rail that relates to the stopped fluting fashionable at the time. The screen is adjustable which is an unusual feature on such a delicate piece (the material panel is of a later date).
JOHN BLY

Above
Early 19th century continental chinoiserie screen, the four panels of painted leather decorated with exotic birds and flowers in gilt and polychrome colouring on a black background. Like many leather screens the back has been relined.
H 198 cm (6 ft 6 in)
DAVID MARTIN TAYLOR

Above
Melanesian (South Sea Islands) tarpa screen with native decoration in brown and white. Dated around 1920. Two fold.
BIBI HARRIS

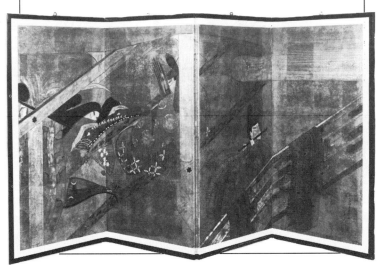

Below detail
19th century double sided 4-fold English screen made up of various 18th century parchment land deeds complete with seals.
H 137 cm (4 ft 6 in)
DAVID MARTIN TAYLOR

Right
19th century Japanese 4-fold bedroom screen in subtle tones of golds and brown copying an earlier style. Signed. The vogue for Japonaism was particularly strong at the end of the 19th century with the rise of aesthetic movement and the artefacts of Japan were swiftly assimilated into the architectural, painting and furniture designs of the 1860s and 70s.
H 91 cm (3 ft)
W 122 cm (4 ft)
LENNOX MONEY

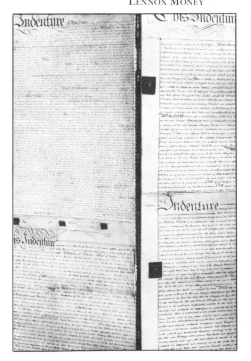

Colour near right and detail left
Very important and rare early 18th century Chinese Export lacquer screen commissioned by the Burghers of Amsterdam. The 9-folds are extremely unusual for their concave form and the top of the screen is surmounted by a bold carving in gilt of scrolls and acanthus leaves. The screen itself on a deep maroon background depicts a Dutch canal scene with superb raised decoration all built up out of layers of lacquer. The high price of this screen is determined by the early date, historical value, and exceptional quality. Photograph by courtesy of Mallett & Son (Antiques) Ltd H 193 cm (6 ft 4 in)
MALLETT & SON

Colour far right (detail)
18th century continental screen (possibly Dutch) of six panels, decorated with an interesting combination of a rustic and classical landscape, the top of each fold being surmounted by a classical bust. This is a very early example of a painted screen and is in surprisingly good condition for its age.
H 214 cm (7 ft)
RENDLESHAM & DARK

Left

Victorian 4-fold 'scrap' screen with brightly coloured applied cut-outs stuck on to both sides of a canvas ground. These collage screens became very popular during the 19th century and were generally coated in varnish to protect the paper. Although they are susceptible to damage they are easy to repair and are found especially in country junk shops and sales.
PRIVATE COLLECTION

Right (detail)

Mid 17th century Japanese 6-fold screen depicting four chapters of Genji Monogatari, the most famous novel in Japan which was much illustrated by Japanese artists as it expressed the height of noble sentiment. Decorated in ink polychrome and gold leaf. Kambun period.
H 162.5 cm (5 ft 4 in)
JOHN MILNE HENDERSON

Far right

Regency papier-mâché fire screen decorated with an attractive mother of pearl inlay. All types of screens appealed to the Victorian love of ornamentation and gave the artist a chance to show off his versatility.
H 76 cm (30 in)
W 61 cm (24 in)
ROBIN GAGE

35

Below

*Regency games, writing and work table in
calamander wood, about 1800. The height of the
leather-lined writing panel is adjustable. The
backgammon board is also of leather and the chess
board slides out from below. The work bag has been
removed. H 76 W 74 D 41 cm.*
STAIR & COMPANY LTD.

Games and Card Tables

Colour

Top

Late 18th century mahogany games and writing table with a detachable sliding top with plain mahogany on one side and a chess board on the other. H 75 cm W 109 cm D 56 cm.

H. C. BAXTER

Middle

Late 18th century partridge wood games table. The removable board has a chess board on one side and a painted board for Game of the Jew, which is played with dice. Below the removable board is a leather backgammon board. H 71 cm W 55 cm D 46 cm.

ANTHONY FORTESCUE

Bottom

Late 17th century walnut games table of outstanding quality. The chess board is veneered in walnut of contrasting colours and the backgammon board is cross banded in holly and inlaid with ivory. Its open twist legs are very much rarer than the more usual barley twist legs so often found on furniture of this date. H 78 cm W 115 cm D 61 cm.

THORPE & FOSTER LTD.

'There is nothing that wears out a fine face like the Vigils of the Card Table' claimed *The Guardian* of 1713 on the subject of women gamesters. This could well have been aimed directly at Georgiana, the Duchess of Devonshire who surely must have aged considerably during the short space of time in which she took to gamble away £1,000,000 of her husband's money. But these lamentable happenings were not exclusive to women or even the 18th century, as even as early as the 17th century the Earl of Sunderland played for £5,000 a night at basset.

However, at least the cabinet makers who made games and card tables were not as stupid as many of those who played at them, for to make even the simplest of games tables required considerable skill. The first games tables were made about 1600, although chess, dice and tables (backgammon) had been played for centuries before. These had either parquetry, needlework or very occasionally velvet tops. Towards the end of the century the introduction of many different sorts of new games to this country brought about tables made specifically for one game. 'Euen or Odde' was played on a table with compartments market E and O into which the dice fell, and ombre, introduced about 1660 was played by three people around a three-sided table which was usually tripod.

But it was not until the very end of the century, and almost exactly two centuries after they had been introduced to this country, that tables were made exclusively for cards. At first cards were considered 'an invention of the devil', and it was not until Queen Elizabeth I took up playing primero that the playing of cards became an acceptable pastime, so much so in fact that soon afterwards children were expected to be proficient whist players by the time they were ten years old. These tables were typical of the style of the late 17th century, being of walnut veneer with two back legs which swung out to support the folding circular top. Basset, loo and picquet became popular, and the latter, being for two players only, was played on small and elegant tables which were often similar to pembroke tables.

The increasing interest of gaming and cards at the end of the 17th century became a mania in the 18th century, which came to be known as the age of clubs. Everyone from royalty to peasants gambled, but particularly the aristocracy who played every night until dawn losing or gaining literally thousands of pounds in a single hand. However, whereas George II encouraged gambling, George III strongly disapproved and forbade it in the royal palaces. Although this did not have much effect at the time, it was the first step towards ending the national obsession. Certainly far fewer card tables were commissioned in the Regency period. Faro, however, became popular and was played on tables with a series of deep oval wells for counters round the edge and a recess to one side to enable the croupier to be nearer the play. Games tables of this period were also often combined with work tables.

The late 18th and early 19th century games tables are remarkable for their ingenious craftsmanship, often accommodating many different games in one table. These are of course very expensive, but are a much safer buy than the cheaper and plainer varieties, especially those with a games board inset on the top which is often a later addition. But whatever sort of antique games or card table you are looking for, they are all equally intriguing in their guarded secrets of the fortunes which have been won or lost over them.

Where to Buy

There are no specialist games table dealers as such, but the following list gives a guide to those who are likely to have some in stock:

THE ANTIQUE TRADER, 357 Upper Street, London N1 (01-226 3802)

H. C. BAXTER & SONS, 191/3 Fulham Road, London SW3 (01-352 0807)

SUSAN BECKER ANTIQUES, 18 Lower Richmond Road, Putney, London SW15 (01-788 9082)

WILLIAM BEDFORD ANTIQUES, 327 Upper Street, Islington, London N1 (01-226 9648)

ADRIAN BOWYER ANTIQUES, 30 London End, Beaconsfield, Buckinghamshire (Beaconsfield 71316)

ANTHONY FORTESCUE, 19 Walton Street, London SW3 (01-584 7586)

ROGER KING ANTIQUES, 111 High Street, Hungerford, Berkshire (Hungerford 2256)

PHILLIPS OF HITCHIN (ANTIQUES) LTD., The Manor House, Hitchin, Hertfordshire (Hitchin 2067)

STAIR & COMPANY, 120 Mount Street, London W1 (01-499 1785)

THORPE & FOSTER LTD., 13 Grafton Street, New Bond Street, London W1 (01-499 7396)

WOBURN ANTIQUE GALLERIES, 69 Leighton Street, Woburn, Milton Keynes, Beds (Woburn 200)   S.B.

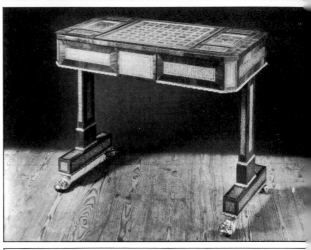

Above

Sheraton 'Harlequin' pembroke games table in harewood with mahogany bandings, about 1790. The removable top has an oval amboyna panel on one side with an inlaid chess board on the other. The backgammon board inside is removable. Harlequin tables, invented towards the end of the 18th century, were so called because of the box-like structure fitted with small drawers or compartments which was concealed in the structure and made to rise by means of weights. H 72 cm W (flaps down) 52 cm (flaps up) 98 cm D 67 cm.
Stair & Company Ltd.

Left

This is a superb example of everything to look out for when buying a games table. At first glance it is obvious that the top is a box and was not originally intended for a stand. But a closer look at the stand will reveal that the pillar, which probably came from a tripod kettle or urn stand of about 1780, has been married to the legs of a tripod table made about thirty years later and which do not even have their original feet. A closer look at the box will also reveal that it is in the same state as the stand. The drawer does not fit and its decoration does not correspond to the carcass, suggesting that they do not belong to each other. Its height of 51 cm is another dubious feature. But if, as in this case, you are willing to overlook these features first pointed out by the dealer, this would make an ideal games table for a small flat.
Susan Becker Antiques

Left

Triple leaf George II mahogany card table with guinea wells, the top embroidered in red, blue, green and brown petit-point. H 69 cm., W (open) 81 cm., W (closed) 41 cm., D 81 cm. Mahogany was first used for card tables in George I's reign, and by the time George II ascended the throne it had completely superseded walnut in popularity. Card tables with square corners were first introduced in about 1730, at about the same time as scroll feet became fashionable. This table can therefore be dated to about 1730-35 because of its ball and claw feet which were popular throughout the first quarter of the 18th century.
THE ANTIQUE TRADER

Left

Regency rosewood games table with Bombay inlay panels, about 1820. H 75 cm., W 84 cm., D 53 cm. Bombay inlay is a technique which originated in Persia in the late 18th century and was taken to British India in about 1800 It was made by chopping bundles of strips of ivory, green wood and steel into thin slices which were inset into the surface. It is often found inlaid in boxes and tea caddies. This table is obviously of English craftsmanship, and it is likely that the Bombay inlay was brought from India in bundles and cut and inlaid over here.
PHILLIPS OF HITCHIN (ANTIQUES) LTD.

Left

Regency rosewood card table with swivel top covered in its original baize with a solid ebony base with brass binding and mounts, about 1815. H 74 cm., W 91 cm., D 44 cm. Probably because of the discouragement begun by George III, the mania for cards had waned considerably by the Regency period, although games, and in particular faro, were as heavily indulged in as ever. Consequently, far fewer card tables were made in the Regency period, and these were usually rosewood with inlay of different woods.
WILLIAM BEDFORD ANTIQUES

Left

George III mahogany card table with concertina-action legs and sliding counter slide beneath the folding top, about 1770. H 72 cm., W 97 cm., D 47 cm. Until 1715, the folding flap was supported when open by swinging legs at the back of the table which often looked rather unsightly. However, the problem was solved after that date with the invention of the concertina action which enabled the support of the back legs to fold neatly away. Tables with concertina action usually have a counter slide similar to the one illustrated, which also helps to brace the legs. Square, fluted legs were made between 1755 and 1770.
WILLIAM BEDFORD ANTIQUES

Left

Oak card table on carved quadruped cabriole stand, with a folding oval top, about 1860. H 74 cm W 87 cm D (closed) 47 cm (open) 92 cm. It is likely that this table was made by a provincial craftsman for a country house.
ADRIAN BOWYER

Left

Victorian papier mâché chess table with inlaid mother-of-pearl board, on a single tripod stand with hand-painted decoration. H 68 cm D 70 cm. The production of papier mâché flourished in the 19th century and these tables tend to be inexpensive.
ROGER KING ANTIQUES

Left

Edwardian satinwood and mahogany patience table with swivel top. H 73 cm W 53½ cm D (closed) 38 cm D (open) 75½ cm.
ADRIAN BOWYER

Furniture of the Chippendale Period

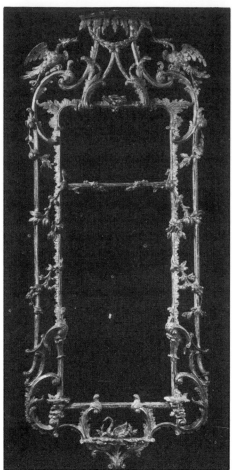

Below and left

Thomas Chippendale described this as a 'tea chest', and it is larger than the expected caddy case. As can be seen, the mahogany example here corresponds almost exactly with the illustration in Plate CLIX of The Director. *The carving is sharp and the handle is gilded brass, and finely chiselled. A direct attribution is understandable in this rare instance.*
MALLETT

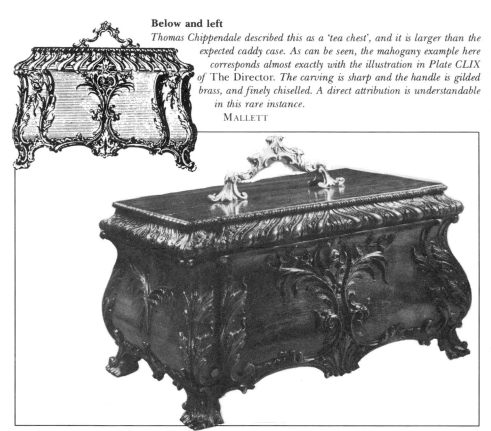

Above

One of a pair of Chippendale giltwood rectangular mirrors retaining the original gilding. It has a double framework united with garlands and sprays. The crest serves as a ledge beneath which on either side are resting grotesque birds with wings outspread. A swan centres the lower ledge at the base.
H 183 cm (72 in) W 81 cm (32 in)
PARTRIDGE FINE ARTS

The decade immediately preceding 1760 was a period of extraordinary activity with which the name Thomas Chippendale is inextricably associated. There was, and continues to be, a strong propensity to describe any piece of furniture bearing the characteristics of this period as Chippendale, suggesting a production line worthy of Henry Ford. So powerful and pervasive was his influence (through the successive editions of his book *The Gentleman and Cabinet-maker's Director*, 1754, 1755, and 1762) that the expression, 'the Chippendale style', is thought to be a comprehensive term for all the furniture constructed in England in the mid to late 18th century. Modern studies, starting in 1929, but much quickened in the last 20 years, show this to be an untenable position. Now many famous pieces enjoying a generally accepted attribution to Chippendale have been passed over to the cor-

pora of works of cabinetmakers equally deserving. The best example, because it is so memorable a piece of furniture, is the Chinese bed from Badminton in the Victoria and Albert Museum, now ascribed to John Linnell (it had usually been thought, on a balance of probabilities, to be by Chippendale).

The styles

The Director is the highest expression of the rococo taste, often wildly extravagant asymmetrical forms of which Chippendale coolly says, 'I frankly confess, that in executing many of the drawings, my pencil has but faintly copied out those images that my fancy suggested'. Look for 'C' and 'S' scrolls, for beneath the profusion of ornament simple design gives a unifying coherence. Closely connected with the rococo are the separate tastes for the Chinese and the Gothick, the latter drawing its inspiration from the Strawberry

Hill fantasy of Horace Walpole (the pieces are rare) and the former from the occasional remembrance of the Chinese which characterises the history of English furniture from 1660. Then in the 1760s the predictable swing in fashion heralded the neo-classical delights of Robert Adam, which Chippendale for his part meekly accepted with the eye of the born businessman. The French taste also cannot be ignored; the French cabinetmaker, Pierre Langlois, made fine pieces in the continental style, whereas English cabinetmakers assimilated the style rather than imitated it. Most important of all, for the collector, is the permission (rather than the suggestion) that Chippendale gives, for the simplification of ornament 'if thought superfluous', and his furniture for Nostell Priory (1766-1771) for Sir Rowland Winn, are models of that simplicity. The plates for *The Director* frequently

Right and detail below

Fine Chippendale period mahogany stool dated about 1760. What is especially fine about this stool is the quality of the carved legs joined with well-moulded stretchers. The detail shows the good patination of the piece.
H 47 cm (18½ in) w 60 cm (23½ in)
D 44 cm (17½ in)
JOHN KEIL

Below and detail above

A difficult feature to illustrate is the quality of the timber in the finest pieces of mid-18th century furniture. The simplicity of design in this fine bureau bookcase shows the beautiful figure of the mahogany used. This example has affinities with pieces supplied by Chippendale himself to Aske Hall, Paxton Hall and Mersham le Hatch. The cupboard doors enclose sliding trays covered with marbled paper, a feature of Chippendale's case furniture at Nostell Priory.
H 246 cm (97 in) w 124 cm (49 in)
D 63 cm (24¾ in)
HOTSPUR

Right

This small table is attributed to Pierre Langlois and has an unmistakably French quality to it. Langlois anglicised the French style by eschewing the use of marble for tops and similarly the use of gilt metal mounts. The result is a greater use of wood than is characteristic of the French equivalents.
GLAISHER AND NASH

show chairs with one leg fretted and the other severely plain, giving the patron a visual alternative.

The problem of attribution

Even worse than painting: few pieces of English furniture can be safely attributed; the cabinetmakers, particularly those in the *Champs Elysées* of English furniture, St Martin's Lane, rarely signed or stamped their finest productions. Mere congruence to any illustrated design is not conclusive, and documentary evidence has to be peculiarly specific (a mere bill usually is vague in its descriptions). The position is extremely difficult, and the thorough modern studies, while they provide a mass of new information, point to increasing complexity in the future attribution of articles as they come to light.

The makers

Do not expect to see illustrated here the work of all the makers working between 1750 and 1780. The list is very surprisingly extensive. There is a commonly held view that William Vile (d. 1767), maker to the Crown, produced the finest pieces of carved mahogany; indeed it is this writer's view that in the history of English furniture he knew no peer. The jewel cabinet of Queen Charlotte (in the Royal Collection) is a sparkling example of his work. He worked in partnership with William Cobb (d. 1778) whose furniture, which later shows the influence of neo-classicism, was quite as fine as the luxurious dress of this overweening tradesman. Pierre Langlois, a French trained ébéniste, produced essentially French furniture in England, from his Tottenham Court Road premises from about 1760. Recent researches suggest that there is a deal to the name of John Channon (1737-1783) although no authenticated piece exists. At the risk of producing an unwieldy list, the following

Above

Fine Chippendale period serpentine chest with the original swan-neck handles. The corners have blind fretwork panels. The top drawer is fitted with compartments for powders and writing materials including a folding mirror and a writing slide.
H 88 cm (34½ in) W 103 cm (40½ in)
D 53 cm (21 in)
NORMAN ADAMS

Below

Tripod tables can be oppressively ordinary, but this example is of extremely high quality. What is especially fine is the acanthus carving on the knees of the three legs, which terminate in ball-and-claw feet. The gallery top, with small turned balusters, is now most uncommon.
H 75 cm (29½ in)
NORMAN ADAMS

Above

Fine Chippendale period overmantle mirror in gilded beechwood. The oval centre glass is flanked by smaller shaped panels in a rococo framework of scrolling foliage and pierced stalactite decoration.
H 117 cm (46 in) W 130 cm (51 in)
PARTRIDGE FINE ARTS

Left

Mid 18th century giltwood wall table in the Chinese taste with a pierced frieze set with panels containing bell-shaped flowers. The legs have typically Chinese fretwork and terminate in plain feet. The marble slab is later in date. Chippendale describes this type of furniture as a 'Frame for a Marble Slab'.
H 79 cm (31 in) W 80 cm (31½ in)
D 50 cm (19½ in)
PARTRIDGE FINE ARTS

names are thrown into the arena, names uncovered by the researches of the Sir Ambrose Heal and later scholars. Giles Grendy (1693-1780), most of whose work, especially lacquer, is memorable before 1755; the partnership of Bradshaw and Saunders (fl. 1736-1772); the Linnells, whose sketches are in the Victoria and Albert Museum; and George Seddon (1727-1801). Provincial makers of quality are known, especially two Scotsmen, George Sandeman of Perth (1724-1805) and James Cullen. It is safely predicted that discoveries will in future be slow.

Then comes Thomas Chippendale himself (1718-1779), Yorkshire born, who gravitated slowly from Long Acre and the Strand, to *The Sign of the Chair* (now Nos. 60-62) St Martin's Lane, London. There is little doubt he was a great entrepreneur, drawing on existing designs, and certainly on his own considerable inventiveness, who produced furniture always up-to-date, notwithstanding the fluctuations in popular taste. Indeed in his last years he

was wholly at home under the powerful influence of Robert Adam. He was succeeded by his son, Thomas, and the firm continued into the 19th century.

The design books

Foremost is *The Director*, in all its editions closely followed by cabinetmakers and arbiters of taste (in the latter case the list of subscribers is powerful testimony to the extent of his influence). But it may not be the first, chronologically, as studies have shown. The English rococo, which is the French taste subsumed, had been illustrated before in the works of Thomas Johnson and Matthias Lock. (Lock was employed by Chippendale in the illustrations to *The Director*.) Even before Lock, John Vardy produced an illustrated book of the baroque designs of Inigo Jones and William Kent. A comparison of the designs in this book with those in Lock, Johnson and Chippendale, give the student an excellent idea of the gradual change in styles. Another important book of design is that of Ince and Mayhew, *The*

Above

One of a pair of carved giltwood brackets, probably to display busts. An exotic bird, standing on rococo foliage, supports with raised wings the carved shelf. Chippendale period, about 1765.
H 36 cm (14 in) W 25 cm (10 in) D 17 cm (6½ in)
STAIR

Above

Large Chippendale period mahogany partner's desk, with a reading slope set in to the leather top. This is later Chippendale, and is a desk of classic simplicity and restraint. The colour is most attractive.
H 78 cm (31 in) W 201 cm (79 in) D 140 cm (55 in)
JOHN KEIL

Below

Gothic furniture is very scarce and this mahogany hall mirror is in the manner of the Ince and Mayhew. The rectangular plate glass is headed by a panel of blind frets, and is flanked by pierced niches with well carved crockets and spires backed by mirrors.
Dated about 1765.
ASPREY

Left

One of a pair of Chippendale period 'Chinese chairs', with geometrical chair backs in the oriental taste. The legs of these chairs are particularly fine; with four turned columns topped with square capitals inset with carved foliage. The legs terminate in square plinths.
MALLETT

Below

It is known that Chippendale worked at Harewood House in Yorkshire, and it is with some confidence that a pair of stools in mahogany, one of which is illustrated here, are assigned to Thomas Chippendale. They are in his 'French Manner', with moulded serpentine seat rails. The carving is crisp, and of acanthus leaves. The legs terminate in scroll feet. They remained at Harewood until recently, thus an impeccable provenance. L 120 cm (47 in)
ASPREY

Universal System of Household Furniture (1759-1762), the greater part of the plates being by Mathias Darly and were much influenced by Thomas Johnson. From 1760 the study cannot be contemplated without a knowledge of the designs of Robert Adam, but the first publication of his designs did not appear until 1773.

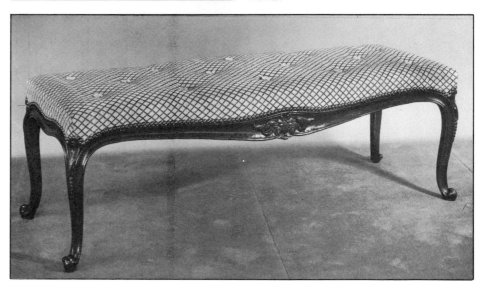

43

Above

One of a pair of 'French Chairs' as Chippendale would describe them. They are in fact for a library and are in the rococo Director manner. The back is pierced and the knees to the cabriole legs are carved with blind ribbon fretwork.
ASPREY

Below

Mid 18th century low chest of drawers of simple proportions standing on bracket feet. It is made of straight-grained mahogany of good colour.
H 75 cm (29½ in) W 104 cm (41 in)
D 75 cm (29½ in)
THE GENERAL TRADING COMPANY

Above

Chippendale arm chair dated about 1760 with finely carved cabriole legs and blind fretted seat rail. The acanthus carving on the arms is very fine.
H 97 cm (38 in) W 66 cm (26 in)
STAIR

Left and detail right

By a continued study of Chippendale's Director, it becomes apparent that this 'Lady's Writing Table and Bookcase' is very much in his manner, and the details indicate the exquisite quality of the carving. The upper stage is breakfront surmounted with carved scrolls and a pierced fret gallery. Below there is pagoda moulding above the three drawers, and the arcaded frieze in the lower stage conceals a fitted writing drawer. The corners to the writing table are concave and the hexagonal legs terminate in block feet. From the collection of the Marquess of Sligo. About 1760.
H 221 cm (87 in) W 124 cm (49 in) D 66 cm (26 in)
ASPREY

Left

One of a set of four Chippendale period mahogany chairs in the Director *manner, although the precise design of the back is not found in the book. The cabriole legs, which terminate in scroll feet are crisply carved with acanthus ornament.*
ASPREY

Below and right

Chair from a set of eight (six chairs, two carvers) of exceptional quality, the model being taken from plate XIII of The Director, *the legs being plain rather than cabriole. Dated about 1755. A great number of chairs look as though they might have come from a design in* The Director, *but they are very scarce that in fact do.*
ASPREY

Below and detail below right

Chippendale period mahogany wing chair of about 1765. A trained eye has to be directed to the wing chair in terms of dating, as it was popular for the greater part of the 18th century. It is the carving of the legs, which is of very fine quality, that points to the date assigned to this example.
H 112 cm (44 in) W 81 cm (32 in) D 72 cm (28½ in)
JOHN KEIL

Where to see the Chippendale style

It is most important to see Chippendale furniture in the setting for which it was intended, either the rococo interiors of the 1750s and 60s or in the neo-classic taste of Adam. These you can expect to see in most of the great English country houses of the mid- to late 18th century. However, as in this chapter, you will find that few are specifically ascribed to Chippendale or his contemporaries. But especially to be recommended are Nostell Priory, Wakefield, Harewood House, Yorkshire, Osterley Park, Middlesex, and Temple Newsam House, Nr. Leeds.

WHERE TO BUY

The furniture illustrated in this article is of a uniformly high quality and is rare. The dealers mentioned are among the principal in the country. To see any large quantity of these pieces in one place, then one of the great museums, or a fair, such as The Grosvenor House Fair, are recommended. If you find that the piece has no provenance, then you will find that the reputation of the dealer to be your best guide.
NORMAN ADAMS LTD, 8-10 Hans Road, London SW3 (01-589 5266)
ASPREY AND COMPANY, 165-9 New Bond Street, London W1 (01-493 6767)
ARTHUR BRETT AND SONS LTD, 42 St Giles' Street, Norwich (0603 28171)
THE GENERAL TRADING COMPANY (MAYFAIR) LTD, 144 Sloane Street, London SW1 (01-730 0411)
GLAISHER AND NASH LTD, Lowndes Lodge, Cadogan Place, London SW1 (01-235 2285)
JOHN KEIL LTD, 154 Brompton Road, London SW3 (01-589 6454)
MALLETT AND SON (ANTIQUES) LTD, 40 New Bond Street, London W1 (01-499 7411)
PARTRIDGE (FINE ARTS) LTD, 144-146 New Bond Street, London W1 (01-629 0834)
SPINK AND SONS LTD, 5-7 King Street, London SW1 (01-930 7880)
STAIR AND COMPANY, 120 Mount Street, London W1 (01-499 1784)
G.S.

SILVER

Silver has been used constantly for ornamental objects and personal adornment since the ancient worlds; the craft of the goldsmith has been highly respected and admired throughout the centuries of its history; and the use of silver table ware has long been an important sign of wealth and social status. For these reasons and more the brilliant white metal has been worked by the most skilful hands, with an artist's attention to form and decoration, to produce some of the finest expressions of the art and craft of each age.

Antique silver represents one of the most esteemed branches of collecting and even while prices rise continually, it is one that has grown enormously in popularity. Apart from those who prefer to choose their silver candlesticks or cutlery from the products of an earlier age, there are always some collectors who wish to gather around them examples of the silversmith's art, and through them to study its history and development.

Now, when the idea of 'collecting' is far removed from the image of the untouchable glass cabinet, many of the new generation of collectors are still drawn to decorative silver.

Over the past few years, the silver market has widened its spheres to cater for this new demand, while continuing to serve more conventional customers. In spite of this encouragement it is always difficult for newcomers to embark on a silver collection, and the four articles in this section aim to give a brief historical outline and some buying confidence for the beginner.

Deciding what to collect

It is important to look at and examine as many different pieces of silver as possible, in antique shops and markets, to get an idea of the range of goods available. Handle the pieces, ask about them and their age and use, and look at condition, decoration and quality of the piercing or chasing. This should help you to identify decorative styles with periods, to distinguish the most sought-after makers or patterns, and also to find friendly, helpful dealers. After a while your collection will probably follow a more definite direction: you might concentrate on a particular object, or collect by year or different assay offices. The article on salts and peppers (page 60) shows you the possibilities of collecting one favourite object, and you could apply the same technique to teaspoons, candlesticks, or photograph frames, depending on your pocket.

The article on Sheffield plate (page 48) approaches the subject from a different and slightly more specialised angle. It suggests a way of collecting superb workmanship and elegant designs through the famous plated wares made in Sheffield from the middle of the 18th century until the invention of electroplate about 100 years later. This offers opportunities for the more modest collector, and introduces the idea of smaller silver items, in the form of the boxes and buckles; the first objects made in Sheffield plate. These tiny but fascinating personal accessories have become very popular with modern collectors, and there is an enormous and amusing variety in 19th and early 20th century small silver: pencils, card cases, pincushions or matchcases, known as vestas. All can be collected for around £50 ($90).

Victorian and Edwardian reproductions of earlier silver (page 52) provide an interesting and relatively inexpensive area of silver collecting, and encourage you not to reject out of hand the idea of reproductions or imitations, as long as they are well made, fine quality pieces in their own right. Your pleasure in collecting will increase with the knowledge you gradually accumulate, as shapes and styles become more familiar, and you are able to identify pieces more accurately.

The study of hallmarks (page 56) is intriguing, but so often its importance is exaggerated. It is far better to concentrate on developing your own instincts and tastes while searching for a new addition to your collection, and in that way valuable information on hallmarks, and makers will be absorbed. All those suspicious buyers who wander around markets clutching their hallmark books are perhaps missing the real pleasure of collecting silver, and certainly nothing can replace the experience of the true collector's eye.

Antique and 'old' silver of some form is sold throughout the country, from specialist shops in London to country bric-à-brac shops, and each has something to offer different kinds of collectors. Beginners who may need a little reassurance of the quality and authenticity of their first purchases should find a helpful and reputable dealer to set them off on the right foot. Your own taste and judgement will be your best guides, but at the crucial moment, remember to look for fine workmanship, distinctive styles and for the best quality and condition you can afford.

PRICES
Sheffield Plate

Although this will never be as expensive as the original silver wares it imitated, its value rises correspondingly. As prices for silver candlesticks become higher, those for Sheffield plate will probably also increase. When a fine set of Sheffield plate candlesticks could be bought for around £500 ($900), prices for silver equivalents were perhaps double, or more. Strong styles, particularly Adam designs, fine workmanship and well-known makers will command highest prices, and early period plate will also be expensive.

A large demand for conventional items such as salvers, trays, entrée dishes keeps their prices high, while some of the smaller objects can be found around the £50 ($90) mark, like the wine funnel (page 49) or jug and mustard pot. More unusual and real collectors' items such as the nutmeg grater case (page 49) will always be more expensive and prices for these vary enormously, according to the amount the dealer had to give for them and the amount a particular collector is willing to pay for them.

Victorian and Edwardian reproductions
Prices should be reasonable for the quality of work they represent, which can only be judged by experience and close examination. The silver gilt teaspoons (page 53) celebrating George V's accession, small peppers and seal top spoons might well be under or around £100 ($180). Superb pieces, involving a great deal of skill, that recall the work of silversmiths like Paul de Lamerie are the highest in price, as well as those executed by well-known names such as Charles Fox, D. & J. Wellby and Garrard. Early and rare reproductions like the early 19th century pair of silver gilt salts (page 53) are always amongst the most expensive. A large amount of silver used in the making of objects, raises the cost, so that punchbowls and salvers are always expensive items, but even the grandest of objects can be bought in an Edwardian reproduction for the price of a small but original early piece, like a salt.

Salts and Peppers
Collecting an object in this way means that there is a wide choice of dates, as well as both standard and special patterns, and therefore a large range of prices. Generally, salts are more expensive than peppers: for example, the urn-shaped castors (page 61) by a good maker and from the best period are relatively low in price, compared to salts of the same quality. Mid 19th century salts like those made by Robert Hennell III (page 62) are some of the least expensive illustrated, at prices around £200 ($360). Early 18th century individual salts made

by leading silversmiths will always rise in value and prices could start from £400 ($720) upwards. Some of the more standard patterns, many early 19th century, oval or boat-shaped, might be lower in price, such as the pair by David Hennell I, or the tub-shaped salt of 1804 (page 61). 19th century novelties like the champagne cork or gothic towers (page 63) are around the £100-£150 ($180-270) price range, but again this could be the area for the cheaper purchases. The most expensive salts illustrated (page 62) are the impressive examples of Paul Storr's work, at prices of £1500 ($2700) upwards, when the customer is paying for the very best in quality, design and workmanship.

VIVIENNE BECKER

Old Sheffield Plate

Above
Since Sheffield plating was intended as a substitute for silver, it was wholly in imitation of current silver designs that the first plated wares were made. This tapering cylindrical tankard and cover, made about 1760, has a high domed cover, spreading foot, moulded rib round the body and – a rococo touch – a shell at the junction of the handle socket. Note the marks of the maker, Henry Tudor of Sheffield, struck four times in imitation of hallmarks.
C. J. VANDER LTD

Fused rolled plate was first discovered by a Sheffield haft-maker, Thomas Bolsover, about 1743. He found that a layer of sterling silver could most effectively be fused to a layer of copper by rolling the two together, and from this new 'metal' he made buttons, which he sold at a good profit around a guinea a dozen. He was soon followed by other smallworkers making boxes, buckles and other smallwares, and by 1752 his neighbour Joseph Hancock began to produce the first Sheffield plated wares for domestic use.

It is really no exaggeration to say that the finest Sheffield Plate rivals silver in its design and craftsmanship. It has, of course, the great advantage over its later rival, electroplated ware, which finally extinguished the industry, that the covering layer is of sterling silver, and not the harsher more highly polished pure silver that is deposited thinly on plated wares. The colour of the sterling alloy applied, at first in particular, fairly thickly on the copper core, is of the same fine lustre as silver, and in the best work it is almost indistinguishable from silver – indeed, when it was first made, detection must have been even more difficult, for the parts most susceptible to wear which today may show 'bleeding' (as the uncovering of the core is known) were still in fine condition, and the high standard of tooling gave the substitute Sheffield Plate a very creditable appearance. Even today it is not always easy to detect that a well-preserved piece, especially a finely pierced example, is not silver but its imitator.

Imitation marks at first also helped to deceive the unwary, but by 1784 rules were laid down that Sheffield Platers were to use their full names, with a symbol, which had to be registered at the Sheffield Assay Office. This was the year, too, of a duty once again being laid on silver, so that the platers were much at an advantage.

The early period plate, which lasted until about 1790, saw many advances. The first, about 1763, was the invention of double-plating, which meant that both sides of an article could be covered with the layer of sterling silver – especially advantageous for trays, salvers, chamber candlesticks and the like. Then about 1785

came the introduction of silver edges so that the joint between the silver and copper was concealed, followed within a year or two by the filled mounts, using tin and lead to give body to the hollow stampings used for edge wires. An early and very important development was plated wire – the two metals actually being drawn together so that all sorts of baskets, cruet frames and so on could be made by the platers. Another important advance was the method of piercing, using a fly-press to squeeze the edges of the metal over to hide the raw edges, enabling the manufacturers to make some exceptionally fine baskets, fish slices, strainers and salts, all in the latest London silver styles.

From about 1790 onwards, the Sheffield Plating trade was at its zenith. Huge quantities were sold both at home and abroad. Few examples were, however, marked, and much plate can only be dated by its style – usually, fortunately, fairly obvious because of its adherence to silver fashions. There are many examples, however, that have been re-plated by electrolysis, ruining their inherent quality, and there are also a number of fakes in circulation: mostly detectable because of their poor workmanship. The Sheffield platers were noted for the high quality of the die-stamping, the silver shields which were rubbed-in during the fusing process ready for engraved armorials, and for the excellent finish of their goods. Reproductions rarely show any of these qualities.

During the early 1800s, Sheffield Plate maintained a nice balance between simplicity and ornament, relying largely on superbly stamped mounts for ornament. Gradually more elaborate patterns appeared, as tastes in the 1820s veered towards a rococo revival. However, so much ornament meant that there was some tendency for the copper core to show through, especially as the silver layer was sometimes rather lighter than it had been in the early days. White alloys such as those containing nickel began to replace the copper as the base metal about 1830/1835, but within a decade the end of the era of fine Sheffield plating came with the invention of plating by electrolysis.
J.B.

Above
The earliest Sheffield Plate salver was made by the inventor of the process, Thomas Bolsover, for his daughter Mary on the occasion of her marriage to Joseph Mitchell in 1760. A year or two later, the process of double-plating gave a fillip to the salver makers, for it meant that the undersides could be made to look as though they were silver throughout, instead of being tinned and polished. The mounts, however, were still hollow stampings, as in this fine 13-inch waiter with a shell and shaped gadroon rim made about 1765.
H. OLIVER & CO LTD

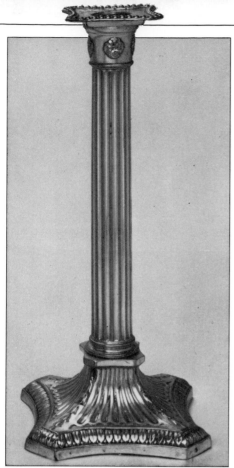

Left

In many ways it must have been galling to the Birmingham industrialist Matthew Boulton to have his plated wares called after the city to the north, but whether that was true or not, the Soho Works produced some of the best fused plate to designs that were often inspired by Boulton's friend and collaborator, Robert Adam. Here typical Adamesque themes – fluting and paterae, formal foliage borders and husk details – are interpreted by the Soho platers for a pair of 27 cm (10¾ in) candlesticks made about 1775.
HARVEY & GORE LTD

Below

Wine strainers or funnels were indispensable to the connoisseur of fine wines, for wine from the cellar needed decanting for the table. Funnels made in Sheffield Plate followed silver styles in general, though this example of about 1810 has an unusual ribbed strengthening section applied down the spout, and also features finely applied and chased foliage motifs round the reeded rim.
SIMON KAYE LTD

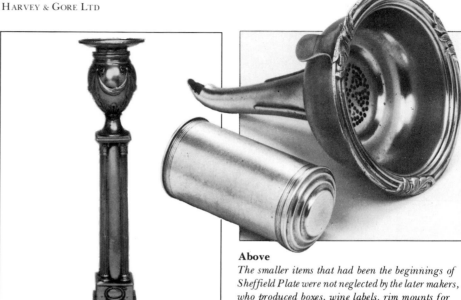

Above

The smaller items that had been the beginnings of Sheffield Plate were not neglected by the later makers, who produced boxes, wine labels, rim mounts for pottery, extinguishers, snuffers and other wares. An unusual and rare survival is this Sheffield plated cylindrical nutmeg grater case with circular grater inside, and thread edge decoration below the stepped cover. It dates from about 1790.
SIMON KAYE LTD

Above

London influences on Sheffield Plate even extended to the manufacturers' taking up designs by the leading artists of the day, among them John Flaxman, who designed – or at least, inspired – this square-based candlestick from a pair perhaps made by John Winter & Co, a leading firm of Sheffield candlestick specialists, about 1779. The 29 cm (11½ in) candlesticks are also very unusual in being fire-gilt, while the detail of the shell and spray designs on the pedestal, the coiled snake, pilaster stems and festooned urn sockets are indicative of the superb craftsmanship of the Sheffield die-sinkers and stampers.
HARVEY & GORE LTD

Below

The Sheffield Plate manufacturers must to some extent have been relieved when tastes veered away from the expensively decorated rococo styles to the more formal ovals of the 1780s. This oval tea caddy, 11.5 cm wide, 8.75 cm high (4½ × 3⅜ in), is decorated with bright-cut engraving, with narrow borders in the manner of contemporary silver, but with perhaps rather more flamboyance in the style of the foliage calyx on the cover and the wreath and ribbon motifs around the vacant cartouche – its lack of armorials perhaps indicating a landless owner, though even so one might have expected initials or a monogram, for the layer of plate was still thick enough to take them, as the bright-cut engraving itself shows.
S. J. SHRUBSOLE LTD

Left

Sheffield-made candlesticks in both silver and plate were often struck from the same dies, and are usually of very distinctive styles, quite unlike the cast 'sticks made in silver in London and elsewhere. The earliest Sheffield Plate examples owe much, however, to the London silver designs, as this fine 12-inch example from a set of four made in about 1765. The heavily gadrooned base and boldly modelled Corinthian capital nicely balance the spiral and flower-engraved stem – detail that is clearly not of London origin.
HARVEY & GORE LTD

Above

The imposition of a new duty on sterling silver in 1784 greatly increased the demand for the untaxed Sheffield Plate, and during the 1780s and 1790s the range of plated wares was considerably expanded, and families who might buy, say, a silver teapot and salver would perhaps have larger items such as wine coolers or candelabra in plate. Indeed, the same arms, of the Scottish family of Cunningham, have been noted on a silver salver of 1786 as on this pair of tub-shaped wine coolers, made about the same date but of Sheffield Plate, with gadrooned rims and attractive scroll and shell filled handles.

THOMAS LUMLEY LTD

Detail and below

The tremendous amount of work that went into this large Sheffield Plate tea tray can hardly have been economical even about 1820, though at that time the price of silver had risen and the duty stood at about 1/6 an ounce. The cost of the rich gadroon, shell and foliage borders, the turned ivory handles and the intricate and detailed flat-chased border must, even with plentiful labour, have been quite costly. The tray is 86 cm long by 61 cm wide (34 × 24 in), and has a let-in silver shield engraved with a rococo cartouche for armorials that have never been engraved.

S. J. SHRUBSOLE LTD

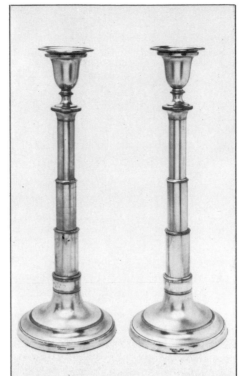

Above

By the end of the 18th century, tea was a far more popular drink than coffee, and most coffee-pots simply formed parts of larger tea and coffee services, or took the form of the percolator or biggin, sometimes on a spirit lamp stand. Occasionally, however, coffee-pots in Sheffield Plate were made exactly in the manner of contemporary silver ones, often of very heavy quality plate. This tall vase-shaped example, made about 1795, with fine heavy gadrooned mounts, shows the gauge of the silver 'skin' fused on to the copper base by extensive use of engraving simulating fluting and for the cartouche for the crest. It stands 28 cm (11 in) high.

HANCOCK & CO

Left

The Sheffield Plate manufacturers were nothing if not inventive, and the Telescopic Candlestick was a product of many firms, each making its own patented versions, and proudly announcing its name on the 'sticks: an invaluable guide to dating. Some were raised by a twist-action, others by a sliding device. This pair, made by A. Goodman & Co who registered their mark in 1800, rise by three extensions to a total height of 40 cm (15¾ in).

S. J. SHRUBSOLE LTD

Above

Fine example of a boat-shaped cake basket of about 1790, with the borders of the chased flutes picked out with bright-cut scallops and wrigglework and thread-edge swing handle with an applied disc for the owner's initials on the top. 35.5 cm (14 in) long.

H. OLIVER & CO LTD

Above

All the ingredients of the designer of bright-cut silver but perhaps a little clumsily interpreted for a milk or cream jug on four ball feet – an early 19th century example unusual in having a broad band of engraved rather than chased ornament. The mustard pot on four paw feet, with egg-and-tongue mount is representative of some of the last examples of Sheffield Plate before the whole trade was overtaken by the new process of electro-plating invented by Elkington in 1840 and fully productive on a commercial scale by the late 1850s.

HANCOCKS

Below

An unusual and practical shape for the argyle – in the form of a covered sauceboat with short spout and wooden handle. The aperture through which the hot water is poured into the outer jacket is hinged on the handle side of the cover. The crest is on an applied silver disc. With reeded rim and a matching border of reeded on the oval foot, the argyle was made about 1800.
WILLIAM WALTER

Above

Gadrooned borders were particularly effective on old Sheffield Plate, as this fine entrée dish and covers show: simple yet dignified with just a touch of Regency grandeur about the elaborate foliage handles. They date from about 1815.
OLIVER & SONS

Left

Despite Frederick Bradbury's note that Sheffield-plated argyles, or jacketed vessels for keeping the gravy hot, are difficult to repair, it seems that almost as many have survived in Sheffield Plate as in silver, and certainly their variety of designs is most appealing. The neoclassical vase-shape was a favourite one, on a high foot to keep the hot jacketed section away from the table-top. This example, with its hinged cover over the jacket aperture to the side of the wood handle, has a sensibly broader spout than usual. A band of bright-cut engraving at the shoulder and the applied shield for the armorials are typical of its date, about 1790.
WILLIAM WALTER

Where to Buy

HANCOCKS & CO LTD, 1 Burlington Gardens, London W1 (01-493 8904)
HARVEY & GORE, 4 Burlington Gardens, London W1 (01-493 2714)
SIMON KAYE LTD, 1½ Albemarle Street, London W1 (01-493 7658)
S. J. SHRUBSOLE LTD, 43 Museum Street, London WC1 (01-405 2712)
WILLIAM WALTER, London Silver Vaults, 53-63 Chancery Lane, London WC2 (01-242 3248)

Right

Since every member of the household needed a chamber candlestick, there was a ready sale for those in the less expensive Sheffield Plate – but of course, as with most other wares, in styles that closely followed those of the silversmith, and since Sheffield was renowned for candlesticks many were made there. This example, from a pair of about 1815, shows the gradually increasing use of shell, scroll and foliage ornament, while even the conical extinguisher has a shelly mount at the hook and a flame finial. The space in the centre of the stem is for the snuffers.
OLIVER & SONS

Left

In the grand vein, but still relatively plain, one of a pair of vase-shaped wine coolers with half-fluted bodies, the foliate border to the rim echoing the decorative side handles.
C. J. VANDER LTD

Below

A neat and attractive decanter trolley of about 1810 with a pair of trays for small-size decanters – note the small stopper rings – has nicely finished paterae terminals on the wheels and a turned ivory handle.
SIMON KAYE LTD

Below

A fine example of how the practical and the decorative could be combined: a breakfast dish and cover with a simple gadrooned rim on a burner and stand with rococo-revival scroll and foliage feet. Made about 1820, the armorials are engraved on a silver shield that has been 'rubbed into' the silver layer of the plate so that there is no fear of the copper core being revealed by the graving tool.
C. J. VANDER LTD

Victorian and Edwardian Reproduction Silver

While every age of art has developed from and borrowed from its predecessors, the conscious reproduction of earlier silver designs was rare before the early 19th century. Then the leading copyists of original earlier silver were Robert Garrard, successor to the long-established firm founded by George Wickes, and their competitors in the City, Rundell, Bridge & Rundell. Garrard's were perhaps most noted for their replicas of pieces by Paul de Lamerie and of the firm's own predecessor Edward Wakelin, but many of these early to mid-19th century reproductions were rather cold imitations.

By the end of the century the ever-changing enthusiasms of the Victorians for a succession of styles, old, new and intermingled, finally found a new expression in the Paris-born Art Nouveau. It was not, however, to everyone's taste, and while most collectors searched the antique shops for Tudor and early Stuart treasures, others began to collect late 17th and early 18th century domestic silver. Those who could not afford or chose not to collect old silver often preferred new silver made to the old patterns, and so the still very much alive fashion for reproduction silver swept in. Besides the reproductions of earlier silver, much of it English silver rather than of 15th and 16th century Continental treasures, the Royal occasions of the period encouraged the production of replicas. Queen Victoria's two great Jubilees, the accession of Edward VII and then of George V, and the latter's Silver Jubilee in 1935, were all celebrated with silver, and many manufacturers chose suitably grand antiques to commemorate the occasions: a custom that lives on.

Though patently copies, the great attraction of Victorian and Edwardian replicas and reproductions is their superb quality. Not only is the gauge of silver heavy and the making of the pieces generally excellent, but the attention to the detail of decoration – applied work, flat chasing, engraving and piercing – is almost infallibly good: though many of the best decorative skills were later to be lost by the inter-war years.

Many of the makers and sponsors of these replicas and reproductions were the leading antique silver dealers of the day –

some of them still in business, such as A. & E. Parsons of Tessiers, R. & S. Garrard, Spink & Son, D. & J. Wellby, Crichton Bros. and, out of London, firms such as Hamilton & Inches of Edinburgh, Edward and Son of Glasgow, Payne & Sons of Oxford, Reid & Sons of Newcastle, and many others. Often it was the retailer's mark that was struck, though in fact, as now, many of the pieces must have been the work of the specialist manufacturers such as Wakely & Wheeler, Comyns & Sons, H. & A. Vander and so on. Again and again, the actual originals can be found – no doubt because the years from about 1895 to 1914 saw the dispersal of many fine silver collections in the salerooms. The silversmiths were quick to reproduce the best that came their way and cater for the new interest, much promoted by the new textbooks, such as Sir Charles Jackson's monumental *History of English Plate*, in the collection of the best of English and other antique silver.   J.B.

Where to Buy

J. H. BOURDON-SMITH LTD, 26a Conduit Street, London W1 (01-629 0434)
GARRARD & CO LTD, 112 Regent Street, London W1 (01-734 7020)
HANCOCKS & CO LTD, 1 Burlington Gardens, London W1 (01-493 8904)
SIMON KAYE LTD, 1½ Albemarle Street, London W1 (01-493 7658)
THOMAS LUMLEY LTD, Standbrook House, 2-5 Old Bond Street, London W1 (01-629 2493)
M. MCALEER, 1a St Christopher's Place, London W1 (01-486 1171)
PARKHOUSE ANTIQUES, 45 Jewry Street, Winchester (0962 67276)
TESSIERS LTD, 26 New Bond Street, London W1 (01-629 0458)
WILLIAM WALTER, London Silver Vaults, 53-63 Chancery Lane, London WC2 (01-242 3248)

Above
In recent times, the first great occasion for silver replicas was the Golden Jubilee of Queen Victoria in 1887. The Mercers' Company, the foremost in precedence and one of the wealthiest Livery Companies of the City of London had replicas made of the pair of silver-gilt standing cups that had been given them in the 17th century by the Bank of England in return to their having been allowed to hold their first meeting at Mercers' Hall. The replicas vary slightly from the originals in bearing only the Arms of the Company in a wreath in a reserve on the matted sides, and some have the presentation inscription on the reverse, others on the base. The cups, all engraved 'The Gift of the Mercers' Company to Commemorate the Jubilee of Queen Victoria, 1887' were presented to the Liverymen of the Company. Each weighs between 17 oz and 18 oz. This is one of a pair and is silver-gilt.
HANCOCKS

Right
Edward VII's Coronation also brought a spate of reproduction silver to celebrate the occasion. This salt is a replica of one of the pair given to the Innholders' Company, engraved 'This Salt is the Gifte of John Waterworth 1626'. The replica is further engraved 'Edward VII, 1902' around the rim, and in size approximate to the original. It was one of several made in 1901/1902 by Elkington & Co. of Birmingham, who also marked many of their wares in London.
J. H. BOURDON-SMITH LTD

Below:

The Jubilee of King George V and Queen Mary in 1935 was another occasion for celebration with silver, as will The Queen's Silver Jubilee be in 1977. This small cup, 4¼ in high and 4½ in in diameter, weighing 10 oz, is an exact copy of the Holms Cup of 1521, formerly in the Dunn-Gardner Collection. With a Latin inscription on a hatched ground around the lip, and with a scale design chased on the bowl, the cup is typical of pre-Renaissance standing cups of the late Gothic period. The replica, made by S. Blankensee of Birmingham in 1936, was sent for assay and hallmarking to Chester, an office that was finally closed in 1962.
HANCOCKS

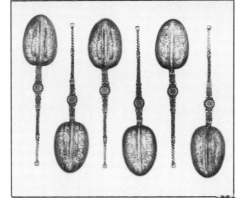

Left and detail below

Another Royal reason for silver replicas was the Accession of King George V in 1910, and his Coronation the following year. The historic Anointing Spoon of the sovereigns of England appealed to the public then as at other Coronations since, and the pattern was adapted in miniature for sets of teaspoons. This set of six silver-gilt spoons was made in 1911 by the London firm of Wakely & Wheeler.
M. MCALEER

Above

The early years of the 20th century were notable for some of the finest collections of early domestic silver, and for those who did not like the decorated styles of late Victorian silver or the new craze for 'art nouveau' reproductions of the plain and elegant designs of the early 18th century were welcome. This pair of small peppers, their vase-shaped octagonal bodies based on casters of about 1715/1720, were made by Barnard & Co of London in 1907.
M. MCALEER

Above

For Irish collectors, the dish rings of the 18th century were a favourite subject, and the Dublin silversmiths West & Son, whose business was founded in the 18th century, produced numbers of replicas of original early rings at the turn of the 19th/20th centuries. This example, typical of Irish pierced rings of about 1755/1760 was made in 1897. 6½ in in diameter, smaller than average, and 3 in high, it weighs 9 oz.
M. MCALEER

Left and below

Also harking back to the early 18th century, this reproduction tea service set a style for tea-table elegance that continues today. Bearing the mark of Crichton Brothers, who were for many years leading antique silver dealers in London, it was no doubt reproduced from authentic originals of about 1710 to 1730 – a period when in fact matched services were almost unknown. Made in 1908, this four-piece service weighs in all 28 oz. The engraved decoration on the teapot suggests a date about 1730, while the cream ewer and basin follow the old style of initialling silver, with the surname below the initials of the Christian names of the owners.
PARKHOUSE ANTIQUES

Above

An early example of reproduction silver – one of a pair of silver-gilt salts in mid-18th century taste with corded rims and bellied bodies, on three hoof feet, 2½ in in diameter. They date from 1827 and were made by Charles Fox, one of the finest makers of the period.
T. LUMLEY LTD

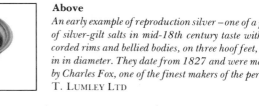

Above

In the same year, 1911, the Lincoln retail jewellers, J. Usher & Son, had replicas of seal-top spoons made in Sheffield. Struck in the bowl with a fleur-de-lys within a double circle of pellets, a mark at that time associated with old Lincoln silver, the set bear the firm's mark and the Sheffield marks for 1911 on the reverse of the stems.
M. MCALEER

Above

Lamerie-inspired again, a beautiful pair of silver butter shells or 'scallops for oysters' as they were known in the mid-18th century. Each on three cast dolphin feet, and with flying scroll handles enriched with scrolls, shells, flowers and intertwined serpents' tails, the dishes measure 5½ in across and weigh together 20 oz. Made by J. E. Gillot & Son, they were assayed and marked in Birmingham in 1920 and 1921 respectively.
SIMON KAYE

Left

This copy of a William & Mary period porringer of about 1690/1700 was perhaps based on an original made after 1696, as the makers, Lambert & Co, have chosen to use the higher Britannia standard of silver for their reproduction of 1891. The porringer is of large size, 9½ in high overall, 6 in high to the rim, and weighs no less than 39 oz. The arms appear to be those of Stevenson.
SIMON KAYE LTD

Above

A subject for a replica that caught the imagination of Lambert & Co of London was the Bacon Cup, one of three made from the Great Seal of Mary I and Philip of Spain in 1573. The three were bequeathed to the three houses of Sir Nicholas Bacon – to Redgrave, bequeathed to the British Museum in 1915, to Gorhambury, which passed to Lord Verulam, and Stewkey, which was one of the Townsend heirlooms and was sold by the family at Christie's in 1904, and from which Henry Lambert made the copy. This example, 11¼ in high and weighing 43 oz 3 dwt – slightly more than the original – was made in 1907 and engraved with an inscription recording its origin.
J. H. BOURDON-SMITH LTD

Below right and detail

The reproduction silver of the Edwardian period was usually very well made and mostly accurately copied original antiques. This porringer and cover in the style of about 1675/1685 closely follows the flat-chased chinoiseries of the period, and the chaser was almost certainly copying an original. Made by D. & J. Wellby in 1908, it was a pattern that the firm continued to make from time to time during the next four or five years. This example, weighs 24 oz. GARRARD & CO

Right

There is absolutely no doubt that H. & A. Vander had before them a footed salver of 1685 when they made this replica in 1909. Every detail of the finely chased chinoiseries is identical to that of a 12¼ in wide footed period salver sold at Christie's in 1971, and even the weight of the copy, 26 oz 16 dwt is the same as the original.
GARRARD & CO

Left

Lamerie is known for the originator of sugar bowl and cover, of which A. & E. Parsons, of the firm of Tessiers, made this superb heavy replica in 1910. Cast and chased strapwork of exceptional quality is applied to the hemispherical bowl and cover, which has a rim foot, presumably so that it could be inverted for use as a spoon-tray. The Edwardian replica weighs 15 oz.
TESSIERS LTD

Below

The antiquarian interests of the collectors of the second half of the 19th century inspired numerous pieces 'in the Renaissance manner'. In Europe, the goldsmiths of Vienna were leading exponents of this taste, and it was probably there that an unknown craftsman produced this set of six silver-gilt spoons. Note the Tudor-style dress of the terminal figures.
M. MCALEER

Above

Mappin & Webb's reproduction of an antique punch bowl dates from 1909 and shows a typical adaptation of the original. The bowl, which can be compared with an almost identical plain bowl of 1716 by Edmund Pearce, is, however, much smaller, measuring only some 8 ½ in across. The rim is fixed, not detachable as in most early punch bowls, and the definition of the lion mask and ring handles is less free than the original. However the bowl is of good weight, 22 oz 10 dwt, and of heavy gauge silver.
GARRARD & CO

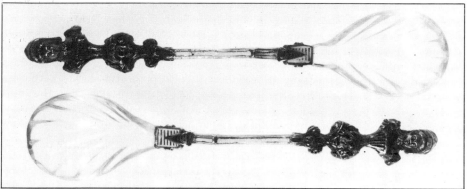

Below

In Dublin, West & Son continued the tradition of making fine reproductions of Irish silver, and in 1911 produced this swirl-fluted sugar bowl with a shaped and beaded rim. Note the particularly fine lion mask knuckles and paw feet. 4¾ in in diameter, it weighs 3 oz.
SIMON KAYE LTD

Left

The name and fame of Paul de Lamerie remained undiminished throughout the 19th century, and by Edwardian times the makers of fine reproduction silver were eager to find the best of his work to copy. Though a precedent for this silver-gilt ewer has not been identified, the style of the cast caryatid handle and the applied scrollwork cartouches and musical trophies round the top of the body and the finely cast and chased mask below the lip suggest an original by Lamerie or one of his able contemporaries, dating from about 1745. Weighing 13 oz this fine piece has been classified as a work of art.
TESSIERS LTD

Right

Today, many fine replicas of early silver are chosen for prizes and presentation pieces – cups, rosebowls, porringers and many other reproduction silverwares find their way to presentation ceremonies. In 1914, this version of a Charles II period porringer and cover made its appearance at the Chelsea Show, and is engraved with the badge of the Royal Horticultural Society. The formality of the detail of the foliate chasing perhaps betrays its actual date, but the quality of the cup is very fine, and it weighs no less than 33 oz for its overall height of 7 ½ in to the top of the acanthus bud finial. It is silver-gilt, and was stamped with the maker's name and address, Johnson, Walker & Tolhurst, 80 Aldersgate Street, London, as well as the London hallmarks for 1913.
WILLIAM WALTER

Hallmarking on Silver

1977 was a remarkable year in the long history of hallmarking in Britain: one of those rare years when a special additional mark was struck on all British-made silver over 15 g. in weight – Her Majesty's head in profile, after a design by the distinguished silversmith Leslie Durbin, C.B.E., was used throughout the year to celebrate her Silver Jubilee. It was also the 650th anniversary of the incorporation of the Guild of London Goldsmiths by Royal Charter, which made the Wardens and Commonalty of the Mystery of Goldsmiths in the City of London responsible for the proper conduct of the assay, or testing, of precious metals, with various privileges that were balanced against those duties which gave them jurisdiction throughout the realm.

In 1300 the 'gardiens' of the craft were ordered to assay every piece of gold or silver before it left the hands of the workmen and to mark it with the leopard's head. Until 1363 this appears to have been the only essential mark, though even before it was made obligatory in that year, most goldsmiths probably applied their own maker's or workshop mark, if only so that the Wardens could trace the makers of substandard wares.

The standards of silver

Since very early times goldsmiths (the term was until recently equally applicable to craftsmen in both gold and silver) recognised the need to harden the pure metal by alloying it with another, most commonly copper. In different countries, different standards of alloy have applied, most approximating more or less to the 92.5 per cent sterling standard, which was accepted in Britain as early as Anglo-Saxon times when the moneyers found it a durable alloy for the coinage. And since both coinage and silverwares were basically regarded as bullion, the use of the same standard for money and silverwares was convenient, and by 1238 it was laid down as the minimum acceptable standard of fineness in England. Elsewhere, however, there were variant standards – in Scotland, for instance, even after the Act of Union in 1706, goldsmiths were using silver only 91.66 per cent pure, and continued to do so until 1720, while in Paris, the standard from 1554 onwards was 95.8 per cent, with many variants in the provinces, while in many countries very much lower grades are still permitted, down to 83.5 per cent and even 80 per cent.

The date letter

During the 15th century, the Keeper of the Touch at London's Goldsmiths' Hall and his fellow wardens devised that beautifully simple and, for the collector, incidentally, so invaluable system of year marks. Using consecutive letters of the alphabet, changed annually on May 19, the day of the goldsmiths' patron saint St Dunstan, the letter was struck alongside the leopard's head crowned and the maker's mark. Possibly instituted before 1478, by then it was fully established, and the 20-year cycles have been unbroken since then with the exceptions of 1696/7 and 1975 (see below). The style of the letter and the stamp within which it is contained are changed from cycle to cycle, so that the year of manufacture can immediately be identified – a system that was, again with many variations, adopted in Scotland, Ireland, France, the Netherlands, and Sweden.

The lion passant

The maker's mark and the two guaranteeing hallmarks applied by the wardens at Goldsmiths' Hall, which gave the system

its name, sufficed until 1544, during the reign of Henry VIII. The King, faced with dire economic troubles even after dissolving the monasteries and filling his treasury with their riches, had debased the currency. The goldsmiths, adhering to their ancient customs and the statutes laid down during the previous 200 years, continued to ensure that silver for church and home was still of the sterling standard. They continued to use the leopard's head crowned, which was sometimes known as the King's mark, but added another – a lion passant (walking to the left, with a paw raised) and gardant (in the same position but looking over its shoulder). This is thought to be the Company's stamp of authority, and ever since has, in England, represented the sterling standard mark, while the leopard's head crowned has, by transference, become the place mark of London. The leopard's head was also used in several of the provincial assay offices of England – at Chester, York, Newcastle, Exeter and Bristol – and, in smaller provincial centres, often in a debased form, by local silversmiths presumably to suggest that they were under the jurisdiction of the London Company.

The Britannia Standard

The return of the Court of Charles II from exile coincided with a national – or at least a metropolitan – taste for show, a revulsion against the stricter puritan ideas that had been foisted on many during the Commonwealth. Merchants grew rich, and so did the goldsmiths, though not a few were ruined by the closing of the Exchequer in 1672. Bullion soon became in short supply, and so extensive was the practice of melting down and 'clipping' the coinage that William III in 1696 passed 'An Act for encouraging the bringing in of wrought plate to be coined'. One of its conditions was the raising of the standard for wrought plate to 95.8 per cent pure (equivalent to the Paris standard). Sterling was abolished, and new marks instituted to indicate the higher standard – a lion's head erased (i.e. represented with a jagged edge) and 'the figure of a woman commonly called Britannia'. A new series of date letters was started in March 1697 – the first therefore only in use for a mere three months until the end of May. Since the date letter had been changed on 29 May, in celebration of the Restoration of Charles II. Makers were also commanded to re-register their marks in a new form – the first two initials of their surname, instead of the former style of initials of forename and surname, a single initial, a monogram or other device.

Parliament in London, then as now, often tended to overlook the provinces, and it was not until 1700 that the anomalous position of Chester, York, Exeter and Norwich was recognised and the new standard marks introduced there, while Newcastle was ignored until 1701. New cycles of date letters were instituted, of varying lengths and the local offices, other than Norwich which was almost defunct even in 1700, continued well into the 19th century, while Chester, which had become an overflow office for Midlands makers and importers, survived until 1962.

Since the Britannia silver cost more than sterling, the silversmiths soon began to clamour for a return to the old standard, though a few, especially those with a thriving export business and some of the French-trained craftsmen used to the Paris standard, counter-petitioned for its retention. On 1 June 1720, both had their way. The old sterling was restored, with a sting in the tail of a duty of 6d. an ounce on wrought plate, while those who preferred it could still work in the Better Nine, and have it marked with the lion's head erased and the figure of Britannia instead of the leopard's head crowned and the lion passant.

The Duty Mark

The 6d. an ounce duty was equally unpopular with both silversmiths and patrons, and from 1720 onwards even otherwise highly reputable craftsmen were not immune to the temptation of 'duty-dodging'. Rather than pay out on, say, an 80-ounce cup and cover, the silversmith would use a small, properly assayed piece of silver and insert it in his new work, avoiding payment of duty and with no one any the wiser. These duty-dodgers have caused considerable trouble for modern collectors, as their sale is officially illegal unless they are re-submitted for assay and marking – a factor that for many mars their original appeal. It must be noted, however, that many of them are of fine intrinsic quality and, apart from their improper marks, do not usually break the standard laws.

In 1758, the abolition of duty rectified the situation, for the government recognised that they were getting very little duty paid in, although patently the trade was flourishing. Instead, they instituted a £2 plate licence and made the counterfeiting of hallmarks a felony, punishable by death.

When, a quarter of a century later, the question of duty was raised again, the authorities avoided the 1720 trap and recorded that duty had been paid at the time of assay by instituting the sovereign's head duty mark. At first, from 1 December 1784 to May 1786, the head of George III was shown incuse (hammered or stamped in), after that it was in cameo (raised, in relief). The profiles of George III, George IV and William IV all face to the right, that of Queen Victoria to the left. The duty mark was also struck at all the provincial offices, which from 1773 included the new ones at Sheffield and Birmingham, though it did not appear in Dublin until 1807 and in Glasgow, on its official revival, in 1819. Not all the offices changed the punch used immediately on the accession of the new sovereign, and William IV's head appears on quantities of Victorian silver marked in York, Chester, Edinburgh, Glasgow, Newcastle and Sheffield as late as 1840/1841.

In 1797, the King's Head mark is sometimes found struck twice, to indicate that the duty had been doubled. This practice was shortlived, however, and the official punch, which was not cut by the Asssay Offices themselves but supplied by the Government, was struck in association with the other marks just once, although the rates of duty varied from time to time, reaching 1s. 6d. an ounce in 1815.

The town marks of England, Scotland and Ireland

Originally, Edward I's ordinance of 1300 that laid down the standard of fineness for silver and gold had specified that 'in all good towns of England where there are goldsmiths . . . one shall go . . . to London to seek their sure touch'. Though under the overall jurisdiction of the London goldsmiths, each town tended to use a locally significant mark or, in small places, the local goldsmiths seem to have agreed to use a 'standard' mark. Later statutes referred to specific towns as 'assay towns' to which, presumably, goldsmiths from the surrounding areas could take their work for assay and marking rather than send it on the hazardous and lengthy journey to London.

The marks used in the minor towns of England, Scotland and Ireland have proved tantalising and stimulating subjects for research, and every year more and more detail is uncovered of the men who made and marked their wares in the towns from Truro to Aberdeen, and Inverness to Bury St Edmunds.

The larger centres, while still leaving much room for further research, are less problematical, and readily available tables can be consulted for Chester, Dublin, Edinburgh, Glasgow, Exeter, Birmingham, Sheffield, York, Newcastle and

Norwich. Each had or has its own distinctive mark, used in association with the standard mark, the date letter and in some cases the leopard's head crowned as well.

Outside Britain

In the past, many European countries and states used systems of hallmarking, often jealously guarded by the goldsmiths' guilds. In France, for instance, every town came under strict jurisdiction and, despite the complications of wars and conquests, many other countries were able to maintain their own hallmarking systems, usually on a local municipal basis. By the early years of the 19th century, the sweeping changes in the map of Europe also swept away many of the old groupings, and today few countries other than Britain and Ireland retain so complete a system, though they acknowledge the superiority of the sterling standard.

The importance and significance of the British system has, of course, led to imitation. In Canada, America and India, for example, imitation hallmarks have long been used unofficially, some of them suspiciously close in style to the lion passant, the Birmingham anchor and even the leopard's head. Here again is a wide and interesting field for research which has received much attention in recent years.

Recent legislation

The entry of Great Britain and of the Republic of Ireland into the European Community caused some consternation as to the position of the system, since few other of the member countries used any real form of assay and marking. The Joint Committee of the Assay Offices of Great Britain and the Company of Goldsmiths of Dublin prevailed in their efforts to leave the system untouched, and, indeed, a new Hallmarking Act has cleared up some of the problem points, adding platinum to the traditionally marked gold and silver and unifying throughout the country the date letter cycles, which were all revised to start with 'a' on 1 January 1975. Another alteration was the Sheffield mark, formerly a crown, but now replaced by a Yorkshire rose, to avoid confusion with the crown used on goldwares.

Today, only four British assay offices remain – London, still denoted by the leopard's head, which curiously and sadly lost its crown as long ago as 1821; Birmingham, founded in 1773, and using an anchor; Sheffield with a Yorkshire rose, founded along with Birmingham largely due to the efforts of that great entrepreneur, Matthew Boulton; and Edinburgh, with its time-honoured Castle

mark and for which the Lion Rampant (on its hind legs) has been introduced instead of the thistle, as the standard mark. In Ireland, the figure of Hibernia and the crowned harp remain the standard assay marks.

From June 1976, a series of 'Convention hallmarks' have been approved for use in addition to the maker's or sponsor's mark and the assay office marks. This shows a balance with the fineness shown in Arabic numerals giving the parts per thousand pure. They have been accepted not only in Britain but in Austria, Finland, Sweden and Switzerland.

A very rare mark

While the Britannia standard was obligatory from 1696 until 1720, it has since then always been a permitted standard and is still marked with the traditional figure, though since 1975 the lion's head erased has been dropped. For nine months, from 1 December 1784 to July 1785, the figure of Britannia was used, in an incuse mark, to denote the drawback of duty of exported gold and silver.

Since it was struck after the ware had been finished – polishing, engraving and other decoration are usually completed after assay and marking – there was some danger of damage to the finished piece, and the practice was withdrawn, the duty repayable simply being claimed from the Customs department against shipping bills.

OFFICIAL COMMEMORATIVE MARKS

In recent years it has become the practice, both in Great Britain and in the Irish Republic, to sponsor special marks to celebrate notable occasions. These are properly restricted to events of national consequence, reflecting the popular interest in official celebrations.

In Great Britain, the first such special commemorative mark was struck on the occasion of the Silver Jubilee of King George V and Queen Mary in 1935, and showed Their Majesties' heads in profile. Since at that time the various Assay Offices changed their date letters in different months, the marks in practice covered the years 1933 to 1936, though the Jubilee actually fell in 1935. Only silver was struck with this mark, which today, over 40 years later, does add a small premium to the price of what would otherwise merely be 'secondhand'.

The next mark, used from 1952 to 1953, commemorated Her Majesty's Coronation and showed the Queen's head in profile facing to the right. As in the '30s

the special additional mark helped to boost the trade, and a good many specially designed souvenirs and other commemorative pieces were made, some in limited editions that have showed an increase on basic prices for silver of the period.

Even more limited in its time of use was the special Queen's Head Jubilee mark on silver weighing more than 15 g. (about 0.5 oz.) made in Great Britain between January 1 and December 31, 1977. The mark, in a shaped punch following the outline of the Queen's head in profile, facing toward the left, was personally approved by Her Majesty. Again, most manufacturers of silver prepared their special 'jubilee collections', many of them being decorated with the Royal cypher, which was permitted to be used until October of that year, and some in special limited editions.

In Ireland, there have been two special marks to date, the first of national importance, the second of international significance. In 1966, the 50th anniversary of the Easter Rising in 1916, which brought independence to southern Ireland, was commemorated by a punch showing a hand holding a flaming brand and the dates 1916 and 1966. In 1973, the Company of Goldsmiths of Dublin authorised a special mark for gold and silver to commemorate the entry of the Republic of Ireland into the European Community. Present and past were linked by the punch, which shows the bronze-age gold Gleninsheen collar, dating to about 700 BC, enclosing the date 1973. Gold and silver bearing both these marks is understandably rare and they have rapidly become sought-after collectors' pieces commanding good prices.

Using hallmarks

With so much to intrigue and fascinate the collector, and with so much intrinsic information, it is perhaps all too easy to overstate the importance of the hallmarks. Indeed, taking them at their face value can be dangerous. Good marks may appear on the least desirable silverwares, a really fine and exceptional piece may carry nothing more than the maker's mark, while, even worse, the marks may not even be what they purport, but the product of the faker – for though the death penalty may have disappeared for the misdemeanour, the perpetrators have not.

Always, the collector's first task is to look at the piece and not the marks. Could you date it if it were unmarked? Is the decoration in keeping with the form? Is the form acceptable? Could any part have been altered – a handle removed for repair, a spout added, a coat-of-arms erased? Is it of sound metal, free of wear, free of modern restoration that may tidy up, say, the expected solder on the base?

Having satisfied oneself of the quality of the piece, then the marks can be scrutinised. Where to find them should soon become second nature – to the right of the handle and across the cover of a 17th century tankard, for example; scattered on the base of a mid-18th century candlestick, or along its rim by the 1770s when most were filled, not cast; near the bowl on a spoon stem before 1781, at the top of the stem after that – each age and each assay office had its own methods and practices. Incidentally, most British assay offices have always taken their scrapings from a fairly hidden area, though on the base of salvers, teapot stands and tea caddies in the second half of the 18th century a fairly noticeable area of scraping can often be detected. On Continental silver, from early times, a characteristic zigzag mark denotes the scrape used for assay.

On most silver made before the middle of the 19th century (except for spoons and forks after 1781) the marks were struck individually, so that it would be very unlikely that those on two pieces would appear in identical positions. If they do appear to be, suspicions should at once be roused, for the one may be a casting of the other – a nasty habit of the tableware faker. The marks may then, however, tend to show rather softened edges, not the rubbed look due to wear, but rather shallow, and occasionally pitted, details. Soft hallmarks, so called because they are usually cut in copper or other easily worked metal instead of the hard steel used for true punches, are detectable by their indistinct appearance – though it should be remembered that many makers' marks show a rather less pronounced crispness than the hallmarks, since they were applied by the maker and were not always replaced as soon as they began to wear.

During the middle years of the 18th century – and, of course, earlier – it must be admitted that hallmarking was not always as distinct or as widespread as it later became. Many pieces, on the score that they were light in weight, small, or generally considered insignificant, were struck only with the maker's mark and lion passant, applied presumably on batch-tested wares such as wine labels. By 1790, however, there was a great tightening up, and most silver subsequently made in Britain is fully marked, sometimes even to astounding numbers of times, such as a

carriage lamp bearing 21 separate marks.

In Birmingham, great attention was – and still is – paid to marking each separate part. True, it had always been the law, and cups, coffee pots, teapots, tankards and other covered silver should always bear at least the lion passant in the cover. But Birmingham made certain, even on such small items as snuff boxes and vinaigrettes, which are almost invariably marked on base and lid, the marks split up between the two: woe betide the careless 'renovator' who mixed up two boxes, or for that matter the careless collector – a recent sale in New York produced a porringer and cover of different dates and makers which, it was noted, had obviously been switched with another porringer and cover in the '30s, when the porringer, by Christopher Shaw, 1659, appeared with a cover of 1663, maker H – obviously the two that should have matched up with the New York example. But then, hallmarks have not always been so absorbing a subject of study, and the cover did fit well enough, though a more careful look at both hallmarks and porringer might quickly have revealed the difference.

J.B.

Left
The town mark for Sheffield was changed from a crown to a rose in 1975.

Left
Marks on a London spoon of 1804, by Soloman Hougham, near the top of the stem, showing that it was made after 1781. This example is stamped twice because the assay master's hand apparently slipped!

Above: left and right
Two of Paul de Lamerie's marks: his Britannia standard mark which he continued to use right up until 1732, and his Sterling mark used thereafter.

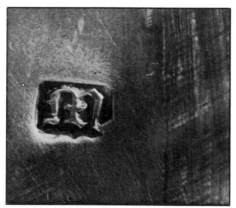

Above
To the right of this date letter, on the base of a cake basket, can be seen the 'assay scrape'.

Above
Tankard, about 1670. The marks, to the right of the handle and across the cover, are where you would expect to find them at that period.

Below
Imitation hallmarks struck in Calcutta, about 1840, and in Madras, about 1828.

Silver Salts and Peppers

The importance of common salt in diet was one of the earliest of man's scientific discoveries, and it is small wonder that in due course many magical, religious and ceremonial attributes were accorded to it. Biblical references abound, and 'eating the salt of the Palace' may have suggested to medieval monarchs the idea of creating the standing salts which, grand and often extremely large, actually enclosed only very small salt-wells – usually no bigger than the small salts common from the mid-17th century onwards. From Cellini's unsurpassed gold salt for François I of France, through the few surviving medieval examples such as the Huntsman Salt at All Souls' College, Oxford and the architectural salts of the 16th century, to the simpler, but still ceremonial drum salts and their successors the bell and the capstan salts of the early 17th century, the history is not only one of ceremony but of silver styles as well.

In less courtly households, salt still held its place of importance, though usually a well, carved at the corner of the wooden trencher, would suffice to hold the precious mineral – and, indeed, was probably far more practical than silver, which quickly corrodes in contact with salt that is at all damp. But silver was the cynosure of every householder, and by the second half of the 17th century the custom of making small, or trencher, salts in silver, to be placed by each diner, became firmly established.

Early trenchers were always simple – small receptacles on a spreading foot, round, oval, octagonal or square. The round salts were sometimes quite shallow, and by the baroque period of the 1680s, usually heavily gadrooned. Some of these salts with knurled rims were made taller and waisted, but by the early 18th century, most were shallow round or octagonal cast cellars. About 1725, they were heightened by placing a shallow circular bowl on a stepped foot – the pedestal salt – and soon the bellied salt on three or four feet – sometimes with decorative knuckles such as lion masks, more rarely applied with rococo ornament – followed. During the high rococo period about 1740, shells and other exceptional shapes made their appearance, extravaganza by such masters as Lamerie, Crespin and Sprimont, but for most patrons, the more or less standard trenchers and bellied salts of the specialist makers, like Edward Wood and David Hennell sufficed. Firms such as Norman

Above

Smaller casters than those made for sugar were used for pepper, dry mustard and other spices from the last quarter of the 17th century onwards. Early examples often have rather coarsely pierced covers, suitable for coarsely ground pepper: for mustard an inner sleeve was sometimes fitted. The earliest were cylindrical, a pattern ousted by the Huguenot immigrants who introduced the baluster form. By 1714 the octagonal vase shape was established, with the cover sprung in instead of having a bayonet fixing. This fine plain caster, engraved with armorials, is 5½ in (14 cm) high and weighs 6.3 oz (196 g). It was made, in Britannia standard silver, by Gabriel Sleath in 1719.
ASPREY & CO

Above

Spice dredgers, often called 'kitchen peppers' because they look like the usual culinary type, of straight-sided cylindrical form with a simple dot-pierced domed cover and loop handle, were popular from the beginning of the 18th century for about 20 years, when they were generally superseded by the handleless 'bun pepper'. The earliest examples sometimes had the cover secured by a bayonet fastening, and about 1714 many appeared in the fashionable octagonal form. This example of 1721, however, reverts to the older cylindrical type. Just 2 in (5 cm) high, it weighs 1.4 oz (44 g).
S. J. SHRUBSOLE

Left

The typical trencher, or small salt of the early 18th century was of oblong octagonal form with incurved sides and spreading base. It was cast, and marked usually in the well – a factor that often means worn marks, as the constant use of salt, especially if allowed to get damp, inevitably corrodes the silver. Care must also be taken that the salt is not itself cast from others. Good examples are today fairly hard to come by. One of a pair, by specialist salt-maker Edward Wood, made in 1729. They measure 3 × 2½ in (7.5 × 6.3 cm) and weigh 3.15 oz (98 g) the pair.
S. J. SHRUBSOLE

Left

About 1726, the salt, still placed beside the individual diner, gradually became rather more imposing – a circular hemispherical bowl set on a raised stepped foot. These pedestal salts were sometimes quite plain, sometimes applied with chased foliage or even more elaborate detail. Pedestal, or spool salts as they are sometimes called, were made by many of the leading silversmiths of the day, including David Willaume, Paul de Lamerie, Anne Tanqueray and John Le Sage. This is one of a fine pair also made by the specialist maker Edward Wood, which date from 1732.
GARRARD & CO

Left

A dozen years later, the taste for decorative silver meant that even such functional pieces as salts were enriched with applied cast and chased detail. Edward Wood remained a leading maker of salts – he himself had been trained by Gundry Roode, who specialised in them, and he was master to David Hennell, whose family dominated salt-making for the rest of the century. Here Wood interprets the rococo in a set of salts superbly applied with festoons of flowers between the three paw feet with their finely modelled lion mask knuckles. One, from a set of four, made in 1744, weigh in all 20 oz (622 g).
ASPREY & CO

Above

Oblong, circular or oval dishes of the turn of the 18th century are sometimes mistakenly said to be ash-trays or sweet dishes. Most were, however, stands for cut-glass salts, and here is one of four gadroon and shell stands which retain their original cut-glass cellars. Made by Samuel Whitford in 1815, the stands alone weigh 15.3 oz (476 g).
GARRARD & CO

Above

David Hennell I, who had been apprenticed to Edward Wood, entered his mark in 1736 and began the family business that still exists today. He made every conceivable pattern of salt, plain or ornamental, and in 1763 he entered a joint mark with his son Robert, whom he had trained himself. This was the period of pierced salts, enhanced by blue glass liners, and the Hennells were pre-eminent in making them, first of all in the rococo style, later in the more formal neoclassical manner. This paw-footed oval salt of 1766, with wavy gadrooned rim, is 3¼ in long, one of a pair that hints at the new formality.
HENNELLS

Below

Circular bombé salts, on three or four shell-shaped supports, continued to be made in large numbers alongside the pierced neoclassical oval patterns throughout the 1760s and 1770s – a simple and practical design that was usually gilded inside to obviate corrosion. This large example, 3¼ in diameter, is from a late pair made in 1778 by Robert Hennell I, grandson of the founder of the firm.
HENNELLS

Below

By the 1780s, a new and graceful style of salt made its appearance – the oval boat shape, with rising loop handles – miniature counterparts of the soup and sauce tureens of the period. Sometimes with gadrooned or beaded rims, occasionally with bright-cut borders, these salts were usually made in sets of four or more and again were often gilded inside. These two from a set of four are of good size, measuring 5 in (13 cm) long over the handles and weigh a sturdy 11.2 oz (348 g). The applied thread rims, reeded handles and thread-edge oval supports are typical of work by Henry Chawner, who made them in 1791.
S. J. SHRUBSOLE

Left

The neoclassical urn and vase shapes were well suited for the small casters, almost always called muffineers in contemporary records: in size very much conforming to the dredgers of the early part of the century, but now invariably with simply dot-pierced covers. These two small peppers, of 1784 and 1786, are unusual in having bun-shaped covers instead of taller domed covers with a flame or baluster finial. They were both made by Robert Hennell I.
M. McALEER

Left

Made in the same year, 1804, one of a pair of tub-shaped oval salts with gadrooned rims, the bombé bodies engraved with a crest. The pair weigh 5 oz (155 g) and were made by Abstainando King.
HEFFERNAN & JONES

Right

A most unusual silver and parcel-gilt salt with two cellars supported on four cabriole legs. 6 in (15 cm) long overall, it dates from 1796. Maker's mark WF, either for William Frisbee, the former partner of Paul Storr, or William Fountain.
GARRARD & CO

Below

The Hennells again – this time Robert I with his son Samuel, their joint mark entered in 1802 – for a capacious oval salt, slightly bellied below the gadrooned rim with scroll handles, and gadrooned foot. Measuring 5 in (12.5 cm) long, from a pair made in 1804.
HENNELLS

Above

By Robert Hennell III, one of the fourth generation of silversmiths in the family, one of a set of three deep hemispherical salts with beaded edges and a shaped border of chased and matted work imitative of the early 18th century Regence style. Measuring 2¾ in (7 cm) in diameter, they date from 1856.
HENNELLS

Below

Grandeur in silver-gilt, a pair of impressive circular salts that hark back to the rococo but still remain firmly 19th century and typical of Paul Storr's best work. The shaped gadroon rims, the bold and well-modelled lion mask and paw supports, and the festoons of different shells – a shoreline lesson in silver – recall Lamerie's marine creations, yet have the grandiose treatment beloved of the Regency and the years after Waterloo. Made in 1820, when Storr was at last working on his own and not for Rundell, Bridge & Rundell, they typify his best work at a time when often he failed to design to the highest standards. The set, accompanied by pair of 'rococo revival' salt spoons, weigh 22 oz (684 g).
SPINK & SON

Below

Vase-shaped muffineer – a style that was much copied in Calcutta, Madras and elsewhere in the East – with gadrooned rim and a border of rope-plait round the foot, is a sturdy piece of silver made in 1826 by William Fountain. It weighs 4 oz (124 g).
HEFFERNAN & JONES

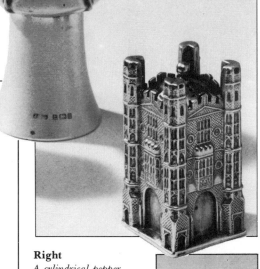

Left

Probably more than any other silver for the table, condiment sets were made in amusing designs during the late Victorian period – cats, chickens, gargoyles, military drums, rabbits, seated lions, frogs and parakeets. It was almost as though the Birmingham toymakers, who specialised in so many smallwares for pocket and purse, should have lived up to their traditional name. The tower pepper dates from 1889 and was made by S. W. Smith of Birmingham. The Champagne cork pepper mill, a patented design made for a wine firm, Peugeot Frères dates from 1900.
M. McALEER

Right

A cylindrical pepper with drum-shaped body and low domed cover in the early 18th century style but with three wholly Victorian ball feet. Just over a century old now, it was made in 1873 (maker's mark worn).
M. McALEER

Appleton and Anne Smith, the Hennells and the Batemans produced quantities of circular, pierced oval and boat-shaped salts for a wide market. Always, of course, there were unusual salts made to special order by the leading makers – Wakelin & Taylor, Scott and Smith, Paul Storr, Philip Rundell, Robert Garrard – so that the collector has a wide choice of standard and special patterns.

Whatever one's taste, in buying salts, the first consideration should be to ensure that the metal is still in good condition. Salt is ruthless in its capacity for destroying silver, and where inside gilding is very thin, or non-existent, marks are often badly worn away and the surface pitted. Care should also be taken to see that liners, preferably of contemporary blue glass and not replacements, fit well and are unchipped, and that the pierced frames are in good condition, not repaired. On bellied salts, a tell-tale bruise on the inside often reveals that a foot has been off and soldered back. Salts vary tremendously in weight – two pairs of the same year by the same maker may be of very different qualities – one pair perhaps may weigh a mere two or three ounces, another as much as seven or eight. But the sheer variety and the relative availability of salts of many different dates and styles makes them a worthwhile – and useful subject for the silver collector.
J.B.

Left

One of a pair of salts in revived style – looking back to the 1790s. Boat-shaped, weighing a good 8.9 oz (277 g) made in 1863 by James Franklin.
GARRARD & CO

Left

'Water-leaves' had first appeared in English silver in the early 19th century, and during the next 20 years, lily pattern flatware and hollow-ware became popular, as in this lily salt, chased with overlapping lily leaves. Made in 1849 by J. C. Edington, the pair weigh 9.3 oz (290 g)
GARRARD & CO

WHERE TO BUY

PICTURES

Pleasure should always be the deciding factor when buying a picture. It is only by satisfying this purely subjective need, and having to live with the result, that you can build up a really interesting collection. It is for this reason that serious collectors will constantly rehang or sell part of their collection in exchange for new acquisitions. For an individual's taste is constantly developing; this development should be based upon the attitude that 'all pictures are interesting, but some are more interesting than others'. As the eye becomes more experienced it should be constantly appreciating good qualities in mediocre paintings whilst marvelling at, and when possible buying, paintings which fulfil all expectations.

A heightened perception

Just as collecting pictures makes you perceive them more astutely, so pictures make us perceive our everyday lives with greater awareness. And herein lies the chief satisfaction of collecting. Living with pictures does not mean standing in front of them reverentially for ten minutes every day; it means glancing at them by chance as you rush to the office, or noticing them whilst doing the housework, or scanning them rapidly whilst locking up for the night. If they are pictures of quality they will reveal more as time goes on: some unexpected detail or subtle use of colour will emerge. And as we begin to understand how certain artists interpreted the world around them, so we begin to see the world around us from their point of view; it might be in a stretch of rolling landscape, or a bowl of apples or a patch of shadow on grass. In every case your perception of the natural world is heightened and your enjoyment increased.

As you grow more fascinated by painting, so you will find yourself becoming more interested not only in your own collection but also in those of museums, other private collections and of course the picture dealers' stock. It is important to feed this curiosity, which will make any visit whether to a National Gallery or a junk shop an exciting occasion. For the more you see and question, the more your visual education is increased. It has to be faced that when it comes to collecting pictures of quality (and they are the ones of value) there is no substitute for an educated eye, and it is for this reason that it is impossible to collect purely for investment. For no amount of studying market trends or deciphering signatures will guarantee that your purchase will go up in value; only if your eye likes it and learns from it can you be sure of a good buy.

PRICES

Painting is the most pure of all the fine and decorative arts and you should never compare the price of a picture to that of an everyday, practical object. For example a small 19th century oil painting might well cost the same as a washing machine, so you must accept a different scale of values when deciding to buy the former. Invariably the more you buy the easier it becomes to recognise and adopt these values.

There are two ways to buy pictures (excluding directly from an artist's studio): from a dealer or from an auction room. Far too many people distrust dealers. This is nearly always completely unfounded. Generally they enter the business because they like paintings; and the best dealers are also scholars, who often rescue artists from total oblivion. Every dealer will have a bargain, and every dealer (unless it is the first day of an exhibition) will be prepared to give money 'off': that is, provided one asks. It is sometimes tempting to stick to one particular dealer, but remember, no one has a monopoly over the type of picture you may want to buy. In theory the advantage of the auction room is that you can by-pass the dealer's markup and buy straight from the source of the art market. This is fine if you have both the time to view and the confidence to bid. It is too easy to snap up a cheap picture at an auction only to find that you have to pay twice the sum to have it restored and reframed. The excitement of an auction can often make you do stupid things (as it must be admitted can too much wine at a private view) and this is likely to make you bid up and pay more for a picture you do not really want.

Themes, schools or media

The articles in this chapter reveal the three different ways to collect pictures; those on views of London and on ruined abbeys (pages 66 and 77) show how one can collect a theme; those on icons, Dutch drawings and British marine painting (pages 82, 93 and 71) show how one can collect a school; and that on inexpensive watercolours (page 89) shows how one can collect a medium. Undoubtedly the cheapest approach is to collect themes as this ensures that one can buy not only oils and watercolours but much cheaper media such as drawing and engraving. Thus in the article on views of London all the prints illustrated have an average price of £30 ($54), apart from the very early print by Wolffy; its value would be around £230 ($414). The pen and ink sketches and simple watercolours average £40 ($72) to £50 ($90) but the much grander highly finished water colours such as *Fish Street Hill and the Monument* (page 69) would cost approximately £1400 ($2520). The price range of pictures of abbeys fall into the same categories. The prints such as *West View of Mount Grace Priory* (page 78) could start as low as £5 ($9) with the etchings around £15 ($27) and aquatints at £50 ($90). Small watercolours all average around £50 ($90) whilst the most valuable picture in the article would be the marvellous watercolour of *Buildwas Abbey* (page 80); its value would be around £700 ($1260).

Collecting schools is much more expensive as so often they are subject to fashion. For example the price of icons has rocketed in the last ten years due to fashion whereas the price of Dutch drawings and marine paintings, although they have always been high, have remained stable. The lowest value of an icon illustrated is the Russian 17th century icon of *The Ascension* (page 83); its value is approximately £750 ($1350). The average price is around £2000 ($3600); this is the value of examples such as the *Old Testament Trinity* (Page 82). And the highest prices are £7000 ($12600) to £10,000 ($18 000).

The articles on Dutch drawing and marine paintings are nicely interlinked, as it was the Dutch who first perfected the genre of marine painting in the 17th century. Both have always been popular with the English. Dutch drawings are naturally cheaper. They range from as little as £150 ($270) to as high as £7000 ($12 600). The cheaper drawings include the study of hounds by Peter Boel, the river scene near Rademaker (both on page 96) and the study of peasants (page 95). The most expensive drawing with a value of around £7000 ($12 600) is the brilliant study of birds by Saftleven (page 94). Marine paintings vary according to date. The cheapest examples are of the late 19th century, for example *Full Sail* (page 72) by Kershaw Schofield is worth approximately £140 ($252) whilst other late watercolours such as *St. Ives, Evening* is worth approximately £250 ($450). 18th century examples are much rarer and more expensive particularly the oil paintings and prices range from approximately £4000 ($7200) for *Off the Kent Coast* (page 73) by Thomas Witcombe to approximately £8000 ($14 400) for *The Royal William and other Shipping in the Thames Estuary* by Richard Paton

Finally, the article on watercolours shows how it is possible to collect attractive pictures on a very limited budget, as all of the examples illustrated cost less than £50 ($90). This proves that a collector with a good eye and determination can still pick up remarkable bargains. This is all the more astonishing as one remembers that watercolours have been very fashionable with collectors for the past 200 years.

JAMES KNOX

London in Watercolours, Drawings and Prints

In the early hours of Sunday morning on 1st September, 1666, a baker's shop in Pudding Lane, near London Bridge, caught fire. It seemed nothing at first. When the Lord Mayor was pointed out the blaze from his house in Gracechurch Street he remarked: 'Pish, a woman might piss it out.' But contrary to mayoral opinion the blaze did spread and by Tuesday evening the ancient city of London had been almost totally destroyed. In visual terms, the city that was rebuilt upon the groundplan of the old marked a total break with medieval London: every building was now made of stone or brick; the streets were wider; and the dominant architectural style was that practised by Sir Christopher Wren.

As the new city arose from the ashes and as its elegant suburbs began to spread towards the West, the hectic spectacle of London captivated the imagination of artists and inspired them to depict every aspect of its life. The mist and stink of the river, the commercial bedlam of the city, the parks, the gothic relics of Westminster, and the dome of St. Paul's, were all vividly portrayed by artists representing a whole spectrum of talent and practising in every medium known to their craft.

London is in her time of dotage. In August 1940 the Blitz began; one raid was so heavy (29th Dec, 1940) that it was described as the second great fire of London, and by the end of the war two thirds of the City had been destroyed, not to mention the destruction in the East and West ends. Since 1945 the banality and intolerance of modern architecture has continued the disfigurement of London and tarnished her reputation as one of the most beautiful cities in the world. There is all the more reason

therefore for collecting pictures of her past, for London is one of the most fascinating palimpsests in existence: evoking layers of historical and personal associations, which haunt her buildings, streets and squares even now.   J.K.

Where to buy
All these views have come from dealers in London, although there is nothing more satisfying than finding a London scene in some remote shire, so it is strongly advised to pursue the quarry wherever you go. The shops mentioned in the text are listed below:
BAYNTON-WILLIAMS, 18 Lowndes St., London SW1 (01-235 6595)
THE BROTHERTON GALLERY, 77 Walton St., London SW3 (01-589 6848)
ERIKA BRUCE, 124 New Bond St., London W1 (01-499 4728)
THE FINE ART SOCIETY LTD., 148 New Bond St., London W1 (01-629 5116)
MARTYN GREGORY, **34 Bury St.,** London W1 **(01-839 3731)**
OSCAR & PETER JOHNSON LTD, Lowndes Lodge Gallery, 27 Lowndes St., SW1 (01-235 6464)
THE PARKER GALLERY, 2 Albemarle St., London W1 (01-499 5906)
THE PARKIN GALLERY, 11 Motcomb St., London SW1 (01-235 8144)
ROYAL EXCHANGE GALLERY, 14 Royal Exchange, London EC3 (01-283 4400)
FRANK T. SABIN LTD., 4 New Bond St., London W1 (01-499 5553)
THE SABIN GALLERIES, 4 Cork St., London W1 (01-734 6186)

Right
Henry VII's chapel, Westminster Abbey, aquatint, 37.5 × 27 cm (14.75 × 10.75 in)
Baedeker in his guide to London writes: 'The airiness, elegance, and richness of this exquisite work can hardly be overpraised.' It was started by Henry VII in 1503 on the site of the old Lady chapel, and he lies buried there.
THE PARKER GALLERY

Left
Highgate and the road to Kentish town, anonymous, about 1780, pen and ink and watercolour, 35.5 × 50 cm (14 × 20 in)
The milkmaid and the cow indicate the rural quality of London suburbs in the 18th century.
SABIN GALLERIES LTD

CROSS-READINGS AT CHARING-CROSS.

Left
Cross-readings at Charing Cross (with a view of the new National Gallery), mixed media, published by Hunt 1838, 22 × 38 cm (8.75 × 15 in)
The original cross was erected by Edward I in 1291 to commemorate the place where the funeral cortege of his wife rested before she was buried in Westminster Abbey. Over three-hundred years later the Parliamentary regicides were executed upon the same spot and ironically the statue of their victim, Charles I, was re-erected there, where it remains to this day. The area around Trafalgar Square and Charing Cross was originally conceived in its present form by the Regency architect Nash, although the final plans were perfected by Barry. The National Gallery was designed by Wilkins and he had to incorporate the enormous portico from the demolished Carlton House into his facade. Such a complicated case history of one small patch of London is indicative of the layers of history to be found in the city. The inspiration for this amusing print was probably John Parry's London Street Scene with Posters painted in 1835.
THE PARKER GALLERY

Left
The building of the County Council Building by Charles Dixon (1872-1934) pencil and gouache and watercolour, inscribed and dated 1913, 36 × 25 cm (14.5 × 10 in)
The drama of this painting gives some idea of the Piranesian quality of the final result, which was designed by Ralph Knott and finished in 1922.
OSCAR & PETER JOHNSON

Above
A view of the Palace from the South side of the lake with the temples of Bellona and Aeolus and the House of Confucius in the Royal Gardens of Kew, line engraving, about 1780, 35 × 53 cm (14 × 21 in)
Kew Gardens were first embellished by Queen Caroline, consort of George II, when she and her husband lived in a congerie of palaces in the grounds. Their principle residence was the White House (demolished 1802) and they farmed out their numerous children either in Richmond Lodge or the Dutch House (the latter has just been restored). The temples were designed by the architect Chambers and the majority still exist. The lake was the work of Capability Brown, unfortunately it swamped one of Queen Caroline's favourite follies, Merlin's cave, where she had installed Stephen Duck, the peasant poet, as curator. The swan seen in this picture is an exotic boat fashionable at the time.
BAYNTON WILLIAMS

Left
A view of Nelson's column by William Gaunt (b. 1900) pen and watercolour, signed and dated 1928, 19 × 35 cm (7.75 × 13.75 in)
This drawing was executed by one of the best known writers on London. His works, which are strongly recommended, include a general book on London and two specific books, one on Kensington and the other on Chelsea. In this picture Nelson's column (185 ft H) dominates the skyline. It was erected between 1832-42, the statue, which is 17 ft high was by E. H. Baily and the capital was cast from a cannon from the Royal George, which sank off Spithead in 1792.
THE PARKIN GALLERY

WINE OFFICE COURT

Left
Wine Court Office by Joseph Pennell (1858-1926), pen and ink, 28 × 20 cm (11 × 8 in)
This is an American's view of one of the literary corners of London. It shows the Old Cheshire Cheese pub, which still exists and although he never mentioned it, is reputed to have been used by Samuel Johnson. It is known however, that the rhyming club met there in the 1890s, which included Arthur Symons, W. B. Yeats and Richard le Gallienne. Oliver Goldsmith lived in the court and the poet Richard Lovelace (1618-1651) died just round the corner.
THE FINE ART SOCIETY

Below

View of London Bridge by Yates (fl 1790-1837), watercolour pen and ink, signed and dated 1829, 33 × 53 cm (13 × 21 in)

This picturesque view shows the medieval London bridge after it had been modernised in 1763. The original structure had been erected in 1176 and with its fortified gate, church and houses, rapidly became one of the wonders of the medieval world. In the modernisation the houses were swept away and the central arch widened. Even then the rapid flow between the arches was extremely dangerous to negotiate, but a Frenchman who took the risk exclaimed: 'Marbleu C'est le plus grand plaisir de monde.' Between 1824-31 it was demolished and replaced by a new bridge. This was dismantled and sold to America in 1973.
THE ROYAL EXCHANGE GALLERY

Above

London, a copperplate panorama by J. Wolffy probably published in Augsburg late-17th century, 33 × 104 cm (13 × 41.5 in) detail

The great fire destroyed 88 of the 108 churches of the city of London, 37 were not rebuilt, but the remaining 51 were all designed by Wren. It took much longer than imagined to rebuild the city. St. Paul's was not finished until 1710 (the artist must be allowed some licence here) and more than half the churches were not begun until 1676. When complete they made one of the most memorable skylines in Europe.
BAYNTON WILLIAMS

Above

Jackson's Lane in Highgate by William George Jennings (fl 1797-1843) pencil and watercolour, inscribed and dated 3rd June, 1843, 14 × 9.5 cm (5.75 × 3.75 in)

Jennings exhibited extensively at the Royal Academy where he is described as an Honorary Exhibitor suggesting that he was a rich amateur. This lush view is another example of the proximity of the countryside to London.
MARTYN GREGORY

Above

Imports of Great Britain from France by L. P. Boitard, line engraving, published March 1757, 25.5 × 38.5 cm (10 × 13.5 in)

One theory of the origin of the name London is that it stems from the Celtic Llyn-Din meaning 'the hill by the pool'. True or not this aptly describes the original port of London, which was the Pool just West of the Tower. Here the bulk of the trading was carried out, often in chaotic and overcrowded conditions. Here 'four porters staggering under a chest of birth-night clothes' and 'several emaciated high-lived epicures' may be observed at the scene of the unloading of cargo from France.
BAYNTON WILLIAMS

Colour
Right

Fish Street Hill and the Monument by G. B. Moore (1805-1875) ink and watercolour, signed and dated 1830, exh. R.A. 1830, 53 × 36.8 cm (21 × 14.5 in)

This watercolour gives an impression of the busy world of the 19th century city. Old London Bridge can be seen in the distance with the church of St. Magnus, by Wren (once described by T. S. Eliot as 'Inexplicable splendour of Ionian white and gold'), beside it. In the foreground is the Monument erected to celebrate the rebuilding of the City after the fire. Christopher Wren wanted to place a statue of Charles II on top, but the King dissented saying: 'After all I didn't start the fire'.
FRANK SABIN

Top centre and detail right

George and Bill of Deptford by Francis Dodd (b. 1874), watercolour and pencil, inscribed, 21 × 21.5 cm (8.25 × 8.5 in)

Francis Dodd admirably conveyed the variety and character of Londoners; here two East-enders are trying their luck in a West end park.
G. M. NORMAN GALLERY

Centre

A front view of the Royal palace of Kensington, copper plate handcoloured engraving published 1751, 26 × 39 cm (10.25 × 15.5 in)

William III believed that the site of Kensington Palace would be beneficial to his asthma. It is one of Wren's most sober buildings, where Queen Mary, King William and Queen Ann all died. The gardens were open to the public at weekends as early as George II's reign, although formal dress had to be worn, but by the 19th century as Princess Lieven remarked: 'Good society no longer went there except to drown itself.'
BAYNTON WILLIAMS

Bottom

The International Sculling Match, final heat from Putney to Mortlake by C. A. Fesch, watercolour and pencil, signed and dated 1886, 42 × 76 cm (26.5 × 30 in)

This splendid picture was given to the World Champion sculler William Beach on his birthday. Around the picture are vignettes of London and portraits of other scullers. This particular part of the Thames had been made famous for feats of rowing by the University Boat Race between Oxford and Cambridge, which was founded in 1829 and first held on this stretch of river in 1864. Perhaps one of the most memorable moments in the history of the race occurred when the commentator exclaimed: 'I can't see whose ahead its either Oxford or Cambridge.'
THE BROTHERTON GALLERY

Left

The Drinking Well in Hyde Park, stipple printed in colour by Godby after Spilsbury, 1802, 33 × 61 cm (13 × 24 in)

Hyde Park has always been the grandest of London's four most famous parks. It was given to the people by Charles I in 1637. De Gramont wrote that 'Everyone who has either sparkling eyes or splendid equipage, constantly repaired hither.'
THE PARKER GALLERY

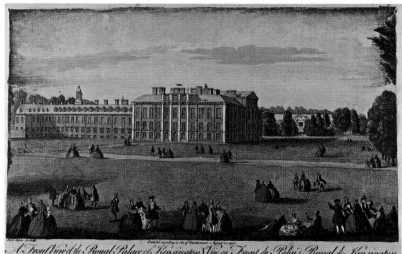

A Front View of the Royal Palace of Kensington. Vue en Front du Palais Royal de Kensington.

Top
The 'Royal William' and other Shipping in the Thames Estuary *by Richard Paton (1717-91), official painter to the Admiralty of the Royal Navy. The artist's concern for detail is evident in the careful delineation of the ship, its railing and crew painted with the utmost of delicacy. 18th century marine paintings are difficult to find today, especially those of such fine quality. About 1770. Oil on canvas.* 76 × 134 cm (30 × 53 in)
DAVID MESSUM

Above
Before the Wind *by E. Aubrey Hunt. French Impressionism of the late 19th century had its influence on British marine artists, both stylistically and in outlook – the sea no longer became just a background for the portrayal of a ship, but a means to explore and study elements of light, air, space and colour. Signed and dated 1884 and inscribed on reverse. Oil on canvas.*
35.5 × 66 cm (14 × 26 in)
PYMS GALLERY

British Marine Painting

The Van de Veldes arrived in London in 1673 and British marine painting was born, so the art historians tell us. Early works, those of the 17th century and many of the 18th century, were Dutch guided and inspired, in terms of composition and style.

Then came Turner and Constable, whose artistic visions had considerable influence on marine artists. The calm, mirror-like waters that dissolved into misty horizons, one of many Dutch 'standards', became lost in the wave of an emerging individual and national art. The study of light and atmosphere became an important artistic consideration; a flatness of surface and a sense of patterning began to replace the beloved Dutch creation of illusionary depth. What resulted was a British style of sea painting, a thriving and commercial art by the 19th century.

Countless numbers of marine paintings were produced during the 19th century, many of them commissioned by trading companies, the navy and yacht owners. The great demand for ship portraits in particular, coupled with the artist's need to produce quickly, ultimately led to a

Below
Shipping off the Humber *by Henry Redmore (1820-87), a Hull School painter who was little known until 1971, when a major exhibition (and televised review) was held in London. Redmore, today, is regarded as one of the finest exponents of late 19th century British marine art; his seas are real and restless and his ships are accurately drawn, achieving a harmony between the elements of sea, sky, wind and man. Signed and dated 1850. Oil on canvas.*
51 × 76 cm (20 × 30 in)
PARKER GALLERY

Above
A Rest Day for the Fleet *by Joseph Parry (1744-1826), also known as 'Old Parry' to avoid confusion with his two sons who were also painters. Although a British style of marine painting evolved during the 18th century, the break from the Van de Velde-type presentation was a gradual one. This example retains much of the Dutch influence – the calm, reflecting waters, the illusion of depth merging into vast and distant skies and the somewhat contrived grouping of figures. Parry exhibited at the Royal Academy in 1803 and an example of his work can be seen at the National Maritime Museum. Signed. Oil on canvas.*
94 × 124 cm (37 × 49 in)
N. R. OMELL GALLERY

Below
An East Indiaman off Hong Kong *by William John Huggins (1781-1845). The art of ship portraiture flourished during the 19th century, not surprising with the success of the ship industry. Huggins is often considered the master of the art during the second and third decades of that century. His time at sea in the service of the East India Company influenced his work, and a great many of his portraits are of vessels owned by that company – often characterized by fresh breezes, distant coastlines and ships broadside on – achieving a light and airy effect that was further enhanced by his use of thin, clear colour. Examples of his work can be seen at Hampton Court and at Greenwich. Signed and dated 1837. Oil on canvas.* 86 × 127 cm (34 × 50 in)
N. R. OMELL GALLERY

standardised type of portrayal. The patron was primarily interested in the detailed and accurate painting of his ship, and although the sea and sky were important, they were also very much of secondary consideration. Thus, the successful artist needed to be something of an expert on ship construction, concentrating fully on its careful delineation and details and satisfying the demands placed on him. This may have inhibited his creative scope, but the art of ship portraiture could hardly foster much experimentation anyway.

The portrayal of other marine subjects, including fishing trawlers at sea, coastal and beach scenes, harbour and port scenes and the painting of sea and sky to the exclusion of all ships, were more susceptible to current artistic trends and allowed a greater freedom of individual expression and exploration.

French Impressionism was one movement that influenced the outlook and style of many British artists. The sea was an excellent place to study elements of (continued on page 75)

Above left
Entrance to Beaulieu River *by Alfred Vickers (1786-1868), a well known landscape artist who painted few marine subjects, some around the Isle of Wight and Solent areas. Signed and dated 1845. Oil on canvas.* 38 × 56 cm (15 × 22 in)
BRENCHLEY GALLERY

Above
St Ives, Evening *by Julius Olsson (1864-1942). As well as coastal scenes, Olsson was capable of producing fine 'pure sea' paintings in the style of Henry Moore. This example illustrates the artist's choice of rich colour, achieving a light and shimmering quality that is reminiscent of impressionist and post-impressionist work done in southern France. Signed. Oil on canvas.*
41 × 51 cm (16 × 20 in)
CIDER HOUSE GALLERIES

Below right
Fresh Breezes Between Guernsey and Jersey *by Henry Moore (1831-95). Collectors of marine paintings sadly tend to ignore the work of this artist, largely because his subjects are often of the sea itself. Many of his paintings are similar to the French Impressionism of Monet and Boudin, and his works were well received in France (he was awarded the Grand Prix at the Paris Exposition Universelle of 1889). By 1870, Moore concentrated almost exclusively on the sea and sky in varying weather conditions; a ship was sometimes included, only to emphasize the great vastness of the sea. His colours are bright and vibrant, painted with energetic brushstrokes. Signed and dated August 2, 1882. Oil on canvas.*
30 × 55 cm (12 × 21.5 in)
RICHARD GREEN

Above
The Spanish Prizes Captured After the Battle of Cape St Vincent on the 11th February 1791, off Lisbon *by Thomas Butterworth (exhib. 1798-1827). Butterworth is of particular interest to American collectors because, together with Robert Salmon, he provided a link between the British marine school and the emerging American school. Although he never travelled to America, several of his paintings portray American naval engagements during the 1812 war. He was appointed marine painter to the East India Company. His paintings are characterised by a blue and green-grey coloration, overcast skies and great detail of ship construction and crew. Many of his works exist today in private American collections and can also be seen at the National Maritime Museum (including his famous painting* Trafalgar). *Paintings by Butterworth are in great demand today, but also most difficult to find. Signed. Oil on canvas.*
86 × 142 cm (34 × 56 in)
N. R. OMELL GALLERY

Above
19th century ship portrait at Hong Kong harbour of the Elmstone, *by an anonymous Chinese painter. These artists often received commissions from those on board, and satisfied the demand by producing works that were both detailed and British in style. About 1880. Oil on canvas.*
44.5 × 58 cm (17.5 × 23 in)
PARKER GALLERY

Above
Full Sail *by Kershaw Schofield (1875-1941). A Bradford painter, Schofield exhibited at the Royal Academy from 1900-1940. His work was strongly influenced by the Impressionists, although his treatment of the sea, with activated brushwork and thick paint, is almost expressionistic in quality. Along with other Yorkshire artists of the period, a definite school became recognised. Signed. Oil on canvas.*
61 × 76 cm (24 × 30 in)
CAMBRIDGE FINE ART

Below
32 Gun Frigate off Plymouth *by Nicholas Matthew Condy (fl. 1842-45). Condy was a well established Plymouth artist and many of his marine paintings were executed in this area. He died at the early age of 35. He is regarded today as one of the most prominent of Devonshire artists. Many of his paintings are quite small in size; this is a rare exception. Signed twice and dated 1838. Oil on canvas.*
56 × 76 cm (22 × 30 in)
DAVID MESSUM

Left
View From the Beach *by Arthur Meade (exhib. from 1880). This painting again serves to illustrate the extent to which French Impressionism influenced a large number of British artists during the late 19th century. The study and effects of light, a prime concern of the movement, can hardly be better pursued than with its interaction with water. Signed. Oil on canvas.*
71 × 91 cm (28 × 36 in)
CIDER HOUSE GALLERIES

Right
Battle of the Saints *by William Elliott (exhib. 1784-91). Like many naval officers, Captain Elliott painted in his spare time, especially naval engagements and the Eastern ports that he visited on his travels. He was an honourary exhibitor at the Free Society and the Royal Academy. Examples of his work can be seen at Hampton Court. Signed, late 18th century. Oil on canvas.*
77.5 × 105.5 cm (30.5 × 41.5 in)
CIDER HOUSE GALLERIES

Above
The New York Yacht Club Schooner 'Columbia' off Governor's Island, Upper Bay, New York *by William Howard Yorke (fl. 1858-92). Yorke specialised in ship portraits, demonstrating a gift for detail in the portrayal of both ship and crew (who were often conceived of in a naive manner) and an individuality of style in both the sea and sky. Yorke's dates and the extent of his work have not yet been fully researched, but all known works are ship portraits. (There are 10 in the National Maritime Museum, one in the Liverpool Museum and one in the Manx Museum, Isle of Man.) Yorke was a Liverpool artist, but there is some confusion as to whether he remained one after 1870 . . . it is possible that he worked in North America thereafter. Oil on canvas.*
66 × 91 cm (26 × 36 in)
N. R. OMELL GALLERY

Left
Off the Kent Coast *by Thomas Whitcombe (1752-1824). Very little is known about Whitcombe, although he was a prolific artist, painting ship portraits, sea battles, harbour scenes and dramatic stormy weather seas. His ship portraits are artistically conveyed in a traditional manner, and although the Dutch influence began to disappear during the 18th century, traces of it remain here. Whitcombe's seas are usually restless (and like many of his contemporaries, the artist favoured a dark foreground) with cloudy skies, fresh winds – a romantic atmosphere that appeals to many collectors today. Signed, about 1800. Oil on canvas.*
71 × 106 cm (28 × 42 in)
DAVID MESSUM

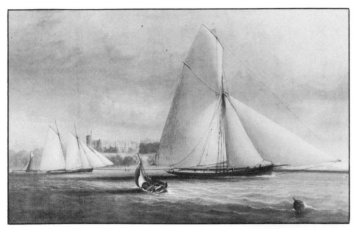

Above

The Yacht, the Gossamer *by John Lynn (fl. 1826-38). His life has been little recorded and he does not appear to have been a prolific artist – but all known works are sea pieces. The fine detail and accuracy of drawing would account for his adeptness in this field. Pictures by Lynn are fairly rare. Examples are in the National Maritime Museum. Signed and dated 1832. Oil on canvas. 66 × 99 cm (26 × 39 in)*
PARKER GALLERY

Above

The Rescue *by A. T. Broom. The stormy weather reflected by this ominous dark grey sky and rough sea is a fine example of Victorian marine painting, that probably little appealed to the ladies of the day who could barely stomach more than choppy water. But storms have become quite popular today and are in demand. Signed and dated 1867. Oil on canvas. 76 × 127 cm (30 × 50 in)*
CIDER HOUSE GALLERIES

Above

A Frigate in Squally Weather *by Thomas Luny (1759-1837). In spite of 30 years of life in a bath chair, rheumatoid arthritis and paralysis of the lower limbs and fingers, Luny was a courageous and prolific painter. His work is uneven in quality although his 'middle period' is regarded as having produced the finest paintings. His best work is characterised by an attractive palette, well drawn ships and a fluidity of brushwork. His portrayal of the ocean, however, has been criticised for its stylised, un-life-like waves. Much of his work exists in private collections although there are some fine examples at Greenwich. Signed and dated 1803. Oil on canvas. 76 × 114 cm (30 × 45 in)*
PARKER GALLERY

Above

Schooner in Scottish Loch *by H. Forrest. Little is recorded about this artist, but several of his yacht portrayals are known. Many of his paintings were executed in Scotland and it is possible that the artist was Scottish – in which case, it is not surprising that he is neglected by marine art historians, as the entire Scottish school of marine artists has yet to be researched and accounted for. Signed and dated 1874. Oil on canvas. 35.5 × 61 cm (14 × 24 in)*
PARKER GALLERY

Below left

Dutch Barges in an Estuary *by Edward Fletcher (1857-1945) who sometimes painted under the name John Hayes. A little recorded 19th century artist, Fletcher's work often turns up at the salerooms, his best work reminicent of W. L. Wyllie. Although some of his paintings are of rather poor quality, this is a particularly fine example. Here, his treatment of light, with distant ships dissolving in the mist, captures something of Turner. Signed. Oil on canvas. 61 × 91 cm (24 × 36 in)*
THE OLD CUSTOMS HOUSE

Below

Fishing Boats off Yarmouth *by John Cantiloe Joy (1806-66), brother of William Joy (1803-67), both Norwich School artists and among the few to paint marine subjects. John Joy preferred more tranquil subjects than his brother and usually worked in watercolours. Although not the most famous exponents of the school, both were accomplished marine artists with a sound knowledge of ship construction, usually confined to studies by the beach or quayside. Examples of John Joy's work can be seen at the British Museum and the National Maritime Museum. Signed. Watercolour. 15 × 24 cm (6 × 9.5 in)*
MANDELL'S GALLERY

Above

Sailing Vessels off a Harbour Entrance by John Moore of Ipswich (1820-1902). One of the finest exponents of the Norwich School, Moore's best marine paintings are vibrant with their transparent, active waters and skies – his treatment of light is, in particular, reminiscent of Constable. Moore was also a landscape artist although those that have appeared for sale recently are of rather poor quality. Some copies and inferior works are in circulation. Dated 1872. Oil on canvas. 56 × 76 cm (22 × 30 in)
THE OLD CUSTOMS HOUSE

Below

The Thames at Woolwich by Edward Hoyer (fl. 1870-90). A little recorded artist, Hoyer worked at the end of the 19th century. He did not exhibit although his work is known to collectors and salerooms. It has been written that Hoyer often portrayed dramatic seas, although this example is perhaps better reflective of the realist approach on a calm day. Signed and dated 1880, inscribed on stretcher. Oil on canvas. 76 × 127 cm (30 × 50 in)
CAMBRIDGE FINE ART

Right

The Barque Nola off the South Foreland by Thomas G. Dutton (fl. 1845-79). He executed many ship portrait paintings (including clipper ships, yachts and steamships) for the purpose of his lithographs. His work is becoming most difficult to find today, much of it having been collected over the past century. Signed and dated 1871. Oil on canvas. 74 × 119 cm (29 × 47 in)
THE OLD CUSTOMS HOUSE

Below

Brigs off Tynemouth in Stiff Breeze, one of a pair of paintings by W. H. Doust (fl. 1859-80). Although Doust was a prolific painter, his works are difficult to come by today. Both signed and dated 1865. Oil on canvas. 29 × 57 cm (11.5 × 22.5 in)
PYMS GALLERY

Below

Harbour at Night by John Atkinson Grimshaw (1836-93), a Leeds landscape painter especially fond of moonlit dock and harbour scenes. His work has become quite popular recently although it is wise to beware of contemporary copies in circulation. Signed, 1893. Oil on canvas. 20 × 40.5 cm (8 × 16 in)
CIDER HOUSE GALLERIES

light, atmosphere and colour in varying weather conditions, the boats often lending themselves to the study of solid matter in those conditions rather than as vehicles to boast the artist's technical mastery.

Interestingly, British marine art of this century has been almost untouched by the multitude of artistic movements and concepts. 20th century ship portraits are often conveyed in a 19th century manner, the ships themselves often appearing as the old clippers of yesterday. But if there has been little stylistic progression during this century, the reason again is largely dependent on the demand. Collectors and patrons of marine paintings have retained a strong interest in ship detail, coupled with a nostalgia for the romantic old days of seafaring. The standardised ship portrait has little altered because its successful presentation of the 19th century remains the successful presentation of today. F.M.

Where to buy

Many galleries deal in marine paintings as well as other varieties, while other galleries specialise exclusively in marine art – the galleries listed below represent both.

17th century British sea paintings are virtually impossible to find (except in museum collections) and 18th century examples are fairly scarce. 19th century examples are the easiest to find although much is of poor quality and the finer works are being bought up quickly (many going abroad) resulting in their increasing scarcity and the up-marketing of inferior artists.

BOURNE GALLERY, Lesbourne Road, Reigate, Surrey (Reigate 49451)
BRENCHLEY GALLERY, Brenchley, Kent (Brenchley 2016) – specialising exclusively in 19th century marine art.
CAMBRIDGE FINE ART, 68 Trumpington Street, Cambridge (0223-68488)
FRANK CHAPMAN AND SONS, Fishdock Road, Grimsby (51317)
THE CIDER HOUSE GALLERIES, Norfolk House, 80 High Street, Bletchingley, Surrey (Godstone 2198)
DAVID CROSS GALLERY, 3A Boyces Avenue, Clifton, Bristol (0272-32614)
RICHARD GREEN, 44 Dover Street, London w1 (01-493 7997)
MANDELL'S GALLERY, Elm Hill, Norwich, Norfolk (0603-26892)
DAVID MESSUM, 11 Bury Street, London sw1 (01-930 2902)
GERDA NEWMAN GALLERY, 53 Ledbury Road, London w11 (01-221 4185)
THE OLD CUSTOMS HOUSE, Quay Street, Lymington, Hampshire (Lymington 2338) – specialising in 19th century marine art
N. R. OMELL GALLERY, 6 Duke Street, London sw1 (01-839 6223)
THE PARKER GALLERY, 2 Albemarle Street, London w1 (01-499 5906)
PYMS GALLERY, 291 Brompton Road, London sw3 (01-589 8525)
RAFAEL VALLS, 34 Bury Street, London sw1y 6au (01-839 2713)

Above

This view of 'The West Window & Entrance of the Church of Tintern Abbey, Monmouthshire' was engraved by W. Byrne after the original drawing by T. Hearne and published in 1804. It is dedicated to the Duke of Beaufort; this was the usual way of attracting the interest and patronage of an influential person – and of stimulating sales. 26 × 19.5 cm (10¼ × 7½ in)

Baynton Williams

The Theme of the Ruined Abbey: 1722-1970

'Bare ruin'd choirs where late the sweet birds sang.' Who can fail to be moved by Shakespeare's evocation of the wanton destruction of monastic life, by a King hungry for revenue? What scenes of desecration following Henry VIII's decree: the ripping away of roofs, the plunder of stones to make many a comfortable secular dwelling. Yet out of such desolation came forth a kind of beauty – the artist's glory in depicting such ruins. Not only painters, but novelists and poets too, have played their part in opening our eyes to the solemn beauty of these ruins, and to them we owe a debt.

Interest in ruins was first evoked in the 17th century, part of a new interest in old houses, buildings and monuments that resulted from increased travel. Lord Arundel was responsible for bringing

Wenceslaus Hollar over from the Netherlands in 1636 to record the places he visited on his travels in England. It was this same interest in the past that created a market for the illustrations of the *Venerable Remains of above 400 Castles, Monasteries, Palaces, etc, etc* that Samuel Buck produced in the 1720s (see illustration on p.78). Many a country house possessed a collection of engravings of these drawings of antiquities. Drawn in a topographical manner, that is as a straightforward record, without any personal interpretation on the part of the artist, they served to depict those subjects whose interest would persist over the next century.

The Englishman's love of nature has ever been known, and it was this love which inspired that great period of watercolour painting, from the mid 18th to the

Above

Kirkstall Abbey *by John Glover, OWS (1767-1849), pencil and watercolour 42 × 59 cm (16½ × 23½ in).*
Glover was a founder member of the 'Old' Watercolour Society, set up in 1804 – the first society specially dedicated to watercolour. His compositions were largely based on Claude, and Claude's vision of 'ideal landscape' – a style against which Constable was rebelling in the interests of a natural style of painting. Glover was also known for his invention of the split brush technique – by splitting his brush into many parts he was able to paint foliage and water in detail without fatigue.
SPINK & SON LTD

mid 19th century. The development of watercolour was in the main a landscape development because of the peculiar powers of that medium to evoke the moods of nature. But before the great Romantic interpretations of nature by Turner, the path was prepared by the topographical watercolours of abbeys, castles and houses by Paul Sandby, Michel Angelo Rooker and Edward Dayes, working in the mid 18th century. Still straightforward representations as these works are, they are nevertheless more interpretative in that they take into account the natural setting of the particular building. The building and the scenery are seen as part of a whole, unlike the isolated buildings, wooden in style, of the earlier Buck.

The late 18th century saw the rise of the Picturesque interpretation of nature, and in this ruins really came into their own, so much so that they became a cult. The idea, as propounded by the Rev William Gilpin, was that roughness and irregularity had a value preferable to that of the formal and regular in providing the maximum pleasure to the beholder. So a ruin was better artist's material than a smooth Georgian façade; a rugged oak or knotty wych elm was preferred to a smooth beech, a gipsy or beggar to an elegantly dressed gentleman. Mrs Radcliffe epitomises the style in her *The Romance of the Forest*, published in 1791. 'He approached, and perceived the Gothic remains of an abbey: it stood on a kind of rude lawn, overshadowed by high and spreading trees, which seemed coeval with the building and diffused a romantic gloom around. The greater part of the pile appeared to be sinking into ruins, and that which had withstood the ravages of time showed the remaining features of the fabric more awful in decay. The lofty battlements, thickly enwreathed with ivy were half demolished, and became the residence of birds of prey . . .' Here is the Gothic Romance of the abbey *par excellence*.

The Romantic school of painters set out to do away with the contrived style of the Picturesque. Their approach can be summed up in Constable's statement that 'Painting is with me but another word for feeling'. Romanticism was all to do with the emotions. Wordsworth's poem *Lines Composed a Few Miles Above Tintern Abbey*, 1798, demonstrates the spirit:

'The sounding cataract
Haunted me like a passion: the tall rock,
The mountain, and the deep and
    gloomy wood,
Their colours and their forms, were
    then to me
An appetite; . . .'

The appeal of the ruined abbey has not waned. Each year thousands of visitors demonstrate this. Why not mark your visit by purchasing a watercolour or engraving?   F.P.

Above
York Minster *by Alan Edward Everitt (1824-1882), watercolour, 33 × 43 cm (13 × 17 in).*
Everitt sketched in the Midlands and the North of England throughout his life. A Birmingham artist, in his youth he took lessons from David Cox. He was instrumental in setting up the Birmingham City Art Gallery, then the Birmingham Free Gallery.
THOMAS AGNEW & SONS

Above
Tintern Abbey, *the ruins on the River Wye, by George Cumberland (1754-1848), signed with initials and inscribed verso 'Tintern Abbey in the Spring of 1815/apples in blossom', watercolour 15 × 22 cm (6 × 8¾ in).*
A romantic interpretation seen in the light of Spring rather than moonlight.
WILLIAM DRUMMOND, COVENT GARDEN GALLERY

Below
West view of Mount Grace Priory *near Osmotherley, North Yorkshire, drawn and engraved by Samuel Buck (1696-1779) and published 1722, 19 × 35 cm (7½ × 14 in).*
This is a good example of the topographical style – the description of interesting places without the intrusion of strong personal comment. Buck made more than 500 prints of the remains of castles and abbeys, generally travelling round the country drawing them in summer, and engraving them in the winter.
BAYNTON WILLIAMS

Above

Hinton Abbey, *Freshford, Somerset by Alfred Hayward (1875-1971), oil on panel, signed and dated 1921, 30 × 51 cm (12 × 20 in).*
This painting must be seen to be appreciated. Its tones are quiet and harmonious.
BELGRAVE GALLERY

Above

Abbey and Palace of Dumfermline, *coloured aquatint, engraved by C. Catton after a drawing by J. Farington, Published by T. Jukes, London 1792, 46 × 63 cm (18 × 25 in).*
Coloured aquatints aimed at reproducing the effect of watercolour, in large numbers. Dumfermline was immortalised in the ballad of Sir Patrick Spens
   'The King sits in Dumfermline town
   Drinking the blude-red wine' . . .
BAYNTON WILLIAMS Price

Below

Buildwas Abbey, *near Ironbridge, Shropshire by François Louis Francia (1772-1839), watercolour, signed and dated 1809, 20 × 27 cm (7¾ × 10½ in).*
Francia was a fellow student with Thomas Girtin at Dr Monro's Academy, where Turner also drew. His most famous pupil was Richard Parkes Bonington.
STANHOPE SHELTON

Below

The Abbey of Saint Mary, York, *colour lithograph by I. Haghe from a drawing by Miss Atkinson, published by J. and G. Todd, York in 1831, 19 × 25 cm (7½ × 10 in).*
The Picturesque ruin with the rough foreground creates a feeling of ruggedness.
BAYNTON WILLIAMS

Above

Malmesbury Abbey, *with three figures in foreground, by John Hodgson Lobley RBA (1878-?), watercolour, signed, 30 × 25 cm (12 × 10 in).*
Lobley, though working in a topographical tradition, introduces a romantic element with the playing light on the abbey and the figures stopping to look.
ABBOTT AND HOLDER

Below

The Convent Dormitory; A figure lying in bed *by George Cumberland (1754-1848), watercolour, inscribed recto 'one side of the Dormitory of 26 beds at the Convent of Lulworth', 15 × 22 cm (6 × 8¾ in).*
Cumberland was an astonishing man – intensely curious in a scientific way, and equally imaginative, he was amateur geologist, agricultural experimentalist, critic, biographer, novelist and painter. He was also a friend of William Blake. Here he reconstructs the sleeping quarters of the nuns as they would have looked before the Reformation – an expression of the Romantic Mediaevalism of the Blake, Palmer, Linnell circle, with whom Cumberland was friendly.
WILLIAM DRUMMOND, COVENT GARDEN GALLERY

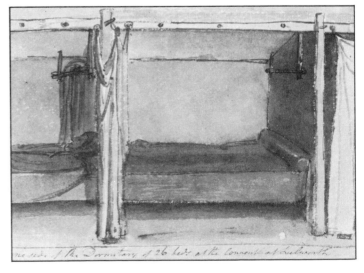

Above

Westminster Abbey *by Ken Howard, born 1932, signed, oil on canvas, 122 × 91 cm (48 × 36 in).* *Howard is a modern war artist, several of his subjects being of Northern Ireland. Here he leaves such horrors behind to paint our most famous abbey.*
LEONIE JONLEIGH STUDIO

Below

Fountains Abbey *by Sir Henry Rushbury RA (1889-1968), etching, signed, 22 × 30 cm (9 × 12 in).* *Rushbury was a watercolourist, etcher and draughtsman of architectural subjects, and keeper of the Royal Academy schools from 1949-1964. Instead of the ivy clad walls of 18th century etchings and the strolling gentlemen, note the scaffolding and the builders.*
ABBOTT & HOLDER

Above

Figures and cattle at Leiston Priory *by Isaac Johnson of Woodbridge (1754-1835), watercolour, 19 × 30 cm (7¾ × 11¾ in).* *An antiquary and surveyor, Johnson worked in the topographical tradition.*
STANHOPE SHELTON

Above

Radford Abbey Gate, *Nottinghamshire, by John Chessell Buckler (1793-1894), watercolour, signed and dated 1813, 20 × 30 cm (8 × 12 in).* *One of a series of watercolour drawings made by Buckler between 1809 and 15 entitled 'Collection of Gateways in England and Wales'. Antiquarian interest was beginning to revive. Michael Bland, himself an antiquarian, commissioned the series.*
THOMAS AGNEW AND SONS

WHERE TO BUY

Eighteenth and 19th century watercolour dealers are fruitful searching grounds. Most artists, amateur and professional, remembered and forgotten, painted ruins at some stage in their life. The print dealers are likely to have the greatest number, since artists often engraved their work, for a wider market. These can be bought at little cost and make an attractive collection. Although they are frequently sold mounted and not framed, all print dealers will provide a simple frame at a small extra cost.

ABBOTT AND HOLDER, 73 Castelnau, Barnes, London SW13 (01-748 2416)
THOMAS AGNEW AND SON LTD, 43 Old Bond Street, London W1 (01-629 6176)
BAYNTON WILLIAMS, 18 Lowndes Street, London SW1 (01-235 6595)
BELGRAVE GALLERY, 17 Motcomb Street, London SW1 (01-235 0066)
CAMBRIDGE FINE ART, 68 Trumpington Street, Cambridge (Cambridge 68488)
CRADDOCK AND BARNARD, 32 Museum Street, London WC1 (01-636 3937)
WILLIAM DRUMMOND, COVENT GARDEN GALLERY LTD, 20 Russell Street, London WC2 (01-836 1139)
LEONIE JONLEIGH STUDIO, Holmefield, Wonersh, Guildford, Surrey (Bramley 3177)
SPINK AND SON LTD, 5-7 King Street, London SW1 (01-930 7888)
STANHOPE SHELTON, Cobbolds Mill, Monks Eleigh, Ipswich, Suffolk (Bildeston 740203)

The Icon: A Focus of Faith

The icon has always, in the Orthodox world, been considered as primarily important because of its religious significance. Icons depict the divine or saintly personage, scenes from the Bible, or events in the lives of particular saints, and vary in size from very large to quite small painted panels. Their essential object was to serve, as it were, as intermediaries between the material world of everyday and the realm of the spirit. They have never been regarded as divine in themselves but they are believed to pertain of divine power through their association with the heavenly world.

Today in the West, on the contrary, they have come to be admired and collected rather on account of their aesthetic importance. But this is something which is not always very easy to determine, for the merits of an icon were gauged not so much on the basis of its originality (as has for many centuries been the criterion for judging paintings in the West) but rather because of the faithfulness with which the painting adhered to a given model. The old set forms were carefully followed throughout the ages, with little variation. In judging them as pictures, it is thus necessary to distinguish between the merits of the original and the skill of the actual painter or copyist, and to estimate how far he has been able to breathe new life into old form.

Icons always have, and no doubt they always will, be prized by the faithful. Today they have suddenly grown in popularity among people of little faith and very large sums of money are paid for them. There are various reasons to account for this. The attraction of the unusual or of the antique constitutes one reason. But more important and of greater basic significance is their appreciation from an artistic standpoint, resulting from changes which have affected criteria of judgment. In the last century and in the earlier years of this icons were wholly disregarded because they did not conform to the tastes of an age in which truth to nature, exactitude of representation or external charm were the things that were most valued, together with a certain degree of originality of conception. But now inner meaning, the expression of emotion, a tendency towards symbolism, even a very abstract

Above
Old Testament Trinity. *The icon is sometimes called the Hospitality of Abraham. The scene is taken from Genesis (ch. 18) where 'three men' appear to Abraham. In the background are the Oak of Mambre and the mountain. In the foreground the three angels are grouped around a table.* Russian. 17th century. 32 × 28 cm (12.5 × 11 in).
MARK GALLERY

Above
The Saviour. *Christ is depicted half-length, holding a gospel in his left hand, his right hand raised in a gesture of blessing. This is a particularly fine icon, formerly belonging to the collection of the late Count Bobrinsky and illustrated in a well known book on icons by V. Lossky called* The Meaning of Icons. Russian. 16th century.
45 × 37 cm (17.7 × 14.5 in).
TEMPLE ICON GALLERY

approach, have become valued aspects and people are ready to pay attention to works of art which would once have been regarded as visually displeasing. So the icon has come into its own.

It would not be correct to claim that every icon is a great work of art, though some most undoubtedly are, but it would be fair to say that until the 19th century, when icons began to be reproduced by purely mechanical means, all were genuinely sincere works, expressive of the faith and belief of those who painted them and as such there was nothing that was meretricious about them. To the believer they were, and always will be, vehicles of the faith; to the discerning collector they can be things of real beauty and profound delight, to be prized as true and lasting value.

How Icons were made and decorated

The first task of the icon painter was to select a suitable wood. In Russia oak, alder and birch were frequently used. In Greece and the East another popular wood was cypress. After cutting and trimming the boards, a depression was made in the wood leaving a slightly raised border. When several boards were fitted together warping was prevented by means of cross-pieces inserted into the back of the wood. The next stage was to apply a canvas to the wooden panel. The canvas was then covered with several thin layers of gesso – chalk and glue. For the actual painting egg-tempera – a mixture of egg yolk, egg white, (or both) and ground colour – was used. When a gold background was used the gold leaf was applied first. The outlines for the figures or scenes were usually taken from earlier models or, at a later date, from a painters manual containing all the standard iconographical types. After completing the painting a layer of olive oil and various resins was applied. This protected the picture from damp but had the disadvantage that this layer easily collected dust and soot from the incense and candles. Over the years the originally fresh and bright colours of the icon darkened and were frequently repainted, one layer over another.

A peculiarity often found in icons, especially Russian ones, is the use of a metal covering. Various types of covering were designed in Russia. A 'basma' merely

Below
Head of the Archangel Michael. *The two archangels, Michael and Gabriel frequently appear in icons and are highly venerated in the Orthodox world.* Russian. 17th century.
39 × 31 cm (15.3 × 12.2 in).
TEMPLE ICON GALLERY

Below
The Ascension. *Christ in Glory surrounded by the mandorla is born up by Cherubim and Seraphim. Below stands the Virgin with two angels and the twelve apostles.*
Russian. 17th century.
31 × 26 cm (12.2 × 10.2 in).
MARIA ANDIPA ICON GALLERY

covered the edge of a picture. If, as happened more frequently from the 15th century onwards, the covering extended over the picture ground until it reached the contours of the figure, it is referred to as a 'riza'. In the 19th century the metal covering came to have a negative effect on painting. Artists often did not bother to paint the whole picture underneath and more attention and importance was given to the decoration of the riza. The riza was usually made of silver, sometimes gilded. They were usually engraved, enamelled or set with precious stones.

Icon Restoration
Most icons that reach the galleries are in need of restoration and the work of the icon restorer is of great importance. It is really only he who can see what lies beneath the layers of dust, soot and paint. The restorer's first task is to inspect the wood. If it is badly warped or damaged by woodworm he injects the wood with consolidating glues. Next cleaning tests are carried out. This is done in order to determine what lies underneath and whether it is necessary to remove upper layers of paint. After cleaning the picture cracks and holes are filled up with gesso and only then does he retouch the paint work. The amount of retouching varies enormously, depending on the state of repair of the icon. Restorers use egg-tempera in the same way as the original

painter did; the difficulty in matching colours is enormous. Finally the icon is covered with a coat of wax varnish.

Dating and schooling
The dating and schooling of icons is made on stylistic grounds. Both present one of the most controversial problems in the whole subject of icon painting. There is no wholly reliable system of dating, only a few guide lines from which the skilled eye can base his system of dating. The same applies to schooling, although this question only arises in Russian icons before the middle of the 15th century when various principalities adopted certain stylistic features peculiar to the region. After the rise of Moscow and the beginning of the process of centralisation it is impossible any longer to speak of specific local schools.

Below
The Virgin of the Sign (Orans). *This method of depicting Our Lady with her arms upraised and Christ Emmanuel in an aureole on her breast is a standard iconographical type. The earliest known version dates from the 4th century but the form, known as orans (the gesture of prayer) is derived from the ancient Graeco-Roman world. It appears for the first time in Russia in the 12th century. In the border two unidentifiable family saints are shown.*
Russian. 17th century.
32 × 27 cm (12.5 × 10.6 in).
MARIA ANDIPA ICON GALLERY

Forgeries

Fortunately it is extremely difficult to forge an icon well. The cracks in the paint which are a result of age are inimitable. However forgeries, recently made in Greece, Turkey, and Russia do appear, though seldom in the showroom or gallery. Places to suspect are small stalls (such as in street markets) and the collector is best advised to deal with reputable galleries.

Collecting today

It is only in the last ten years or so that icons have gained the popularity that they now hold in the West. Consequently the availability is greater but so is the price. The average price is £20 000 ($36 000) for a good, early icon. The connoiseur or devotee will know where to buy and what to expect to pay. For the collector on a limited budget and less well-versed the best place to begin is probably the sale-rooms or to talk to someone at a reputable gallery. Advice is usually given readily.

J.K.

Where to See Exhibitions

Sadly the only public gallery that has a collection of icons is the National Museum of Ireland and these are not of outstanding quality. Icon Galleries in London hold temporary exhibitions at irregular intervals.
MARIA ANDIPA ICON GALLERY, 162 Walton Street, SW3 holds an exhibition annually – usually in the winter months. The Gallery also exhibits icons at the Chelsea Antiques Fair in March and September, and at the Grosvenor House Antique Fair in June.
MARK GALLERY. 9 Porchester Place, W2 exhibits only Russian Icons.
TEMPLE ICON GALLERY. 4, Yeomans Row, SW3 holds exhibitions from time to time (about every 18 months) but always has an excellent collection on view to both buyer and admirer.

Left
St Spiridon. *Spiridon was a native of Cyprus, living in the 4th century. He is venerated, more especially in the Adriatic and Mediterranean areas, as shepherd of sheep and pastor of souls. Iconographically he is easily recognisable because of the strange 'bee-hive' hat which he always wears. This is a good example of cretan style.*
Cretan. 16th century.
34 × 24 cm (13.4 × 9.4 in).
TEMPLE ICON GALLERY

Above
Two Part Icon. *In the upper register, Christ is depicted enthroned flanked by SS. Anthony and Theodosius of Kiev. In the lower register, the Descent into Hell is depicted. In the borders, A Guardian Angel and St Andrew are shown on the right and SS Gregory and Paraskeva on the left.*
Russian. 18th century.
31 × 27 cm (12.2 × 10.6 in).
MARK GALLERY

Below
The Virgin of Kazan. *This method of depicting the Virgin with the child standing upright is a standard iconographical type. It first appeared in 1579. In 1612 the miraculous icon is said to have saved Moscow from the Poles.*
Russian. Late 17th century.
32 × 27 cm (12.6 × 10.6 in).
MARK GALLERY

Above
St Nicholas. *The saint, perhaps Russia's most popular saint, is depicted half-length with The Mother of God and Christ in roundels on either side of him. The icon is covered with an engraved metal riza.*
Russian. 19th century.
30 × 26 cm (11.8 × 10.2 in).
MARINA BOWATER GALLERY

Left
St George and the Dragon. *St George is depicted seated on a white horse slaying the dragon with his lance. The Princess looks on from the castle entrance and her parents and courtiers watch from the castle tower. In the top left hand corner Christ is depicted giving his blessing.*
Russian. 18th century.
36 × 28 cm (14 × 11 in).
MARK GALLERY

Above

St Simeon. *The saint is depicted as a young man holding a gospel in his left hand.*
Cretan. 18th century.
58 × 45 cm (22.8 × 17.7 in).
TEMPLE ICON GALLERY

Above

St Andrew. *The saint is depicted half-length with his right hand raised in a gesture of blessing. This icon is a particularly fine example of the Greek style of icon painting at its best.*
Greek. 17th century.
30 × 23 cm (11.8 × 9 in).
TEMPLE ICON GALLERY

Left

St Andrew. *The saint is depicted half-length holding a gospel in his right hand, his left hand raised in a gesture of blessing.*
Cretan. 18th century.
58 × 45 cm (22.8 × 17.7 in).
TEMPLE ICON GALLERY

Far left and detail left

A Three Part Icon. *In the upper register, St Sophia (Wisdom) is depicted surrounded by assistant saints and cherubims. In the lower register, on the left is an icon of the Blessed Silence and on the right The Mother of God Enthroned with St Anthony and St Theodosius of Kiev standing on either side of Her. In the borders are an Archangel and three family saints.*
Russian. 19th century.
37 × 37 cm (14.5 × 14.5 in).
MARINA BOWATER GALLERY

Where to Buy

The icon market is based in London. To a large extent where one buys is determined by financial factors as prices range widely.
MARIA ANDIPA GALLERY, 162 Walton Street, London SW3 (01-589 2371). A wide range of Greek, Russian and Balkan icons.
MARINA BOWATER GALLERY, 32b Kensington Church Street, W8 (01-937 1594). A small gallery, dealing mostly with Russian icons.
MARK GALLERY, 9 Porchester Place, W2 (01-262 4906). A large range of Russian icons.
TEMPLE ICON GALLERY, 4 Yeoman's Row, SW3 (01-589 6622) deals primarily with first class icons. Dick Temple deals mostly with permanent clients, helping them to build up private collections.
ZACHEIM, Shop 33, The Knightsbridge Pavilion, 112 Brompton Road, SW3 (01-589 5621). A small selection of icons at very reasonable prices.
CHRISTIE MANSON & WOODS LTD, 8 King Street, SW1 (01-839 9060) hold icon sales approximately every two months.
SOTHEBY & CO, 34 & 35 New Bond Street, W1 (01-493 8080) hold icon sales approximately every six weeks.
SOTHEBY PARKE BERNET INC, 980 Madison Avenue, New York, NY10021, hold icon sales approximately every three months.

What to read

The following is a suggested reading list.
M. V. Alpatov, *Art Treasures of Russia,* (London, 1968).
T. Burckhardt, *Sacred Art in East and West: its Principles and Methods,* (London, 1967).
H. P. Gerhard, *The World of Icons,* (London, 1971).
A. Grabar, *Christian Iconography: a Study of its Origins,* (London, 1969).
The 'Painter's Manual' of Dionysius of Fourna, trans. P. Hetherington, (London, 1974).
N. P. Kondakov, *The Russian Icon,* (Oxford, 1927).
V. Lossky & L. Ouspensky, *The Meaning of Icons,* (Basle, 1952).
K. Onasch, *Icons,* (London, 1963).
J. Stuart, *Ikons,* (London, 1975).
D. Talbot-Rice, *Russian Icons,* (London 1963).

Right
St John the Evangelist. *The saint is depicted with
his eyes turned towards heaven whilst he dictates to
Prokhor the scribe. The symbol at the top of the icon
shows a winged lion. A contrary attribution is adopted
in the West, this symbol being used for St Mark and an
eagle for St John. This icon is also illustrated in
Lossky's* The Meaning of Icons *and belonged to the
late Count Bobrinsky.*
Russian. 16th century.
40 × 34 cm (15.7 × 13.3 in).
TEMPLE ICON GALLERY

Above
St Cyril and St Ulita with unidentified saint.
*Both St Cyril and St Ulita are popular Russian
saints. At the top of the icon Christ is shown giving his
blessing.*
Russian. 17th century.
30 × 25 cm (12 × 10 in).
MARINA BOWATER GALLERY

Above
Standing Deesis. *Deesis means prayer and is shown
on icons by the attitude of the Virgin and St John the
Baptist who intercede on behalf of humanity on the
day of Judgment. They are thus placed either side of
Christ.*
Russian. Late 16th century.
36 × 30 cm (14 × 11.8 in).
TEMPLE ICON GALLERY

Colour right
The Baptism. *The naked Christ, standing in the
River Jordan, is baptised by St John. On the opposite
bank are three angels holding garments with which to
receive Christ. Above the Holy Ghost, in the form of a
ray of light descends upon the Head of Christ. Beneath
Christ's feet are the two river gods who signify the old
world giving way to the new. They are named 'The
Sea' and 'Jordan', referring, supposedly, to the words
of a psalm: 'The sea saw it and fled: Jordan was
driven back'. The tree and the axe on the left side
bank are an allusion to a passage in the Gospels
(Matthew 3, 10).*
Cyprus. 17th century.
42 × 29 cm (16.5 × 11.4 in).
TEMPLE ICON GALLERY

Colour top centre
The Prophet Elijah in the Wilderness. *Elijah, the
Old Testament Prophet, is depicted seated in his cave
watching the raven bring him food. The theme is taken
from the Old Testament (3 Kings xvii, 3-6) and is very
popular in Russian iconography.*
Russian. About 1700.
69 × 31 cm (27 × 12.1 in).
TEMPLE ICON GALLERY

Below
The Virgin of Vladimir. *This method of depicting
Our Lady and Christ is probably the most popular and
well-known iconographical type. It follows a
Byzantine prototype and became known as the
'Vladimirskaya Madonna' when, according to the
legend the icon was brought to Russia from
Constantinople after the country's conversion to
Christianity and later set up in the Cathedral of
Vladimir.* Russian. 17th century.
34 × 28 cm (13.3 × 11 in).
MARIA ANDIPA ICON GALLERY

Above
The Saviour. *Christ is depicted half-length, holding
a gospel in his left hand, his right hand raised in
blessing. In the borders are six family saints: SS.
Evdokia, John Vera, Matrona, the Prophet Elijah
and one unidentifiable saint.*
Russian. 18th century. Palekh School.
32 × 29 cm (12.6 × 11.4 in).
MARK GALLERY

Left
St George and St Mary of Egypt. *St George is
depicted, unmounted, together with Mary of Egypt.
Above them Christ is depicted giving his blessing.*
Russian. 17th century.
30 × 26 cm (11.8 × 10.2 in).
MARINA BOWATER GALLERY

Top

The Tichvine Mother of God. *The icon of the Tichvine Mother of God has been venerated in Russia since 1383 when, according to legend, the Virgin appeared on the River Tichvine. This method of depicting the Virgin and Child is a standard iconographical type.* Russian. Late 16th century. 55 × 34 cm (21.6 × 13.3 in)

MARINA BOWATER GALLERY

Above

The Entry into Jerusalem. *Christ, seated on a donkey, is shown entering Jerusalem followed by His apostles. At the gates of the city the Pharisees welcome Him. This is an excellent example of a 19th century icon painted in the style of the 17th century.* Russian. 30 × 26 cm (11.8 × 10.2 in).

TEMPLE ICON GALLERY

Left

The Descent of the Holy Spirit. *Against an architectural background the twelve apostles are depicted sitting in a circle. Below them is a small chamber in which an old man holding a veil stands; he symbolises the World. Above the house is a blue aureole with 12 tongues of flame radiating out of it – the Holy Spirit descending upon the heads of the apostles.* Greek. 17th century.
44 × 33 cm (17.3 × 12.9 in).

MARIA ANDIPA ICON GALLERY

87

The Unassuming Watercolour

'Transparent watercolour allows for a freshness and luminosity in its washes and for a deft calligraphic brushwork that makes it a most alluring medium.' So says the Encyclopaedia Britannica and so I think when looking at pictures and particularly watercolours in the lower price range, fundamental concepts of Art are important. Basic questions should be asked. Is it well painted? Does it decorate and interest? Or in other words, is it alluring? This kind of approach is a good guideline for small collectors and for first time buyers because there will always be a fair amount of 'rubbish' (the term dealers use) on the market priced well under £50 ($90) and tempting for that reason. So it is important to be discriminating and to bear in mind the fact that while fashions and fads in artist, medium and period are continually on the move, a carefully chosen picture, well executed and in good condition, even if unsigned, is always a delight to the initiated and inexperienced alike.

On asking one gallery owner for watercolours which fell into this price bracket, I was rebuked in shocked tones being told that any example to be found under £50 ($90) in his experience was either bad or a fake – his face was a study of disbelief when I told him I had found at least ten good ones already!

It is true that as more and more people find their pockets limiting them to the

buying of drawings and watercolours, so dealers and collectors alike broaden their knowledge and range of interest, thus forcing up prices to meet with the terrific demand. However a print or reproduction of any kind cannot compete in essence with an original work plus the great potential, allied to the possible excitement, of buying unsigned or unattributed pictures. It simply requires a keen, discriminating eye and a fair amount of persevering energy, to find what you are looking for.

Whilst generally thought a better-bet bargain-wise, the country is not necessarily the most rewarding field of research. Many out of London galleries while stocking watercolours in the lower price range may equally well specialise in popular past and present local artists, therefore stimulating an artificially high interest and pricetag. Although more aloof and daunting to the small collector, London galleries dealing in important works of art are often

Left

David Charles Read here gives us a glimpse of not only his Hampshire sketch-pad, but also one feels his sense of humour! From signed and dated sketch-pad, 1822. 11.4 × 16.5 cm (4½ × 6½ in)
SOMERVILLE & SIMPSON

Below

The light yet definitive touch of this Belgian artist M. Huard gives an unusual feel for this date and a great sense of depth and distance. Signed M Huard and dated 1850. 17.8 × 25.4 cm (7 × 10 in)
WILLIAM DRUMMOND

the more satisfactory source, because the proprietors have little time or inclination for detailed research into what they might consider to be less fashionable, amateurish, unsigned or unattributed pictures. It is not unusual to find drawers full of unframed and mounted watercolours and a careful search through these is often profitable and of course great fun. The more helpful dealers keep folders full of what they encouragingly term 'starting points' i.e. drawings, prints, etchings, and watercolours, all modestly priced, and anticipating a lifelong client in the making they are delighted to help the beginner with information and attributions. (But it is important to realise that attributions are essentially uncertain; you will always find it valuable to research them further yourself though the answer may or may not confirm the original opinion.)

If lucky enough to find a sketchbook or even a fragment, these offer a delightfully spontaneous and fresh glimpse of the artist's surroundings and way of life, the drawback being, because of their very nature, a sad lack of signatures, dates and titles; however dealers can usually give some indication and of course prices are low. A good example of work from a sketchbook is to be found in the accompanying illustrations of David Charles Read (1790-1851). They are by no means important to the development of English watercolour art, but are charming miniatures of landscape.

Another idea worth examination is the great interest value attached to the purchase of watercolours by sons of famous fathers. The name lends weight to an already good picture and for those interested in artists' lives and worlds, these insights offered by the children to us of the family house, dog or garden are precious and often offer useful social comment. Two examples of David Cox Junior's work are shown here and I think are certainly attractive enough to collect in their own right. In the same vein, works by a protegé may prove appealing In addition, with the passing of time, it becomes easier to see these kinds of 19th century watercolours in better perspective, and to appreciate

Below

By the popular bird and animal artist Joseph Wolf (1820-99), this grey wash is a wonderfully sympathetic treatment of Orang-utangs. Wolf worked extensively for Lord Lilford and was greatly admired by Landseer. 24.1 × 30 cm (9⅜ × 11¾ in)
WILLIAM DRUMMOND

Above

This sepia watercolour of Carisbrooke Castle is a fine example of the work of the self taught Plymouth artist William Payne (about 1760-1830). Inventing 'Payne's Grey' he specialised in landscapes usually with figures and it is a feature of his work that the colour fades to a distinctive orange brown. Titled and signed Carisbrooke Castle, Isle of Wight. 16.5 × 23.8 cm (6½ × 9⅜ in)
WILLIAM DRUMMOND

Above

This delicate and sensitive study of Salisbury Cathedral is an example of the work of a good lady amateur of the 19th century, and is by Caroline St John Mildmay (1834-1894). Signed. 24.1 × 17.8 cm (9½ × 7 in)
LAWRENCE OXLEY

Above

By the Cheltenham born Robert Thorne Waite R.W.S. (1842-1935) this Shepherd's Caravan masterfully illustrates for us the artist's facility with cloud formation and sky which fall in definition between the rich and sensitive – here the sunset is in tones of yellow and orange. Signed. 14 × 24.1 cm (5½ × 9½ in)
BOURNE GALLERY

Above

Although unattributed, this attractive watercolour drawing of a windmill scene with cows in the foreground is typical of its time. 19th century English school, unsigned. 7.6 × 12.7 cm (3 × 5 in)
BOURNE GALLERY

Above

This French watercolour executed mainly in muted tones of brown is unusual in composition, freely painted with skill and an obvious love of the sea. Signed Heery, and dated 1874.
10.2 × 20.3 cm (4 × 8 in)
ROYAL EXCHANGE GALLERY

Below

A member of the German School, Richard Fehdmer (born 1860) painted this wonderfully poignant and evocative woodland under snow in 1889. It is unusual in that snowscapes falling into our restricted price range are few and far between and always popular. Signed and dated 1889.
28 × 19 cm (11 × 7½ in)
APPLEBY BROTHERS

Above

The View in Ridge Lane near Lancaster, *I feel would stand with dignity beside many of the considered 'greats' of the watercolour world. Technically excellent this picture is by Clark Rampling of Manchester. Titled.*
11.7 × 9.5 cm (4⅝ × 3¾ in)
WILLIAM DRUMMOND

Below

A Cottage in Twineham Lane. One of a pair of appealing cottage landscapes by the Sussex specialist Albert Edward Bowers (1875-93). Signed and titled.
21.6 × 33 cm (8½ × 13 in)
EASTBOURNE FINE ART

Below

This sombre and eerie greywash of Caernarvon Castle *was painted by Charles Parsons Knight (1827-1897). His sky here conveys to us a great sense of drama heightened by the medium used. Signed.*
11.4 × 16.5 cm (4½ × 6½ in)
WILLIAM DRUMMOND

Below

This rather unusual composition by David Cox Jnr (1809-85) is nevertheless a delightful evocation of English village life and the trees are particularly well painted. Rural scene with country church. *Signed.*
11.4 × 12.7 cm (approx 4½ × 5 in)
BOURNE GALLERY

Below

This charming Robert Thorne Waite (1842-1935) will hold appeal for those lovers of harvesting. Here the artist conveys the season of 'mellow fruitfulness' with quiet candour. The Manor Farm, *signed.*
14 × 24.1 cm (5½ × 9½ in)
BOURNE GALLERY

Below
This charming Reclining Boy *will be of interest to admirers of Etty whose work William Edward Frost (1810-77) emulated being an early protégé.*
6.3 × 17.8 cm (2½ × 7 in)
ABBOTT AND HOLDER

Right
From a signed and dated sketchbook 1822, the delicately painted tree shows us the work of the Hampshire artist David Charles Read (1790-1851).
16 × 12.7 cm (6¼ × 5 in)
SOMERVILLE & SIMPSON

them for their true worth. This is why as an added bonus to their intrinsic interest, they may be a particularly good buy today.

Auction rooms and country sales, deserve attention. However, as far as the beginner is concerned, they offer more pitfalls and disappointments, since without access to helpful dealers and reference books, mistakes can be made. T.B-J.

WHERE TO BUY
Contrary to popular belief, I have found that braving the London galleries can be highly rewarding. However, this should not deter you from exploring throughout the country. Here are just a few suggestions.
ABBOTT AND HOLDER, 73 Castlenau, Barnes, London SW13 (01-748 2416)
APPLEBY BROTHERS LTD, 8-10 Ryder Street, London SW1 (01-930 6507)
BOURNE GALLERY, 31-33 Lesbourne Road, Reigate, Surrey (Reigate 49451)
CLARGES GALLERY, 158 Walton Street, London SW3 (01-584 3022)
WILLIAM DRUMMOND, Covent Garden Gallery, 20 Russell Street, London WC2 (01-836 1139)
EASTBOURNE FINE ART, 47 South Street, Eastbourne, Sussex (Eastbourne 25634)
FRY GALLERY, 58 Jermyn Street, London SW1 (01-493 4496)
LAURENCE OXLEY, Broad Street, Alresford, Hampshire (Alresford 2188)
ROYAL EXCHANGE ART GALLERY, 14 Royal Exchange, London EC3 (01-283 4400)
STANHOPE SHELTON PICTURES LTD, Cobbolds Mill, Monks Eleigh, Suffolk (0449 740203)
SOMERVILLE AND SIMPSON LTD, 11 Savile Row, London W1 (01-437 5414)
ANDREW WYLD, 3 Cork Street, London W1 (01-437 2741)

Below
George Barret Jnr (1767-1842) here departs from his usual romantic landscapes to paint with touching simplicity Three Cows. *The younger son of an Irishman who worked with Sawry Gilpin, Barrat Jnr published* Theory and Practice of Watercolour Painting *in 1840 and was a founder member of O.W.C.S. Greywash and pencil. Initialled.*
11.4 × 17.8 cm (4⅜ × 7 in)
WILLIAM DRUMMOND

Below
By Phiz, famed Punch caricaturist and illustrator of Pickwick Papers, David Copperfield, *and* Nicholas Nickleby, *this watercolour and pencil sketch of an embarrassed lady is an unusual subject and an inexpensive 'starting point' for collectors, by Hablot Knight Browne (1815-82). Signed Phiz.*
8.9 × 9.5 cm (3½ × 3¾ in)
WILLIAM DRUMMOND

Above
John Atkinson (1863-1924) considered by many to be one of the finest animal painters of the North East, here draws the observer into his world of horses and Northumberland life with this faithful and candid portrayal of Horses and Caravan at Newcastle Moor. *Signed and dated 1880.*
22.5 × 28.9 cm (8⅞ × 11⅜ in)
FRY GALLERY

Above
This sombre but interesting depiction of Bodiam Castle in Kent is the work of David Cox Jnr (1809-85). A point of interest which lends weight to this attribution is the enclosure of a letter from Cox's daughter donating the watercolour as a wedding present to a friend. Letter enclosed.
19.7 × 49.5 cm (7¾ × 19½ in)
BOURNE GALLERY

Dutch Drawings of the 17th Century

Although Horace Walpole once described Dutch painters as 'those drudging mimics of Nature's uncomely coarseness' the majority of Englishmen both then and since have held the 17th century Dutch school in high regard. This explains the existence of the immensely important collection of Dutch drawings at the British Museum, as well as the large number of superb Dutch paintings in other public and private collections. This taste for Dutch art has inspired successive generations of British artists, so that we can never fully understand English painting without a knowledge of Dutch painting. It is important therefore to look at Dutch 17th century drawing and to appreciate its qualities.

The Golden Age of Dutch painting occurred in the first 75 years of the 17th century. It was then that the seven United Provinces managed to maintain their independence from France as well as greatly expand their mercantile, banking and colonial interests. It was during those years that three of Europe's most renowned artists were working in the United Provinces, Frans Hals (died 1666), Rembrandt (died 1669) and Vermeer (died 1665) as well as scores of minor artists of imagination and sensitivity, all of whom produced seascapes or landscapes or still-lives or portraits or genre scenes in a bewildering multitude.

Peter Mundy visiting Amsterdam in 1640 commented on the love of painting by the people: 'yea many tymes black-smithes, cobblers etts, will have some picture or other by their forge or in their stalle, such is the generall notion, enclination and delight that the countrie natives have to paintings . . .'. The result of such totally novel and generous patronage greatly encouraged painting, but still cannot totally account for such high standards of artistic excellence, which were displayed during this period. It is reflected in the work of the provincial painters of earthy genre scenes as well as in the work of the cosmopolitan artist, who explored the ideas and fashions of the baroque movement. Such diverse and prolific creativity can only be described as a miracle.

What to read

There is no specific book to read on Dutch drawing and the enthusiast has to rely upon a number of specialised catalogues. One of the best is *Inventaire Général des Desseins des Ecoles du Nord* edited by Fritz Lugt, 1929, for a good general book read *Dutch art and architecture 1600-1800 by Rosenberg and Slive* published as part of the Pelican History of Art Series.   J.K.

Where to see

Dutch drawings are extremely well represented in British museums. The best collections may be seen in the British Museum and the Victoria and Albert Museum; and there are also good examples in the Fitzwilliam Museum, Cambridge and the Ashmolean, Oxford. At the National Maritime Museum, Greenwich, there are a number of excellent marine studies by Van de Velde. In Holland the best collections are in the Rijksmuseum, Amsterdam and the Boymans Museum, Rotterdam. The University Collection at Leyden and the Historiche Museum, Amsterdam, are well worth a visit. Finally in Paris, the Institut Néerlandais has a fine collection.

Where to buy

In the last year or so the best place to see good Dutch drawing has been the salerooms. Sotheby's, who bought Mak van Waay, a saleroom in Amsterdam, have recently held a series of outstanding sales (many of the drawings in this article were originally seen there) and hence there is a good supply of drawings on the market at the moment. For lower-priced drawings, London is still the best place to find them: particularly from small dealers such as Christine van Marle and Claude Apcher. Prices for top quality drawings are about the same in London and Amsterdam, possibly slightly higher in the latter. The dealers listed below are those mentioned in the text as well as others, who deal in Old Master drawings and who generally have some in stock.
THOS AGNEW & SONS LTD, 43 Old Bond Street, London W1 (01-629 6176)
C. APCHER, Grays Antique Market, 58 Davies Street, London W1 (01-629 7034)
BASKETT & DAY, 173 New Bond Street, London W1 (01-629 2991)
BROD GALLERY, 24 St James's Street, London W1 (01-839 3871)
CHRISTIE, MANSON & WOODS LTD (saleroom), 8 King Street, London W1 (01-839 9060)
P. & D. COLNAGHI & CO LTD, 14 Old Bond Street, London W1 (01-491 7408)
GEBR. DOUWES, Rokin 46, Amsterdam, Holland (020-23 62 08)
BERNARD HOUTHAKKER, Rokin 98, Amsterdam, Holland (020-23 39 39)
THEO LAURENTIUS, Oenselsestraat 15-17, Zaltbommel, Holland (04180-3515)
CHRISTINE VAN MARLE, 39 Queensdale Road, London W11 (01-603 5731) (by appointment only)
FRANCOIS PARRY, Noordeinde 146, The Hague, Holland (070-60 5886)
SOTHEBY MAK VAN WAAY, Rokin 102, Amsterdam (020-24 62 15)
Y. TAN BUNZL, 25 Montagu Square, London W1 (01-935 1469)
RAFAEL VALLS, 34 Bury Street, London W1 (01-839 2713)

Left and detail below
Ships at anchor near a port by Bonaventura Peeters I (Antwerp 1614-Hoboken 1652), pen and ink with grey wash, 165 × 200 mm (6.5 × 7.8 in).
BRIAN KOETSER

Left
One of a pair of watercolour and black chalk drawings of parrots by Cornelis Saftleven (Corinchem 1607?-Rotterdam 1681), 550 × 320 mm (21.5 × 12.5 in).
This superb study reflects the international courtly baroque of the 17th century as opposed to the more typical homely still-lives.
HOUTHAKKER

Below
Landscape by E. Murant (Amsterdam 1622-Leiden 1700) black chalk, 133 × 190 mm (5.5 × 7.75 in).
It is high-quality drawing such as this by relatively unknown artists that brings the achievement of Dutch 17th century art into focus.
AGNEWS

Left

Study of peasants, anonymous, brown ink and wash, previously part of the Philip Huart collection, 17 × 17 cm sq (6.75 in sq). This good quality drawing is excellent value.

CLAUDE APCHER

Below

Playing 'Kolf' by Allart van Everdingen (Alkmaar 1621-Amsterdam 1675) pencil and wash on grey paper, monogrammed AVE, 150 × 190 mm (6 × 7.5 in).

This artist made a trip to Sweden in 1640 and he is best known for his popularisation of 'Northern' features, such as waterfalls and mountains. This, however, is a typically Dutch scene, showing a group of peasants playing kolf (from German Kolbe meaning club) a precursor of golf.

GEBR DOUWES

Below

Study of weeds, att. Jan van Kessel (Amsterdam 1641-Amsterdam 1680) brush and grey ink, 93 × 145 mm (3.5 × 5.7 in).

The quality of this study leads one to suspect that it could be by the hand of a more talented artist than van Kessel. Possibly van de Velde. (It is interesting to compare the naturalistic detail in his man and woman in a landscape in the Rikjsmuseum, to this study).

HOUTHAKKER

Left

Interior with peasants playing backgammon by Abraham Diepraam, pen and ink with brown wash, 213 ×322 mm (8.3 × 12.5 in).

One of the most popular subjects for Dutch artists was the genre scene: anecdotes, usually of peasant life, painted with an eye for earthy realism and humour. This drawing was executed by a follower of the leading exponent of genre, Adriaan Brouwer.

BRIAN KOETSER GALLERY

Far left

A rocky river landscape with two figures in the foreground by Anthonie Waterloo (1610-1690) coloured chalk, 196 × 154 mm (7.75 × 6 in).

This is one of six drawings from a series, which have appeared on the London art market recently. It is difficult to decide whether they formed part of a sketchbook which Waterloo used on his travels. Waterloo is known almost entirely for his drawings and prints, most of his landscapes show a marked interest in trees.

COLNAGHI

Left

Shipping scene, anonymous, 17th century, watercolour and brown ink, 28.5 × 19.5 cm (11.2 × 7.75 in)

The basis of much of the United Provinces' power rested upon her might at sea, for a short period, during the régime of Johann de Witt (1653-72) she even eclipsed England in maritime power. Naturally a school of marine painters flourished of which this modest drawing is a cheap example.

CLAUDE APCHER

Left and detail above

Landscape with figures attributed to Roland Roghman (b Amsterdam 1597 d Amsterdam 1686), brown ink and wash, inscribed 'le collection Bazot 1817', stamped with Bazot mark, 8.3 × 10 cm (3.3 × 4.1 in).

In the 19th century this drawing was attributed to Rembrandt, certainly the very free use of the pen is reminiscent of his drawing style. It is more likely that it was executed by one of his circle, such as Roland Roghman, who was an intimate friend of Rembrandt and who drew in this manner.

CLAUDE APCHER

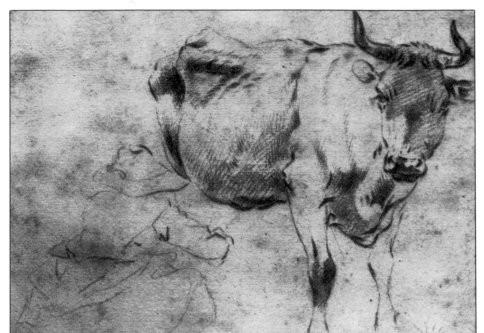

Left
*A peasant milking a cow by Paulus Potter
(1625-1654) black chalk 97 × 126 mm (3.8 × 5 in).
Potter was the most famous of all Dutch animal
painters. His most notorious work is* The Bull *in the
Maurithaus in The Hague. This example shows his
skill and lightness of touch on much smaller, more
intimate compositions.*
AGNEWS

Below
*A cavalier drinking from a glass, by an artist working
in Haarlem or Delft in the mid-1650s, black chalk
heightened with white and with touches of red chalk on
blue paper, bearing an illegible inscription, possibly
Du Ja, 385 × 231 mm (15 × 9 in).
There is a similarity in style between this drawing and
two studies of seated gentlemen in the Teyler's
Foundation, Haarlem. It recalls the pose and
appearance of a figure that appears in paintings by
Gerard Terborch the younger, Jan Steen, and Gabriel
Metsu, and although no firm link can be established
between any painting by one of these artists or their
imitators, it is possible that it came from this school.*
BASKETT & DAY

Left
*River scene near
Rademaker by Frederick
de Moucheron, pen and
brown ink and wash,
165 × 155 mm
(6 × 5 in).
De Moucheron was an
extremely sensitive
interpreter of landscape.*
CHRISTINE VAN
MARLE

Above
*Landscape with a ravine
by Jacob Esselens
(Amsterdam
1629-Amsterdam
1687) pen and brown
ink, 164 × 219 mm
(6.5 × 8.5 in).
This view is so unusual
for Holland that it is
possibly an English
scene.*
HOUTHAKKER

Left
*Study of hounds by Pieter Boel (1622-1674) red
chalk, 240 × 175 mm (9.5 × 7 in).
This compares to a red chalk study of a camel's head
(photo Witt Coll) and it possibly came from the same
sketch book. Boel was a well-known painter of
animals.*
CHRISTINE VAN MARLE

Left
*Dutch landscape by
Albert Flamen (about
1620-after 1664), pen
and wash, signed, 102
× 160 cm (4 × 6 in).*
GEBR DOUWES

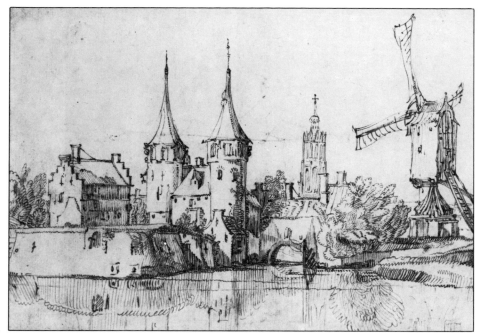

Left

A view of Delft, Rotterdamsche poort by Jan van de Velde II (Rotterdam 1593-Enkhuizen 1641), pen and ink, 147 × 215 mm (5.75 × 8.5 in).
Drawings by this engraver are scarce and this example would have been made direct from nature with a view to working it into an engraving at a later stage. Similarly landscapes in oils were always painted in studios from drawings taken on the spot.
BRIAN KOETSER GALLERY

Below

Riders and dogs resting outside a walled garden by Nicolaes Bercham (Haarlem 1620-Amsterdam 1683) black chalk and grey wash, 215 × 193 mm (8.5 × 7.5 in).
In 1642 Bercham travelled with Jan Baptist Weenix to Italy, where he spent three years. The sketches he made there combined with those made on another trip in the 1650s served him for the rest of his intensely prolific life. He specialised in Italian landscapes and Arcadian scenes.
THEO LAURENTIUS

Right

Young men smoking around a table, a woman and servant drinking, att. to Johann Liss, pen and brown ink, 157 × 203 mm (6 × 8 in).
Liss was a German artist working in Holland about 1615 before he went on to travel in France and Italy.
GEBR DOUWES

Below

Europa and Jupiter in the guise of a bull by Moses van Uytenbroeck (or Wttenbroeck) (The Hague 1590-?1648) pen and grey ink and light grey wash, indented for transfer, 152 × 198 mm (6 × 7.8 in).
The use of mythological figures set in an attractive landscape precurses the Baroque love of such themes in painting. This example is typical of Uytenbroeck's work.
HOUTHAKKER

Right

Young girl skating with a hockey stick by Adam van Breen (The Hague c 1600-1650) pen and ink with grey wash, 70 × 148 mm (2.75 × 5.8 in).
This unfinished drawing was possibly a study for an ice scene. Van Breen was a follower of Avercamp, the artist, who made such typical Dutch scenes famous throughout Europe.
BRIAN KOETSER

Above

Cross bow shooting at a village fair by Anthony van Croos (The Hague ?1606 or 1607-The Hague 1662 or 1663) black chalk, signed and dated 1646, 165 × 225 mm (6.5 × 8.8 in).
It is significant that the monogram on this drawing has been tampered with to make it read as the signature of Jan van Goyen: the master of peasant scenes such as this, and a strong influence upon van Croos. Vogelschieten or crossbow shooting, was and still is a popular pastime in Holland.
HOUTHAKKER

POTTERY & PORCELAIN

Collecting antique pottery and porcelain, invariably thought of as a pastime only for the rich and knowledgeable, is in fact a pleasure that may be enjoyed by anyone. Certainly, the price for some types of ware or article can run into many thousands, but equally there are other fields, and worthwhile fields at that, where the sums involved can be as small as £1 or £2 (under $2 or $3.50). Certainly, too, there are specialist areas where a sound knowledge of the history and technical make-up of the wares is essential; but again there are others where nothing more is needed than a 'good eye' for design and colour – knowledge coming later – and surprisingly it is often in these latter areas that present day prices are the most modest. Probably the three principal questions to be answered by any collector of antique pottery and porcelain are what to buy, where to buy and how to display.

What to buy

So long as the planned collection has some aim or meaning that it follows then it will be a collection that gives pleasure and therefore one which satisfies immediately the primary objective. First and foremost, therefore, the new collector when deciding what to buy must settle for whatever *interests him*. He should not merely follow a fashion – unless it is one with a particular facet for exploration as yet overlooked – and he should aim eventually to look beyond the intrinsic visual beauty of each piece towards a serious study of his subject. It is no exaggeration to say that to know all about one's collection is to increase the pleasure derived from it by at least ten times.

Basically there are two directions a collection of antique pottery and/or porcelain may take. Either it is concerned with one specific kind or make of pottery or porcelain, perhaps early Chinese, perhaps 18th century Worcester, perhaps 19th century English majolica, and so on. Alternatively it is restricted to one specific kind of article, perhaps figures, perhaps tea pots, perhaps tiles, or tureens. A collection of one type of ware has the advantages of uniformity of style, uniformity of provenance and character; a collection of one type of article offers uniformity of scale, and the opportunity to acquire items of totally different materials and character, from different dates and factories. The decision must rest with the collector.

Where to buy

This is a question that is more easily answered. As a general rule it is best in the long run to buy from reputable and established dealers who should (and most do) point out any damage or restoration, and who know the reigning market price. It is possible to beat the market and buy something 'for nothing', either at an auction or in a small out-of-the-way shop. But it is a risky business, especially in this field where condition is of such paramount importance, and, in addition, unless certain of an article's value you can end up paying considerably more than you would to a good dealer. While if you do buy a piece for a price well below the true market value there remains always the thought that the vendor has not received the true market value – a thought that can prick the conscience and spoil the pleasure of a collection each time you look in the cabinet.

How to display

For pottery and porcelain, cabinets are undoubtedly the best way of displaying and looking after a collection. A most attractive sight in any room is a glass cabinet of antique pottery and porcelain, well lighted and not too crowded – wonderful. The cabinet is probably modern (but that is a matter of taste), probably with good quality glass shelves, and may well have some of the excellent perspex stands that there are now available in every shape and form.

One of the exceptions to this are collections of the larger objects, such as tureens, which of course require plenty of space and still have a use around the house, for soup even, or, without their lids, for cut flowers and bulbs.

PRICES

Chinese export porcelain (page 101), is one of the major international fields for collectors; competition is intense, in the heat of the auction rooms in particular, and individual items can fetch prices which put them way beyond the reach of most people. £4000 and £5000 ($7200 and $9000) are the sort of sums required for figures, like those of the Europeans and the seated dogs (page 100); £1500 to £3000 ($2700 to $5400) is required for the more substantial utility items like the fruit stand, after a Meissen original (on the same page), and a good armorial tureen; and plates and dishes with sharply defined decoration *en grisaille* or blue and white of European-inspired subjects are usually priced around £700 or £800 ($1260 or $1440) but will rise to as much as £1700 ($3060) for exceptionally fine examples. In the middle range, £500 to £750

($900 to $1350) is still required for items such as mugs with European ships and hunting scenes. There is though just a glimmer of hope left: very small pieces, like cups without saucers, or perhaps pieces with single hair-line cracks may still be bought for less than £50 ($90).

Parian ware

The prices of the 19th century Parian ware (page 105), made by Copeland, Minton, Wedgwood, Belleek and one or two others, make much more pleasant reading. Even the very finest pieces, with historical and documentary interest, including William Calder Marshall's *Lear and Cordelia* (page 105) and *La Toilette*, the Belleek *Clytie* (both on page 106) and Mintons' *Flower of the Town* (page 107) usually sell for no more than £200 ($360). Good middle-market examples such as John Bell's *Dorothea* and the bust of *Lesbia* (both on page 106) may be bought for under £100 ($180). Portraits, figures and busts, are also quite lowly priced by modern standards: the full-length figure of *Colin Minton Campbell* (page 107) is rare and, at about £125 ($225) is the highest priced of those shown; a large bust of Wellington should be less than £100 ($180) and the smaller busts of Mozart, Spurgeon and Shakespeare (page 106) all under £50 ($90).

Miniature porcelain

If space is the problem then miniatures (page 108) are the answer, although it does not necessarily follow that because the items are small in size the prices are equally diminutive. The productions of the well-known 18th and early 19th century factories, of Bow, Worcester, Caughley and Spode, can be highly priced: a Worcester blue and white tea bowl and saucer (page 111) would cost about £130 ($234); a Caughley one (page 109) with printed rather than painted decoration, in the region of £40 ($72) and Spode's miniature cabaret set (on the same page) as much as £300 ($540), but this is a beautiful little group. Prices become more reasonable as one moves further towards modern times, and things like Wedgwood miniature tea pots, the Victorian doll's dinner services (both on page 110) and fine Coalport mugs (page 109) are priced around £75, £60 and £40 ($135, $108 and $72) respectively. Candlesticks are much in demand and good Spode or Davenport ones (page 111) generally cost about £40 ($72) a piece. But the £10 or £15 ($18 or $27) currently asked for such articles as the excellent Royal Worcester miniatures (pages 108 and 111) seem very fair indeed.

Tureens

These offer a wide price range. £10,000, £20,000 ($18 000, $36 000) and even more may be demanded for a magnificent Chinese goose tureen; £2000 and £3000 ($3600 and $5400) for Chinese *famille rose* tureens – but these are exceptions. The next highest sums likely to be incurred are generally below £1000 ($1800). £500 to £800 ($900 to $1440) should buy the Chelsea flower-painted tureen (with slight damage, page 117), or the Coalport one (page 115) with rich gilding and complete with its stand; a Chinese Nankin blue and white tureen (page 114) is usually priced around £250 ($450) and a well-printed Wedgwood creamware tureen (page 113) around £350

($630). Lower down the price scale a plain Wedgwood creamware tureen (page 113) may be bought for as little as £70 or £80 ($126 or $144) and the same sort of figure should secure almost any 19th century pottery tureen. There are some quite low prices amongst many of the late 19th and early 20th century examples: a Spode or Minton tureen from this period may be bought for about £30 ($54) and a Doulton one for half this amount (pages 113 and 114).

Victorian majolica

A few years ago £20 or £30 ($36 or $54) would buy almost anything in this colourful pottery; today £250 ($450) at least is required for the more important pieces, such as the Wedgwood wine ewer (page 121) and only a little less is required for garden seats – the monkey one, or the simulated bamboo (pages 118 and 120). Bird inkstands by George Jones (page 121) and fruit stands by Minton (page 119) are examples of what may be bought in the £60 to £75 ($108 to $135) range; and single or pairs of Wedgwood green and mottle glazed plates and dishes (page 120) generally cost well under £20 ($36).

English pottery tiles

These offer the greatest scope to the collector of limited funds. Two of the tiles illustrated in colour (page 122) the one by Maw & Co with raised decoration in blue and orange, and the one printed with flowers and bamboo, should be as little as £1 or £2 (under $2 or between $3 and $4). Prices obviously increase for earlier and rarer tiles, yet still not outrageously so: 18th century English delft tiles, including some of the scarce Liverpool transfer-printed ones, cost only £30 or £40 ($54 or $72); and 19th century tiles with decoration by well-known masters of design such as William de Morgan and Walter Crane (the Kingfisher tile and 'Little Brown Betty' – both on page 125 – are examples of their work) may be bought for less than £50 ($90). Even the prices for a complete William de Morgan panel or fireplace (page 124) remain as low as £200 ($360). Finally, for someone inspired to delve far back into history, £20 to £60 ($36 to $108) should buy an interesting slip-decorated tile from the 12th or 13th century – antique beyond dispute.

Note: It cannot be repeated too often that all pottery and porcelain values hang on condition. Perfect pieces, although costing more, always give more pleasure to their owners and are easier to sell if the need arises. It is well worth paying more for anything in perfect condition. If imperfect pieces cannot be avoided, only ones with *minimal* damage or *minimal* repair should be considered.

OLIVER MATHEWS

Chinese Porcelain made for the West

Ever since Chinese porcelain first arrived in the West the finest examples have been counted among the most treasured of material possessions; and from the start Europeans lucky and rich enough to acquire Chinese porcelain had many of their precious pieces mounted in silver and gold – to protect it, and also, no doubt, to put their own 'stamp' on it. It was but a short step, therefore, from passive admiration to active specification, to ordering certain designs and decorations.

The earliest Chinese wares with specifically European decoration were some few domestic articles of blue and white – dishes and ewers painted with the coats of arms of Western dignitaries. These date from the 16th century, from the time when the Portuguese were bringing home the first fruits of a trading post they had established at Macao on the Canton estuary in southern China.

The pioneering Portuguese, the first Europeans to trade with China, were soon followed by others. During the 17th century the English, Dutch and French all started their own East India Companies, with agents at Macao and then Canton itself. (In this respect it is interesting to remember that today on the Continent of Europe Chinese export porcelain is still known as *Compagnie des Indes*.)

After the early armorial blue and white, there came with the increase in trade with Christian countries the most fascinating and strange of all Chinese porcelain with European decoration, the so-called Jesuit-ware, painted with Christian subjects and Christian emblems. Jesuit priests and brothers from the West managed to build-up a unique relationship with the Chinese during the 16th, 17th and 18th centuries. Many of them in the course of spreading the Gospel became fluent in the local language, wore Chinese dress and held influential secular positions – a few even within the courts of power – where their knowledge of science and astronomy, a then neglected area of Chinese experience, was particularly appreciated. While one, Père d'Entrecolles, became a significant figure in the great porcelain manufacturing town of Ching-te Chen. With such a footing, it was not surprising that they also managed to influence much of the decoration on porcelain made for export to the West. Although some Jesuit china was painted in underglaze blue, the great majority, which was produced during the first half of the 18th century, was done *en grisaille*. The Nativity, the Baptism of Christ and the Crucifixion are the most frequently met with subjects.

A good proportion of Chinese porcelain with purely European decoration is *en grisaille*, for the subjects were often directly copied from engravings sent out to China expressly for this purpose. Beyond the rich charm of a European picture with unavoidable Chinese qualities, on such pieces there is the extra pleasure of discovery to be had in spotting Chinese artistic licence (a Nativity scene with a Buddha-like Christ is not infrequent) and in tracing the original prints from which the 18th century Chinese decoration was taken.

Also sent out to China for the ceramic artists to copy on to porcelain were water-colour designs of crests and coats of arms for application to entire services ordered by the Western social elite. Generally in rich *famille rose* enamels, Chinese armorial porcelain remains highly esteemed in the West; the subject of considerable excitement in every auction in which it appears.

Nearly all the porcelain for export to Europe was made at the manufacturing metropolis of Ching-te Chen, further north, but as many of the orders were placed at Canton much of the decoration came to be undertaken there – where the agents received the shippers and their demands and acted as go-between for the Fan Kwaes (foreign devils) and the Cantonese merchants and decorators. F. A. Lloyd Hyde in his *Chinese Export Porcelain*, 1964, quotes a visit by William Hickey in 1769 to a Canton decorating establishment:

In one long gallery we found upwards of a hundred persons at work in sketching or finishing the various ornaments upon each particular piece of ware, some parts being executed by men of very advanced age, and other by children, even so young as six or seven years.

With such activity and skill there were few forms of European decoration not undertaken by the Chinese – from fighting cocks and political propaganda, through allegories, myths, and sailing ships, to flowers, fox-hunting and pastoral

love scenes (sometimes with rather more than just a suggestion of the *risqué*).

European shapes too came to be increasingly copied. In the K'ang Hsi (1662-1722) and Yung Cheng (1723-1735) periods these were mostly confined to helmet jugs, candlesticks and dishes. But in the reign of Ch'ien Lung (1736-1795) the potters themselves responded more and more ambitiously to the requests of the Europeans (perhaps some decadence began to creep in as well) and massive multicoloured tureens in the form of boars' heads and sitting geese headed a list of articles designed for every part of the dining table. These were followed by small tureens in the form of crabs, fruit stands with clambering cherubs (after Meissen originals), such lesser articles of the feast as salt cellars, and even the handles for knives and forks. All were intended directly for Europe, yet all were still unmistakably and essentially Chinese, in character and colour.

Whilst the articles with European decoration make one study; the articles of European shape make another. The first Chinese porcelain to come to Europe was handled by the jewellers and silversmiths, so valuable a commodity was it considered, thus it followed that European silver shapes were the first to be copied by the skilled Chinese potter. In the same way as worthwhile detective work is to be done in unearthing the origin of many of the pictures on Chinese export porcelain, so is there reward to be gained in 're-marrying' Chinese porcelain articles like porringers, tankards and candlesticks to their silver originals which, by bearing accurate dates, bring yet another dimension to the subject and its study.

Following the American War of Independence, the Americans, freed of British duties on most of their imports, were able to trade at Canton unencumbered and in their own right. From the late 1780s they were as active as any of the Western trading nations carrying off wares in the same way as the Europeans, with bespoke decorations including on some occasions portraits of Washington, and on many occasions sailing with flying Stars & Stripes. A type of border decoration composed of a band of blue enamel with gilt stars overlaid is generally thought to be of American origin. This is found in some quantity on porcelain from the late 18th and early 19th centuries and heralds, in fact, the final stages of fine Chinese porcelain with Western decoration.

With the end of the 18th century the original and supremely creative spark seemed to desert the craftsmen; the

Left
Pair of early 18th century candlesticks made in Chinese porcelain after European silver originals, with decoration in the Imari style. Chinese porcelain was considered so precious when it first arrived in the West that it was handled by jewellers and silversmiths, thus some of the earliest 'European' pieces were copied from silver. H 20 cm (7¾ in)
EARLE D. VANDEKAR

Below
Tea pot and cover enamelled with flower sprigs in blue, the border with gold stars on bands of blue. About 1790. This 'blue star' pattern is thought to have been a specifically American order.
S. MARCHANT & SON

Above
Saucer dish painted en grisaille *with a design in the style of Watteau. One of a set of representations of the elements – each one of which is slightly* risqué. *Ch'ien Lung. This is a rare design, although the Victoria & Albert Museum has a set of small circular plaques with the same decoration. Very slight hair crack.*
D 20.5 cm (8 in)
DAVID B. NEWBON

Below
Pair of sauce tureens with covers and stands, painted in underglaze blue with the Fitzhugh pattern. Late 18th century. Of uncertain origin – it seems most likely that one with the name Fitzhugh was the first to order it – this is one of the most sought after of patterns on Chinese export ware. It appears also in overglaze red, green and orange. W 19 cm (7 in)
EARLE D. VANDEKAR

demands of the Westerners themselves became stereotyped (they were in any case by then achieving satisfaction with their home-made porcelain); the East India companies started to sail into warm water (the English East India Co. finally fell to the Crown with the Indian Mutiny of 1857); and Chinese export porcelain as an individual art form came to an end.

How to begin collecting
One glance at the captions to the illustrations is enough to confirm that Chinese export porcelain can command high prices. With one or two minor market fluctuations this has always been the case, and so long as antiques and works of art are collected will remain so. Thus there is the consolation that good money spent in this direction should be money well spent. At the same time it is quite possible to form an interesting, if modest, collection for quite a small outlay – the single tea cup illustrated is in perfect condition, has Meissen-inspired decoration, cost only £18 ($32) and is not an isolated example.

If the plunge is to be taken and it is decided to buy a few pieces – 'few' being the word, as this is not a field in which quantity is necessary – then two things are important. First, as ever, condition: as a rule perfect pieces only should be bought, unless the damage or repair is very slight (the writer has experience of trying to re-sell items bought with damage which appeared of little consequence at the time of purchase). Second, and of particular importance in this sphere, is brilliance of decoration, especially with those items painted *en grisaille* – this decoration by its nature is delicate and 'thin', and pieces with rubbed or dull decoration might just as well be severely broken for the impact it makes to their monetary value. O.M.

WHERE TO BUY
Specialist oriental porcelain dealers certain to have good examples in stock include:
S. MARCHANT & SON, 120 Kensington Church Street, W8 (01-229 5319)
DAVID B. NEWBON, 56 Beauchamp Place, SW3 (01-589 1369)
EARLE D. VANDEKAR, 138 Brompton Road, SW3 (01-589 8481/3398)
General pottery and porcelain dealers likely to have a few examples include:
R. A. BARNES, 16 Lower Richmond Road, SW14 (01-789 3371)
SUSAN BECKER, 18 Lower Richmond Road, SW14 (01-788 9082)
ANDREW DANDO, 4 Wood Street, Bath (Bath 22702)
GEOFFREY GODDEN, CHINAMAN, 17-19 Crescent Road, Worthing, Sussex (0903 35958)
JEAN SEWELL LTD, 3 Campden Street, W8 (01-727 3122)

Parian Ware: 'Statuary Porcelain'

Above

Lear and Cordelia, *after the original by William Calder Marshall, published 1 March 1860 by W. T. Copeland. Lear mourns the death of his daughter, the only one who loved him. The very high quality of the modelling is apparent in the limp hands of Cordelia.* W 30 cm (12 in) H 29 cm (11½ in)
HEMINGWAY ANTIQUES

Mention Parian, and you are quite likely to be met with a blank look. The large quantity of inferior pieces produced in this body has made later generations forgetful of even the very fine quality pieces being made by the Copeland, Minton and Wedgwood factories in the second half of the 19th century. Interest is now starting to revive and there are still numbers of good pieces around, owing to the fact that each model could be produced in large quantities and varying sizes.

Parian is the name given to the soft, white and semi-translucent porcelain body developed in the 1840s by the firms of Copeland and Minton. More a development than an invention, it came into being in an attempt to discover the recipe that the Derby factory had used, in the 18th century, for their biscuit porcelain figures and groups. Parian is different from biscuit, in that it has an ivory creaminess and silky, marble-like quality

quite different from the dead white, chalky appearance of biscuit. Its resemblance to marble particularly appealed to the Victorian middle classes, for marble suggested opulence and wealth, and yet Parian figures and busts could be bought for a fraction of the cost of marble statuary.

Although there is some dispute over which factory – Copeland's or Minton's – discovered Parian first, it is generally agreed that Copeland and Garrett (from 1847 called plain Copeland) were the first to successfully market the new body in

1846. They called it Statuary Porcelain because it was mainly used for producing statuary in miniature. Minton termed it Parian, owing to the likeness it bore to the marble which came from the Isle of Paros, and Wedgwood, commencing production in 1848, christened it Carrara, for they thought it similar to Carrara marble.

Parian varied in colour. Minton pieces are generally less creamy in colour than those of Copeland, and similarly, pieces from the Irish Belleek factory, and the Wedgwood factory, are whiter in tone, but they are all recognisably different from the dead white of biscuit porcelain. In 1853 the Minton factory made experiments in colouring and gilding, and the results are very delicate and pleasing, generally in soft browns, terracottas and pinks. The colour and gilt was applied to the decorative parts of the figure, such as the draperies, and not normally to the body.

In 1846 the first Art Union was formed, to foster sales of works of art. Lotteries were held, offering Parian figures, amongst other things, as prizes. In the same year the Art Union of London commissioned Copeland and Garrett to produce 50 copies of John Gibson's *Narcissus*. The success of this venture persuaded firms to sell directly to the public for the first time. In 1847 further interest in the new body enabled Henry Cole to launch Summerly's Art Manufactures, which existed to commission living sculptors to make original designs for manufacture in Parian.

Parian became enormously popular, reaching its peak in the 1860s, largely because it enabled the middle classes to collect works, albeit scaled down, by leading sculptors of the day. The snob element was also given vent in the reduced models that were made of already famous statuary and sculptures belonging to the aristocracy. One entry in the Copeland and Garrett catalogue of Parian figures reads: 'Apollo as the Shepherd Boy of Admetus; This was modelled from a statue, by Wyatt, for the Duke of Sutherland, who also possesses the original marble'. Queen Victoria took a strong personal interest in Summerly's Art Manufactures, which helped to popularise the ware.

Besides Minton, Wedgwood and Copeland, two other factories must be singled out for their outstanding Parian. The Belleek factory started making porcelain in County Fermanagh about 1860, the type employed being none other than Parian. They chiefly produced baskets and other useful household items which are so delicate that one wonders how they

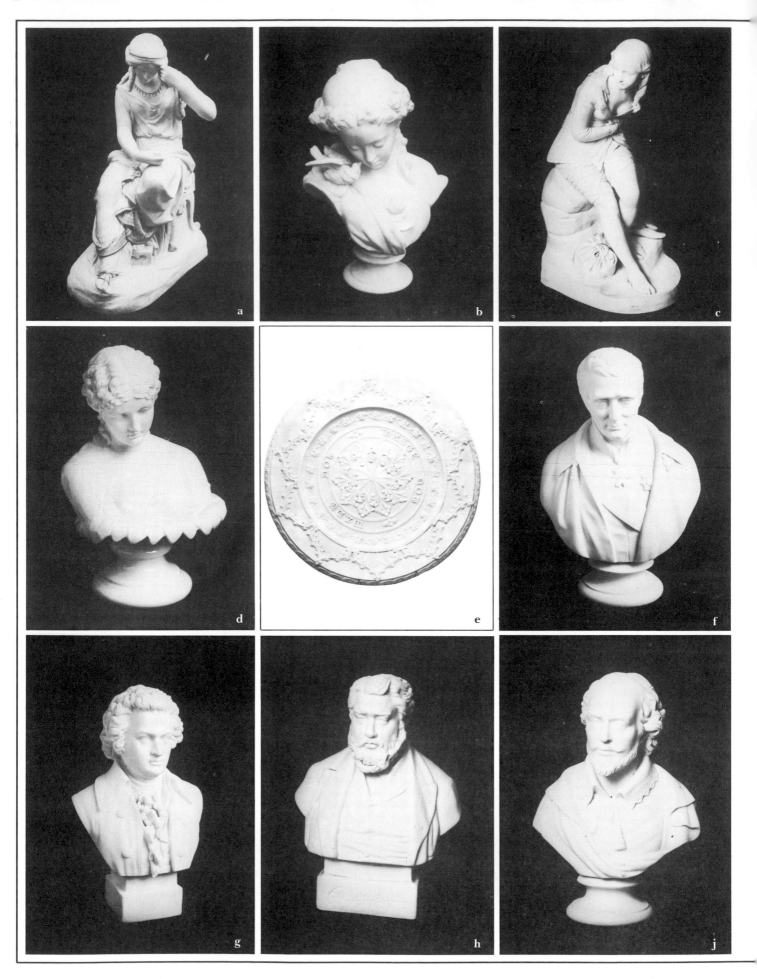

a La Toilette, *with impressed mark 'Copeland' and 'W. C. Marshall R.A. sculpt', and published January 1861. Unfortunately the looking glass in the lady's hand is missing, but this does little to detract from the wonderful quality of the piece. Every detail is finely observed. The robe is decorated with gilt, and two secondary colours (a grey and pale salmon). Even the ladies' earrings are picked out in colour and gilt.* H 43 cm (17 in)
JAY AND GEE ANTIQUES

b Lesbia, *with her little sparrow. The poet Catullus wrote an ode to Lesbia. He wished to be as close to her heart as the little sparrow, of which he was much jealous. Impressed 'J&T.B.' which stands for James and Thomas Bevington (1865-78). Parian figures from the factory of these two brothers are rare.* H 35.5 cm (14 in)
THE BEES, ANTIQUARIUS

c Dorothea, *modelled by John Bell, with impressed 'Minton' and dated for 1847, the year the design was registered. Dorothea from Cervantes' Don Quixote was an immensely popular model and was reproduced over very many years. John Bell was one of the celebrated sculptors (among them Canova and Thorwaldson) commissioned to produce designs by the Summerly Art Manufactures (1847-50), whose works did much to popularise the new Parian ware. Queen Victoria took a great personal interest, and purchased a number of pieces.* H 23 cm (13¾ in) (slight chips on shoulders)
HEMINGWAY ANTIQUES

d *Belleek bust of Clytie. Belleek works are eagerly collected. The part-glazing of figures (in this example, the bodice) was a Belleek speciality, and makes their work instantly distinguishable from that of other factories. Clytie was a subject much favoured by the Victorians. A humble nymph, she fell in love with the great god Apollo. He turned her into a sunflower, that she might always turn to him in adoration, and this is how she is always represented.* H 32 cm (12½ in)
R. A. BARNES

e *Parian ware breadboard, inscribed in relief 'Waste Not Want Not', and decorated with Gothic tracery, also in relief. This very fine piece, impressed 'Minton', bears a striking resemblance to a breadboard by Pugin in the Handley Read Collection. It is likely that this, also, is his work, since we know he undertook a number of designs for Minton.* W 34 cm (13½ in)
Private Collection of RICHARD DENNIS

f *Copeland bust of the Duke of Wellington, the original sculpture by the Comte d'Orsai, with impressed 'Copeland', and dated for 1852. D'Orsai (1801-52), the best known dandy of his day, was surprisingly an extremely hard-working painter and sculptor. Much of his work was reproduced in Parian.* H 30 cm (12 in)
R. A. BARNES

g Mozart, *impressed mark 'R&L', which stands for Robinson and Leadbeater (1865-1924). The firm produced literally hundreds of models, among them Beethoven, Chopin, Byron, Tennyson, Mendelssohn and Mozart. They had a flourishing export trade with the United States.* H 23 cm (9 in)
R. A. BARNES

h *Robinson and Leadbeater Parian bust of the famous Victorian preacher, Charles Haddon Spurgeon, whose sermons regularly attracted 6000 hearers. He was known for his 'rich vein of humour' although it would be difficult to detect it in this portrayal. Robinson and Leadbeater confined their production to Parian ware and were famous for their combination of high quality workmanship and marketable cheapness. Their factory, which was in existence from 1865-1924, was the largest producer of Parian, both for the home market and for export. Inscribed 'J.A. Acton Fecit 1878'.* H 12.5 cm (5 in)
HEMINGWAY ANTIQUES

j Shakespeare, *impressed 'Copeland'. Copeland Parian normally bears the simple impressed mark 'Copeland' until about 1870, when month-and-year potting marks were introduced. This is therefore likely to be prior to 1870. Note the fine modelling of the collar.* H 19 cm (7½ in)
HEMINGWAY ANTIQUES

Above
The Flower of the Town, *impressed 'Minton'. An example of the coloured, or tinted, Parian produced by the Minton factory after 1853. Here it is in terracotta.* H 53 cm (21 in)
SUSAN BECKER ANTIQUES

Below
Colin Minton Campbell, *by Minton, but without the Minton mark. Campbell was a partner in the firm from 1849. He was a nephew of Herbert Minton, under whose aegis the firm became the largest producer of ceramic manufactures of the Victorian period.* H 48 cm (19 in)
RICHARD DENNIS

were ever made. They also made busts, which have the very individual characteristic of being partly glazed (normally the draperies, or hair, would be glazed) and the rest left matt. They are very beautiful, and eagerly sought.

The factory of Robinson and Leadbeater produced the greatest quantity of Parian of all the factories. Most leading figures of the Victorian age were reproduced in bust form, ranging from three inches high to life size, among them Queen Victoria and Price Albert. Their products became very popular in America, and large shipments were sent out. Their style was very realistic and detailed.

The reproduction of sculpture in Parian was greatly facilitated by the invention of a reducing machine by the sculptor Benjamin Cheverton. It became possible to reduce accurately, to scale, the original work. It enabled a great deal of what had previously been very laborious work, necessitating a high degree of skill for its execution, to be avoided completely.

The second half of the century saw Parian employed in the manufacture of every manner of household goods; jugs, butter dishes, spill vases, brooches and ring stands. Whilst the main factories maintained their high standards in these fields, the smaller ones often produced goods of little merit.

Care

It is surprising what a difference a good soap and water wash can make to Parian. If it looks dirty in the window of the shop, you can very easily wash it in tepid water and washing-up liquid and it will immediately take on a new life. If the dirt persists, use Ajax or the equivalent, but it is not a good idea to do this with a scratchy brush, for this may damage the surface sheen. Use a shaving brush very carefully.
F.P.

WHERE TO BUY

Markets are a good hunting ground, and the general type of antique shop which has a bit of everything. Shops which specialise in studio pottery often keep a number of pieces.
R. A. BARNES, 16 Lower Richmond Road, London SW15 (01-789 3371)
SUSAN BECKER ANTIQUES, 18 Lower Richmond Road, London SW15 (01-788 9082)
THE BEES, Stands K1 and 2, Antiquarius, 135 King's Road, London SW3 (01-352 7989)
CORNER ANTIQUES, Coltishall, Norwich, Norfolk (Coltishall 631)
RICHARD DENNIS, 144 Kensington Church Street, London W8 (01-727 2061)
HEMINGWAY ANTIQUES, 12-14 Glendower Place, London SW7 (01-589 6760)
JAY AND GEE ANTIQUES, Stand 56, Antique Hypermarket, 26 Kensington High Street, London W8 (01-937 8426)

Miniature Porcelain

Right
Miniature tea service comprising 17 small plates, 2 large plates and 2 vegetable dishes, and decorated with a transfer pattern of Kate Greenaway prints. Dated around 1910 and probably Austrian or German. These dinner services which are sometimes mistakenly thought of as being made for a dolls' house were used as traveller's samples, although this particular example would probably have been made specially for a child.
D of plate 6.3 cm (2½ in)
R. A. BARNES

Miniature artefacts have existed for many thousands of years from Egyptian funeral bronzes to contemporary dolls' house furniture. Leaving aside the nightmare world of Lilliputia, children and adults alike have always been fascinated by microcosms of a human world – small boys regimenting battalions of soldiers, dolls dressed from rags to riches, and perhaps most interesting of all – the 18th and 19th century dolls' house complete with miniature furniture, paintings, glass, silver and porcelain. The manufacture of miniatures indicates two things: first, as a type of luxury toy they were the reflection of a wealthy leisured class and secondly they show an appreciation for the tremendous amount of skill required to create something on a minute scale. Anyone who has visited the Bethnal Green Museum in London or the Thorne Rooms at the Fine Art Institute of Chicago will know this only too well.

The hand-painted miniature porcelain of the late 18th and 19th centuries demonstrates this superb craftsmanship more than any other medium, except perhaps miniature glass of which very little survives. Although prices might at first astound the new collector, e.g., paying £60-£70 ($108-126) for a tea-pot only 2 inches high, he can be reassured that there are plenty of later examples where transfer printing was used that can still be collected for £5-10 ($9-18).

There has always been an area of confusion over the varying sizes of miniature porcelain, some dealers will say it was all made for the dolls' house, others that it was trade samples. The fact is both types exist (see decreasing sizes of mugs illustrated from 2¾ down to ½ inch) although there are many more of the trade samples around. These served a practical function in that during a period where travel and communication were still very limited, samples could be easily packed up in large numbers to be shown to prospective clients. The earliest examples we know of are the blue and white wares made in the late 18th century most commonly by Caughley and Liverpool and occasionally by Worcester and Bow. The great craze for miniatures really began however at the beginning of the 19th century, starting with individual pieces such as teapots, cups and saucers, ewers and basins and candle holders; ending with large tea, coffee and dinner services often comprising as many as 20 or 30 pieces. All the major pottery and porcelain factories such as Wedgwood, Staffordshire, Spode, Coalport, Minton and Davenport experimented. For checking dates, pattern numbers and marks Geoffrey Godden's *Encyclopaedia of British Pottery and Porcelain Marks* is an invaluable guide.

The prices obviously depend on quality, date and rarity of the item. For example a Wedgwood coffee pot would be more than a teapot of the same date, because there are so few of them about. Continental factories also made miniatures – Sèvres, Limoges and Dresden, to quote just a few. They were particularly fond of the small 'cabaret' set comprising either one or two cups and saucers, teapot, milkjug and sugar basin all on the same tray. These were very popular at the time and some were specially commissioned for display in a Victorian cabinet. The *Catalogue of the Great Exhibition of 1851* mentions the 'Clarendon' miniature teaset. The large dinner services which were made mainly at the end of the century are usually transfer printed and fetch lower prices, being more difficult to display. These stopped being made before World War I and the only miniatures that are still being made today are small cups and saucers made by Spode, Crown Derby and Coalport. S.S.

Where to buy

Because of its popularity miniature porcelain is quite hard to find and more likely to crop up in country antique shops than in London. However these dealers usually carry some examples, although the only specialist is Jill Lewis who deals in every kind of miniature.

R. A. BARNES, 16 Lower Richmond Road, London SW15 (01-789 3371)
CHINA CHOICE, 7 New Cavendish Street, London W1 (01-935 0184)
KLABER AND KLABER, 2b Hans Road, London SW1 (01-589 7728)

Above
Minton miniature teapot decorated with a transfer pattern of scattered flowers and heightened with gilding. Marked 'Mintons England' which dates it between 1890-1910.
H of teapot with lid 5 cm (2 in)
JILL LEWIS

Above
Royal Worcester three-handled loving cup decorated with a transfer flower print. Many of these small mugs, with either one, two or three handles were made in miniature between 1910-1930 and are still quite reasonably priced, and easy to find.
H 3.8 cm (1½ in)
JILL LEWIS

JILL LEWIS, Collector's Corner, Portobello Road, London W11 (Saturdays only)
VENNERS ANTIQUES, New Cavendish Street, London W1 (01-935 0184)
ANNA TRIGG, The Antique Hypermarket, Kensington High Street, London W8 (01-937 4871)

Centre and below

Four miniature mugs illustrating the differing scale: a child's mug with the inscription 'A Present for my dear Boy', H 2⅞ in (7.5 cm); *Coalport mug on a powder blue background with a floral cartouche,* H 1¾ in (4.5 cm) JILL LEWIS; *Coalport mug on a white ground with floral pattern dated around 1840,* H 1¾ in (4.5 cm) JILL LEWIS; *Staffordshire dolls' mug decorated in the Sèvres style with elaborate gilding, dated about 1900,* H ½ in (1.3 cm) JILL LEWIS

Top *Caughley 18th century blue and white cup and saucer decorated with the popular 'fisherman's pattern'. Caughley are the most common examples of 18th century miniature porcelain and are usually marked with a painted 'S'.* D of saucer 7.6 cm (3 in)
PAMELA KLABER

Centre *Spode 'cabaret' set complete with teapot, milk jug, sugar basin and cup and saucer on a tray, decorated on a stippled gilt ground with hand painted enamel flower. Dated 1810-20. Spode miniatures have always been of superb quality and very popular.* H of teapot 5 cm (2 in) L of tray 14 cm (5½ in)
VENNERS ANTIQUES

Below *Royal Crown Derby teapot and cup and saucer decorated with the Japanese 'imari' pattern. Dated about 1900 and marked 'Royal Crown Derby, England'.* H of teapot 3.7 cm (1½ in) D of saucer 5.6 cm (2¼ in)
R. A. BARNES

Above

Crown Staffordshire cup and saucer hand painted with rich blue and gold decoration. Marked and dated around 1910. Hand painted examples will always fetch considerably more than their later transfer counterparts, and although prices seem high, the skill required in decorating these minute objects was remarkable.

D of saucer 5 cm (2 in)
JILL LEWIS

Above and right

Mid 19th century Jasper-ware. Wedgwood tea and coffee pots. Jasper ware was the famous Wedgwood technique whereby the earthenware body was covered over with a solid ground colour and decorated in white relief. Dated around 1890-1900 and marked 'Wedgwood, England'. Blue and white teapot 5.6 cm (2¼ in) Green and white coffee pot 6 cm (2½ in) R. A. BARNES

Right

Staffordshire green and white transfer printed miniature dinner service comprising plates, tureens, vegetable dishes and gravy boat, (approx 56 pieces). Dated around 1840. Unmarked.

D of plate 6.25 cm (2½ in)
R. A. BARNES

Above

Dresden vase and cover on a turquoise ground with a floral cartouche and elaborate gilding together with two late 19th century Limoges plates. These examples show that miniatures were also popular abroad.

H of vase 4.5 cm (1¾ in)
D of plates 3.8 cm (1½ in)
JILL LEWIS

Right

Copeland miniature dinner service comprising 24 pieces – plates, two vegetable dishes and covers, sauce boats on stands, round dish and ladle. Dated around 1850 and the white body heightened with blue leaf design. Marked 'Copeland'.

H of veg dish and cover 6.8 cm (2⅝ in)
ANNA TRIGGS

Left

Royal Worcester miniature mug decorated with an exotic bird and dated around 1890.

H of mug 4.3 cm (1¾ in)

R. A. BARNES

Right

Chinese export miniature tea bowl and saucer made for the European market. Decorated with polychrome enamels and made of hard paste porcelain. Late 18th century. These examples are also quite rare and much sought. D of saucer 9 cm (3½ in)

KLABER

Below

Spode taper stick dated around 1830 and decorated on a white background with floral motifs. These taper sticks which were used for lighting candles were very popular in miniature porcelain, along with little baskets made for holding pot pourri.

H of taper stick 3.7 cm (1½ in)

R. A. BARNES

Below

Worcester blue and white cup and saucer decorated with flowers and marked with a crescent. Dated about 1770. Miniature porcelain of the Dr Wall period is quite rare and therefore likely to command high prices. D of saucer 9 cm (3½ in)

CHINA CHOICE

Above

Two miniature candlesticks which are rare for their early date. The first is decorated with roses and gilding and marked 'Davenport' with an anchor in red. Dated around 1830-40. The second example is Spode pattern 3309 and painted in peach and gold. Both are superbly painted and in very good condition.

H 5 cm (2 in)   H 4.5 cm (1¾ in)

JILL LEWIS

Right

Modern miniature cups and saucers attractively decorated with transfer patterns. D of saucer 2.5 cm (1 in)

PRIVATE COLLECTION

Above

Coalbrookdale ewer in polychrome enamels of about 1840. Examples of miniature porcelain prior to 1850 are quite rare and always expensive. H 3.7 cm (1⅝ in) *Even smaller Coalport or Davenport ewer decorated in the French style* H 3 cm (1¼ in)

JILL LEWIS

Right

Two miniature mugs, one decorated with a cherub and butterflies and marked 'Humblot Paris', the other with gilt lettering and inscribed 'A Present From Leamington'. These mugs began being made as souvenirs at the beginning of this century, and for much less than a true miniature can make an attractive collection.

H 3.8 cm (1½ in)

H 3 cm (1¼ in)

JILL LEWIS

Above

French cabaret set decorated in the Sèvres manner with sprays of flowers banded in blue and unusual for the ormolu mounted tray. Dated about 1840 – this might have been made for a large dolls' house but more likely to have been a miniature sample. Unmarked.

H of teapot 3 cm (1¼ in)

JILL LEWIS

Tureens from the Past

Unlikely as it may seem, it is possible to buy antique porcelain tureens for less than the price of a modern one, despite the fact that they are in greater demand than ever. Seldom does a tureen remain in an antique shop for more than a few days, and yet they seem to have evaded the price-in-ratio-to-demand syndrome which has affected almost every other sort of antique.

The price of porcelain tureens ranges from as little as £10 upwards (and sometimes less if they are damaged) to thousands of pounds. At the cheaper end of this vast price range are the 19th century ironstone or stoneware tureens. This durable type of earthenware, perfected early in that century, can withstand hard treatment as well as intensive heat. Moving up the scale into the lower half of the three figure bracket are the finest ironstone tureens made by Mason's and the ordinary porcelain tureens of the 19th century, after which come the finer examples of that period and the ordinary 18th century examples. Few porcelain tureens survive prior to the Georgian period and finest 18th century tureens are very valuable, in particular if they are Chinese, and preferably armorial or in the shape of a bird or animal. Prices vary enormously according to the manufacturer, type of porcelain, quality and condition of the tureen. They are also more valuable if they are still intact with their original cover and stand; although many have lost them either through breakage or because the stands were retained when the tureens were sold separately out of a dinner service. Perhaps one of the reasons for the recent demand in tureens is because people have found other uses better suited to modern life than their original role as vessels for soups or sauces. They can equally well be filled with flowers or pot-pourri or used as an ornament in the centre of a table.

If you are thinking of buying a porcelain tureen, you are best advised to make your decision soon, as the European tourists who are largely responsible for the demand are increasing the competition.

S.B.

Left
This Mason's Ironstone tureen of Chinese shape is decorated with the pheasant pattern. It was made in about 1815, two years after the founding of the Mason's factory, which became the most successful makers of stoneware. H 26 cm W 32 cm
GRAHAM & OXLEY ANTIQUES

Left
This blue and white onion pattern tureen and stand was made at Meissen in about 1830. The onion pattern was first used by Meissen in about 1740 and is still used throughout Europe today. H 38 cm W 43 cm
ALDBURY ANTIQUES

Left
This urn-shaped tureen was made in about 1818, during the Vienna factory's most prosperous period, having struggled since 1719 with its Meissen-style wares. Vienna wares were not marked until 1751 when the two-bar shield of the arms of Austria was introduced, which was either enamelled, impressed or in underglaze-blue. This tureen is decorated in yellow, mauve, blue and red roses, tulips and forget-me-nots. H 34 cm W 36½ cm
JEAN SEWELL (ANTIQUES) LTD

Right
Much of Wedgwood's 'Queen's Ware' was decorated with overglaze decoration, in this case in the form of transfer printing. This was usually done by outside contractors and it is likely that this tureen went to Sadler & Green in Liverpool in about 1790. H 21 cm W 31 cm
DAVID NEWBON

Right
Ironstone, or stone-china became popular in the early 19th century. One of the most successful makers of this durable ware was John and William Ridgway, who worked together from 1820-30, marking their goods JWR. This hexagonal tureen of that period has a blue floral pattern and gold decoration on the handles and the feet are decorated with relief moulding. H 27 cm W 33 cm
DELOMOSNE & SON LTD

Above
This circular blue printed Spode tureen was made only three years before the factory was purchased by Copeland & Garrett in 1833. Spode factory produced a large range of earthenware, including some of the finest Staffordshire blue printed wares. H 27 cm W 28.5 cm
JEAN SEWELL (ANTIQUES) LTD

Left
Having taken over from Spode in 1833 (see above), Copeland & Garrett were in turn succeeded by Messrs W. T. Copeland in 1847, but the standard and style of Spode survived throughout. This tureen and stand were made in about 1860.
R. A. BARNES

Left

This is an example of extremely good value. Made by Doulton in 1900. These tureens are cheaper than those made by the same factory today.
R. A. Barnes

Left & below

Crown Derby tureen and cover with gold, red and green scroll and leaf decoration, made about 1820.
H 30 cm W 39 cm
Jean Sewell
(Antiques) Ltd

Left

This tureen illustrates the typical shape made by the Chinese. Chinese export porcelain was often referred to in Europe by the name of the port from which it was shipped, which in this case was Nankin. The tureen was made about 1780.
David Newbon

Below

This Minton tureen of about 1868 was made during Minton's finest period. It is typical of the elegant Regency style, particularly with its dome cover.
R. A. Barnes

Right
*One of a pair of Italian Nove pottery tureens
and stands of about 1880.* H 27 cm w 38 cm
IAN G. HASTIE

Below
*Coalport tureen and meat platter of about
1815 decorated with a crested goat's head on
bar, classical orange figures and gold and
sepia trophies and musical instruments.*
H 24 cm w 33 cm
JEAN SEWELL (ANTIQUES) LTD

Above
*One of a pair of Marseilles faïence sauce
tureens and stands of about 1795, decorated
with cartouches and flowers.*
H 19½ cm w 23 cm
ALDBURY ANTIQUES

Right
*Famille rose goose tureen of the Ch'ien Lung
period (1736-95), the upper half of the bird
forming the cover.* H 41 cm
CHRISTIE'S

Above

On the left is a Chinese export porcelain tureen and cover with the arms of Browne and decorated in underglaze blue, about 1770. In the centre background is another Chinese porcelain tureen and cover decorated with flowers in Famille Rose enamels, about 1760. On the right an English porcelain tureen, cover and stand made by Ridgways and printed with flowers, about 1830. Widths 33 cm (12 in); 38 cm (14 in) and 38 cm (14 in)

EARLE D. VANDEKAR

Above & detail right

This tureen and stand decorated in red, pink green, blue and black is believed to have been made by Mason's in about 1830. The tureen, cover and stand are all fluted.
BELINDA COOTE ANTIQUES

Below

This Worcester tureen decorated in gold and pink was only made about five years before the factory became the Worcester Royal Porcelain Co. Ltd in 1889.
R. A. BARNES

Above & detail

This Chelsea tureen of round reeded form with a scalloped edge is painted with insects and flowers in shades of pink, green, yellow and blue. It is marked with the red anchor which dates it from 1752-6, during which time some of the finest Chelsea wares were produced. The apparently random decoration was in fact designed to cover up the spots and cracks in the thick white glaze used at this time. H 22 cm W 25 cm
JEAN SEWELL (ANTIQUES) LTD

Above

Although unmarked, this tureen with acanthus finial and decoration in Pompeii red may well have been made by Coalport in about 1830. If so, it would have been made with the leadless glaze which was a major step forward in the reduction of health risks and for which the Coalport factory was awarded a Society of Arts Medal in 1820. H 25.5 cm W 36 cm
ANDWELL ANTIQUES

Victorian Majolica

Above
Minton majolica game tureen and cover, the lid with a duck and hare modelled in relief. Impressed numeral 668 and date code 1871.
L 34 cm (13½ in).
ALEXANDER GALLERY

Below
Minton majolica garden seat in the form of a hunched monkey holding lemons and supporting a blue and green glazed tasselled cushion. Impressed Minton mark and date code for 1887.
H 48 cm (19 in)
SOTHEBY'S BELGRAVIA

If asked to think what one would define as archetypal Victorian earthenware – the brightly coloured glazes and boldly modelled forms of what we know as Majolica immediately spring to mind. Despite the historical name tag, these countless domestic objects – vegetable dishes, jardinières, fruit stands and candlesticks – have little in common with the original *maiolica* of the Italian Renaissance. It is interesting to trace the connection and see how the word changed its meaning.

The original Italian maiolica was a form of tin glazed earthenware (like faience and delft) decorated with varying Renaissance themes: portrait medallions, istoriato (history painting), armorial bearings and so on. The Victorian cult of revivalism naturally encompassed the Renaissance although this interest was by no means limited to England. Potters throughout Europe, conscious of their increasing technical efficiency, looked back to the past. Maiolica was imitated in France and Germany and naturally by 19th century Italian factories like the Ginori pottery at Doccia, the Torquato Castellani pottery at Rome and the Cantagalli factory in Florence, who reproduced della Robbia sculpture as well as the maiolica of Urbino, Faenza, Deruta and Gubbio. These imitations were exhibited at the Paris Exhibition of 1900.

In England, the development of majolica was due to the interest of Leon Arnoux, the brilliant art director of the Minton factory from 1849 until 1902. He was interested in many aspects of the Renaissance and beautiful imitative wares were produced by two Minton potters in particular, Alfred Stevens and Thomas Kirkby. The two large 16th century maiolica collections (Ralph Bernal and Jacques Soulages) which were acquired by the South Kensington Museum (now the Victoria & Albert Museum) in the 1850s must have aided their endeavours. But what really appealed to popular taste were the coloured 'majolica' glazes developed by Arnoux which combined with lively modelling were first displayed at the 1851 Exhibition. It seemed particularly suited to the production of large domestic

objects: umbrella stands, garden seats, fountains, not to mention life size models of animals, ornamental vases and figures as well as a prolific output of utilitarian everyday objects. By the mid 1860s majolica was an established fashion and other factories besides Minton, notably Wedgwood, George Jones, Adams & Co, Bermontoft, Copeland and even Worcester started production in large quantities. The soft buff coloured earthenware body could be glazed and coloured in a number of different ways and apart from the large sculptural display pieces, no great skill was required. Certain features are very typical: 'marbling' where the coloured glazes run together was often used, plant and vegetable forms such as the strawberry leaf dish and the green glazed leaf plates made by Wedgwood (see p. 120).

The phrase 'for the million' which was soon used of majolica proved that it appealed to the widest possible taste. It was cheap, cheerful and filled the need for mass produced rather than individually designed pieces, although there are examples of the latter such as the fountain over 30 foot high surmounted by a life size figure of St George and the Dragon which was outside the Bethnal Green Museum until the 1920s.   S.S.

The cost of collecting

Comparisons are always odious but the high prices fetched for the original 16th century Italian maiolica contrast with the reasonable prices which are still asked for the beautiful 19th century imitative pieces carried out by the Minton potters and Italian factories. The Minton vase (see p 119) for example would fetch say £40-£50 ($72-$90) though work actually signed would be at least five or six times as much.

The popular range of majolica wares are considerably cheaper and prices can start from £20 ($36). Crazing in the glaze is fairly common and unimportant but chipped pieces should be avoided if possible. Impressed marks were used from the 1860s and the invaluable reference book is Geoffrey Godden's *Encyclopaedia of British Pottery and Porcelain Marks*.

For detailed guidance on how much you must expect to pay for majolica, see introduction to this chapter, p 98 .

Where to buy

Majolica is still relatively uncollected and easy to buy. Salerooms, and country antique shops should provide plenty of utilitarian majolica wares but for the ornamental pieces, I recommend the following:
ALEXANDER GALLERY, 45 Sloane Street, London SW1 (01-235 1813)
R. A. BARNES, 16a Lower Richmond Road, Putney, London SW15 (01-789 3371)
CHINA LOCKER, Georgian Village Arcade, Camden Passage, London N1 (01-226 1571)
CHRISTIE'S, 8 King Street, London SW1 (01-839 9060)
RICHARD DENNIS, 144 Kensington Church Street, London W8 (01-727 2061)
GEOFFREY GODDEN, Chinaman, 15-19 Crescent Road, Worthing, Sussex (Worthing 35958)
SOTHEBY'S BELGRAVIA, 19 Motcombe Street, London SW1 (01-235 4311)

Below

George Jones turquoise blue jug decorated with a circular medallion with fish modelled in relief on a royal blue background, and a grey painted bamboo handle. The two Staffordshire factories of George Jones and Adams & Co produced majolica in large quantities and at a popular level. Jugs, butter dishes, bonbonnières and plant stands are all typical examples. Impressed GJ and numerals 183.
H 17.5 cm (7 in)
R. A. BARNES

Below

Minton majolica fruit stand surmounted by a mythological boy who is flanked by the symbols of sculpture and painting.
H 31.5 cm (12½ in)
RICHARD DENNIS

Above

Minton majolica fruit stand supported by cupid (mythological boy). These putti typify Victorian sentimentality but are not as popular today as the majolica animal and vegetable forms. Minton date code for 1864. H 42.5 cm (16¾ in).
RICHARD DENNIS

Below

Minton majolica vase made for the Crystal Palace Art Union, about 1860. This example is particularly interesting because it imitates the earlier maiolica of the Italian Renaissance with painted putti, classical medallions and grotesques. These Italianate examples were primarily executed by Alfred Stevens and Leon Arnaux of Mintons.
H 22.8 cm (9 in).
GEOFFREY GODDEN

Above

Minton majolica tureen, cover and stand modelled in the form of a boar's head, the fur with a rich aubergine and brown glaze. These animal forms tend to be more popular and amusing than the majolica figures – usually cupid in a variety of different poses. Impressed Mintons registration mark for 1877 and date code for 1878.
L 5 cm (21 in)
SOTHEBY'S BELGRAVIA

Right

Worcester majolica classical figure dated around 1870. Worcester made only a few examples in majolica and their modelling was never as sophisticated as that of Mintons or Wedgwood.
H 5.5 cm (14 in)
R. A. BARNES

Left and right
Wedgwood pair of green glazed leaf dishes and one of three plates. About 1860-70. Impressed Wedgwood mark.
D of plates 8½ in L of dish 4½ in
CHINA LOCKER

Below
Minton majolica cane garden seat decorated on an unusual yellow canework ground and decorated with blue bands and ribbons. Dated about 1855-60. This example is quite rare as most were of one colour.
H 18 in
R. A. BARNES

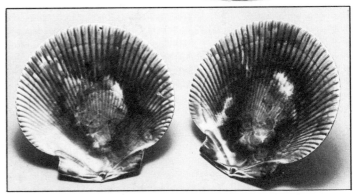

Above
Della Robbia dish, the centre decorated with a leaf pattern the border with deer. From 1894-1906 the Della Robbia pottery produced white opaque glazed ware with painted majolica glazes, and tends to be considered more art pottery. D 25.4 cm (10 in)
ALEXANDER GALLERY

Left
Pair of Sarreguines majolica toby jugs. This French factory very probably influenced the later Minton majolica. The turquoise and pink linings are exactly the same as those used by Minton, although the general colour palette is more faded. H 25 cm (10 in)
R. A. BARNES

Below
Minton majolica asparagus dish, impressed mark and date code 1871.
ALEXANDER GALLERY

Above
Wedgwood pair of shell dessert dishes in marbled brown and green glazes which is a very typical feature of majolica. The colours have again penetrated through to the backs of the dishes. Like faience and delft which have the same soft body and hard glaze, chipping is a problem and the glaze often is quite crazed because the soft paste contracts in the firing. Impressed Wedgwood mark.
D 15 cm (6 in)
R. A. BARNES

Right top

Minton majolica teapot dated between 1860-80.
H 12.7 cm (5 in).
RICHARD DENNIS

Right centre

George Jones majolica sardine dish and stand decorated on a turquoise blue ground, edged with yellow, the inside lined with bright pink, typical of many majolica wares.
D 28.3 cm (8 in)
R. A. BARNES

Right bottom

George Jones majolica inkstand charmingly modelled with two thrushes sitting on their nests representing the two inkstands. The base of the inkstand is decorated with marbled coloured glazes in greens and browns. Because of the soft body the glazes often penetrated through to the reverse side of the object.
L 30.4 cm (12 in)
R. A. BARNES

Below

Wedgwood majolica wine ewer dedicated to Bacchus and decorated in strong blue and green glazes. Dated 1870-80. Impressed Wedgwood mark.
H 27.8 cm (11 in)
R. A. BARNES

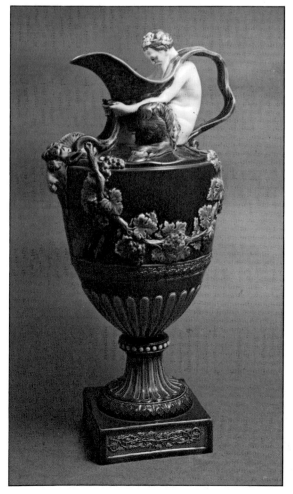

122

English Pottery Tiles

Colour
Far left
The Muse Thalia represented Comedy and Idyllic poetry. Here she is hand-painted on three large Copeland blanks, which are marked B&S. These are probably the initials of the designer, who might have been freelance and bought the blanks direct from the factory. The neo-classical revival led by Lord Leighton is reflected in this design. 30 × 10 in (77 ×25.5 cm).
HASLAM & WHITEWAY

Top centre
This is a typical English polychrome (meaning many coloured) tile of a bird. It was made between 1750-1770, probably in Liverpool.
JONATHAN HORNE

Top right
This is a highly coloured majolica tile by Maw & Co.; a firm who came into full commercial production in 1857 and who by the end of the century were the largest tile manufacturers in the world. Majolica was developed by the Minton art director Lenoux and was first exhibited in 1851. It is characterised by an opaque white glaze.
HASLAM & WHITEWAY

Centre
Millions of tiles were produced in the 19th century, this is a representative example of medium quality transfer printed tile, which can still be seen in many Victorian houses. Tiles were bought from the manufacturer through catalogues, which could be viewed at any ironmongers.
ROBSON & TUDOR

Bottom right
Group of tiles designed by William de Morgan. The watercolour and pencil design is in the Victoria & Albert Museum. It is inscribed WDM & Co/Dec 15 1896, and it was executed for the P & O line ship, the SS Arabia. These particular tiles date from the period when he was in partnership with the architect Ricardo (1888-98). The richness of colour recalls the work he carried out for Lord Leighton in his house at 12 Holland Park Rd., London W14 (now open to the public).
HASLAM & WHITEWAY

There has been no continuous tradition of tile manufacture in Britain. At certain periods since the 12th century demands of convenience as well as fashion have created a taste for ceramic tiles. And there have been three periods in particular when they were produced upon a large scale, the so-called medieval period from the 12th to the early years of the 16th century, the period of English delft largely in the second half of the 18th century, and the prolific boom years from 1840 until the Second World War.

In each period potters have combined the function of tiles with superb decorative effects: the floor of the Chapter House of Westminster Abbey (1253-1259) shows the results achieved with the medieval floor tile (they were rarely used for any other purposes); the few surviving 18th century tile fire-places at Croft Castle, nr. Leominster, Herefordshire or the tiled pictures in the Bristol City Museum and Art Gallery are an indication of the sophisticated use of tiles in that century; and the abundance of 19th and 20th century tiles in hospitals, butcher's shops, churches and private houses illustrate the popularity and versatility of tiles in those years.

The contrast between each period is distinct (although it is interesting to cross-refer certain medieval and Victorian tiles) and it is advisable to concentrate on one period and collect solely that. The choice naturally depends upon the taste and pocket of the collector. Medieval tiles are on average the most expensive, from £20-60, ($36-108) and scarce; delft tiles vary in price; but start at around £10 ($18); whilst Victorian and early 20th century tiles may be had for £1 ($2) upwards. So it is possible for the collector to build up a collection of tiles, which reflect all the decorative trends of their day, whether it be medieval heraldic motifs, 18th century transfer decoration or the fluid lines of art nouveau.

Size of tiles

The basic pottery shape of the tile is called the *blank*. The blanks of medieval tiles vary in size, but are approximately 6 inches (15.2 cm) square, delft tiles are 5 inches (12.7 cm) square and 19th and 20th century tiles are 6 inches (15.2 cm) square. Measurements are only given if the examples vary from these standards.

How to display tiles

The cheapest and most effective way of displaying individual tiles is by adapting 'The perfect plate-hanger' to their shape. These metal braces come in three sizes from the smallest 5-6.75 inches (13-17 cm) to the largest 9.5-14 inches (24-45 cm). They may be bought from most ironmongers, although you are certain to get them at Peter Jones, Sloane Square, London SW1 (01-730 3434). Tiles may also be framed but this is expensive and prevents any inspection of the blank. Groups of tiles may be stuck together on the back of a board and hung as an unframed picture.

J.K.

Where to buy

It is possible to find tiles of all descriptions in junk shops as well as specialist ceramic shops. Listed below are a number of dealers, where you are sure to find them:
ANDREW BORTHWICK, Chelsea Antiques Market, 253 Kings Road, London sw3 (01-352 9695 or 01-603 4245)
BRITANNIA ANTIQUES, Grays Antique Market, 58 Davies Street, London w1 (01-629 7034)
A. J. FILKINS, 25 St. Christopher's Place, Wigmore St., London w1 (01-935 0639)
HARLEY ANTIQUES, South London Antiques Centre, Camberwell Road (01-703 6429)
HASLAM & WHITEWAY, 105 Kensington Church St., London w8 (01-229 1145)
JONATHAN HORNE, 66b Kensington Church St., London w8 (01-221 5658)
ROBSON & TUDOR, 10 Tachbrook St., London sw1 (01-834 5363)
THEODORA, stands M2 & M3 Antiquarius, 135 Kings Rd., London sw3 (01-352 8734 and 01-352 7989)

What to read

E. A. LANE: *A Guide to the collection of tiles in the Victoria & Albert Museum* 1939
A. RAY: *English Delftware Tiles* Faber and Faber 1973
J. BARNARD: *Victorian Ceramic Tiles* Studio Vista 1972

Right

The development (and possible invention) of the transfer process by John Sadler (b. 1720) revolutionised the potter's craft. In 1756 and later from 1757 to 1761 he experimented with first wood and then copper-plate engraved decoration upon tiles. The results enabled him to decorate over twelve hundred tiles in a day. This particular example of copper-plate engraved decoration is one of the fable series representing the tale of Mercury and the woodman. They were produced in the 1770s under the management of Green, who continued the techniques of his partner John Sadler.
JONATHAN HORNE

Above and detail

This is a set of William de Morgan tiles in their original position around a fireplace (the whole is 32 × 32 in (91 × 81 cm). William de Morgan (1839-1917) was a friend and associate of William Morris and an exponent of the Arts and Crafts movement. Most of his designs for tiles were developed during the years when he ran a small pottery in Chelsea, from 1872-1882. They were then continually produced for the next thirty years, and dating is often extremely difficult. This design is typically arresting, it would have been executed by a semi-mechanical process in which the design was painted onto a thin tissue of paper, which was then applied to the blank. When the tile was fired the paper burnt away leaving the painted design.
HASLAM & WHITEWAY

Above

This very fine example of a 13th century inlaid tile was taken from the ruins of Bruton Abbey in Somerset. Others from the same site may be seen in the Taunton Museum. It is interesting to compare this with the Victorian encaustic tiles. This was handmade and thus was perfect neither in shape nor in the moulding of design, whereas in the Victorian tiles the size and design were exact.
By courtesy of A. J. FILKINS

Above

In 1830 Herbert Minton (1793-1858) bought a share in the patent for making encaustic tiles. This involved pressing a moulded design into the square of plastic clay, which was then filled with white pipe clay. The tile was then fired. It was a conscious revival of medieval technique and linked strongly to the Gothic revival in architecture (one of the earliest successes was in 1841 when the floor of the Temple church was restored with encaustic tiles in a design copied from Westminster Abbey Chapter House). Soon the technique was developed still further: the body of the tile was made from compressed dust, which was then sandwiched between two layers of good quality clay. The use of encaustics in churches opened the eyes of 19th-century potters to the possibilities of tiles. This group of tiles was made by Campbell Brick & Tile Co. Ltd. and therefore must have been produced after 1875.
HASLAM & WHITEWAY

Although these tiles are of the highest quality nearly all dealers will say that they are impossible to sell. These would sell for very little individually but would be even cheaper in bulk. They represent therefore some of the most interesting buys on the market at the moment.

Above

This beautiful hand-painted tile in blue, about 1880, was a product of the Doulton factory (1870-1915), who only decorated tiles, they did not make the blanks as well. They were renowned for their hand-painted murals and executed large commissions such as the Harrods Food Hall. (They also faced the exterior of Harrods with terracotta tiles in 1902.)
HASLAM & WHITEWAY

Above

*This is an example of a moulded tile, a technique, where striking effects could be achieved by applying a plain glaze, which would then run into the hollows of the relief and come darker where the glaze was thickest. The subject of this group is Michelangelo and the Sybil, it is marked Flaxman.
16×18 in (45.5×51 cm).*
THEODORA

124

Above

This tile displays a static art nouveau design moulded in green and yellow. It was made by T. & R. Boote Ltd., whose trade mark of a grey hound couchant between laurel leaves, is reputed to have been modelled on Tom Boote's hound, which won the Waterloo Cup.
ANDREW BORTHWICK

Below

De Morgan's designs of animals and monsters allowed his whimsical sense of humour full play. This is the Kingfisher design, which he evolved at Chelsea (1872-1882). It is painted in ruby lustre: a technique perfected by de Morgan, which involved adding a film of metal before firing.
ANDREW BORTHWICK

Above

Little Brown Betty, a tile by the book illustrator and designer Walter Crane, dates from the 1870s. She relates to his illustrations in the Baby's Opera and the Baby's Banquet produced at this time.
ANDREW BORTHWICK

Above

It is presumed that edging tiles were placed around the main tile design in a fire-place, washing recess or any other decorative scheme, although no early tiles are known to exist in situ in England. They are scarce because they were most often destroyed in the process of removing the central tiles. This particular example with scrolling decoration was probably made in Liverpool between 1750 and 1775.
ANDREW BORTHWICK

Left

This medieval tile is reputed to have come from the New Forest. The elementary design indicates that it might be as early as the 12th century. It is possible to see the inlaid technique, whereby the white pipeclay has been poured into the simply moulded surface. 5.2×5.2×0.75 in (13×13×2.85 cm).
A. J. FILKINS

Right

This group of encaustic tiles was made from plastic clay, making them early in date (i.e. about 1845) before the compressed dust process became widespread. 20.75×11.75 in (53×30 cm)
HASLAM & WHITEWAY

GLASS

Glass collecting is a wide and varied field and with so much to choose from, the collector of today possesses a certain freedom and flexibility. You may decide to form your collection on the basis of a particular period or style; you may decide to collect one particular shape, design or colour; your choice may be guided by a technique, for example engraving or etching; or you may form your collection on an historical basis representing glass specimens that date from the ancient worlds of Egypt, Greece and the Roman Empire through to the present day. Whatever factors may guide your preference, about three thousand years of glass production await your personal inspection and selection, with much that is both accessible and inexpensive.

PRICES
Some of the types of glass shown here represent new branches of collecting where prices and availability make them attractive pursuits. Others have been traditionally collected and used by their owners for centuries and form the greater part of very specialised and normally expensively priced collections. Falling between these two extremes, there also exists an enormous quantity of glass wares produced during the 18th and 19th centuries that need not be expensive and indeed, can add tremendously to any collection or interior . . . it is extraordinary what one simple piece of Cranberry or Bristol blue glass can do for a dark corner bookshelf, a window sill or barren table top. The transformation that results may cost as little as £10 ($18) and the glimmer of light and colour will forever be a source of beauty.

Pressed glass
Pressed glass of the 19th century (page 128) is a new area that has only recently become popular with collectors and remains largely untouched by historians. Many attractive examples can be found for as little as £5 ($9) including drinking glasses, tumblers, flasks, plates, salt cellars and jugs. Commemorative wares, sugar bowls and bon-bon dishes tend to be the most popular with collectors as reflected by their higher price tags ranging from £10-£25 ($18-$45). Some pressed glass wares were marked, and in general, marked examples will command slightly higher prices. Those carrying both the Diamond Registration and Trade marks are rare and can cost up to £30 ($54). It is likely that increasing interest will cause prices to rise in the near future.

Ale glasses
Another type of glass that has recently stimulated some interest with collectors are the ale glasses (page 132) that were produced during the 19th century. Prices normally fall below £40 ($72) and it is quite possible for several glasses of the same design, making up a set, to be purchased for that sum.

In general, prices are controlled by two factors. The first is important because it is known to influence the prices of all forms of glass wares, and that is *quality*. In this case, quality is of prime importance and examples that are poorly constructed or damaged should be avoided if possible. The *type* of ale glass, that is its shape, decoration and desirability is the second factor. Pressed ale cans and short ale glasses value from £3-£20 ($5-$35) each while ale tumblers and rummers range from £20-£30 ($35-$55). 'U' bowl and funnel bowl ales can be purchased for as little as £5 ($9) with top quality examples exceeding no more than about £10 ($18). Of course, 17th and 18th century ale glasses are much more expensive and it is because of this, that interest has been diverted to the 19th century and its productions. Examples from this time exist in greater numbers today, but do remember that quality must be your first consideration.

Cranberry glass
Of the many types of Victorian coloured glass, cranberry (page 136) has enjoyed considerable popularity with today's collector. Its versatility of colour and its variety of shape and design are among its most appealing features and it is hardly surprising that prices for this type of glass have greatly increased over the last few years. Domestic wares, that is simple finger bowls, tumblers, glasses and cups are very often free of decoration and because of their simple appearance they are the most inexpensive, ranging from £5-15 ($9-$27) in price. Other examples, namely vases, bon-bon dishes, decanters, wine glasses, 'friggers' and so on, are often decorated by etching, hand painting or applied glass trailing which usually consists of a clear, transparent, colourless glass. Such decoration tends to increase the value of these wares which can normally be purchased from about £20-70 ($36-$126). Cranberry glass with overlay decoration is perhaps the most popular of all its many presentations and prices start from about the £200 ($360) mark depending on the extent and intricacy of the overlay design and the desirability of its shape.

Cranberry glass in particular has a great following both in

126

the United States and in Britain and as examples become more scarce, it is sure that prices will continue to rise. In spite of this, it is still possible to find attractive specimens that are reasonably priced and a small collection consisting of say five or six pieces can cost no more than about £100 ($180).

Decanters
Prices of glass decanters can vary considerably and the reasons for this largely depend on the subtle differences of decoration from one decanter to the next. For example, two decanters produced at the same time, say 1790, and of similar appearance may differ in price by over £100 ($180). It is only after careful inspection that the differences between the two become evident – the decanter with the minimal cut glass decoration will command the higher price than the plainer example even though they may appear identical in every other respect. This is an important point because it affects the prices of most forms of glass wares. Something that is decorated will invariably command the higher price, and this is as true for slightly decorated wares as it is for the most decorative examples. In the case of decanters, decoration is not the only factor guiding values. Signed decanters are expensive because they are rare and pairs of decanters will also be costly, not only because you are paying for two decanters but also because pairs are desirable. Pairs may cost from £100-400 ($180-$720) but you need not pay more than about £50 ($90) for single decanters produced during the late 18th and 19th centuries. Although it is difficult to generalise in this area of the market, prices are greatly bound to factors such as quality, rarity and *condition* – the latter certainly a prime consideration when you realise a chip or star crack can devalue a piece enormously.

Slagware
This is another recently discovered area of glass collecting (page 147) and examples are not only comparatively easy to find but they are also very inexpensive. Top quality items seldom fetch more than about £10 ($18) and these would probably include pieces that are marked and of attractive design and colour. Marked pieces on the whole command the higher prices while un-marked examples fall within a £3-5 ($5-$9) price range. Large and attractive shapes tend to be the most popular with collectors. Always purchase slagware with first-class condition in mind – at present, examples are too plentiful not to demand perfection.

Roman glass
Roman glass (page 148) constitutes a very special area of the market because it attracts collectors who possess a combined interest in glass and in antiquity. Many of the domestic wares that are simple in shape, of plain appearance and coloured the natural greenish-blue are relatively inexpensive. Tear flasks range from about £25-50 ($45-$90) and bowls and other types of flasks start from about £50 ($90). Glass jewellery can also fall amongst the most inexpensive of items and assorted beads and bangle bracelets start from about £10 ($18). Of course, jewellery combined with gold in the form of necklaces, pendants, bracelets and earrings can run into the thousands mark, not only for the materials employed but also because such

items can be attractively worn. Glass that is brilliantly coloured and/or decorated by painting, moulding or applied glass trailing can cost from £100 ($180) to thousands depending on its rarity and attractiveness. Iridescence, the rainbow coloured sparkling surface that covers many glass wares due to chemical reactions during burial, is often thought to be extremely desirable, being particularly highly prized in the United States, and wares with spectacular iridescence again can run into the thousands mark. Damage, as with so many other areas of the glass market, can devalue examples quite considerably even though these pieces may date from the early beginnings of the Christian era. Top market dealers and collectors usually demand perfection except in the case of rare glass wares and they will pay for it. But attractive and slightly damaged pieces can be purchased for much less.

FELICE MEHLMAN

Pressed Glass

The manufacture of glassware was already a thriving industry in Egypt around 1400 BC and objects made from glass believed to date from as long ago as 7000 BC have been found. The art of blowing glass was not discovered until 50 BC and this still remains the only method of producing quality glassware.

Since the invention of blowing the only major innovation in the production of glassware has been the process known as 'pressing'. It was the introduction of pressed glass early in the 19th century which was responsible for a large proportion of the glassware used ever since. Pressing glass is what we would call a mass production process. It has the commercial advantage of superseding the craftsmanship of the blower, and as a result most forms of glassware became both cheaper and more plentiful.

In the past pressed glassware has been neglected by collectors. During the last year however, quite a lot of interest has been shown, and attractive items are rapidly becoming difficult to find. The author considers that, for a reasonable outlay, a collection of 19th century pressed glass can still be made and will provide an interesting and profitable hobby.

Except for a few specialised items little or no research has been carried out on any of the pieces illustrated in this article, which does not pretend to do more than provide an indication of the scope still open to those enthusiastic enough to hoe their own row.

We do not know whether England or America produced the first pressed glassware. We do know however, that Denning Jarves, an American, patented a 'method of pressing glass' in 1828 and that the Americans probably produced more pressed glass early in the 19th century than we did in England.

The Illustrated Encyclopedia of the Great Exhibition of 1851 notes that 'by pressing glass into moulds this elegant material is produced to the public in useful and symmetrical forms at prices considerably lower than those at which cut flint glass could possibly be offered. Many specimens of pressed glass exhibited have a degree of sharpness in all ornamental parts which renders it difficult, without close examination, to say whether or not they have been subjected to the cutters' wheel.

Above, left to right

French pressed drinking glass with conical bowl and knopped stem. Flat foot with pontil mark ground away. Height 7¼ inches (18.4 cm). About 1850-1870.

Pressed sugar bowl, 5¾ inches high, 5¼ inches diameter (14.6 × 13.3 cm). Commemorative with bust of Disraeli on one side and 'Earl Beaconsfield the hero of the Congress of Berlin July 1878' on the other. Greener Trade mark also Diamond Registration mark, about 1878.

Flask 7½ inches high (19 cm), capacity approx: half bottle spirits, moulded hob nail design, cork insert for stopper. Registration No. 274732 for 1896-97.

Below, left to right

Commemorative pressed plate 'Gladstone for the million' 5 inches diameter (12.7 cm). Typical example of dozens of plates, dishes etc. of varying sizes that were produced up to 1937 to commemorate every important event. Prices vary with size and rarity of event.

Pressed plate, 7 inches diameter (17.8 cm), with a 'Granulated' finish, typical of a large number of items produced in this finish, about 1890.

Pressed dish 5 inches diameter (12.7 cm), the plain portions of the design are acid etched to simulate ground glass, many types found. Diamond Registration mark, about 1890.

Pressing or moulding

One of the first problems encountered by the collector is to distinguish between Pressing and Moulding, and further, between these forms of glass when they have been improved by the use of the cutters wheel. The following notes will therefore be of assistance:

Pressed glass. The pattern or design is on the outside, the inside being smooth. The Trade or Registration marks can however be found both inside or out. This method of identification is probably correct for all forms of 19th century pressed glassware. The internal spiral design tumbler p. 130 is, however, an exception to this method of identification.

Moulded glass. This is produced by blowing in the normal manner, the object is however finally inserted and expanded into a mould which has the design cut into it. The result of expanding the glass into the mould is that the inside of the object also carries the outline of the exterior design, and this can easily be detected with the finger.

Pressed and cut. A method used to reproduce economically the skills of the freehand cutter, the bottom of the grooves however, will be seen to be rounded since the wheel does not need to cut to the full depth to reproduce the effect of Cut glass.

Marks

Pontil marks, generally considered to be the prerogative of 17/18th century glasses, are sometimes found on early pressed glass, G. C. Mason writing in 1858 describes the process of pressing and finishing a tumbler and shows why a pontil mark was necessary. The moulded beer glass, page 130, has a pontil mark and the pontil on the French glass, page 128, has been ground away. The pontil is a long iron rod attached to one end of a piece of glass on its removal from a blowpipe; the pontil mark is the scar left after the glass has been worked, then cooled and broken free.

A small amount of 19th century pressed glassware carries a Makers Trade Mark and details of four of these are illustrated. The author has not so far been able to find out the dates when these Trade Marks were in use.

The Diamond Registration Mark which registered the pattern or design with the patent office is also illustrated, this mark came into use in 1842 and continued until 1883. Items carrying both a Trade and a Diamond Registration Mark are rare, two examples are illustrated.

After 1884 a series of Registration numbers was introduced, these started at 1 and had reached 550 000 by 1909. Makers Trade marks as well as Registration numbers are sometimes found.

The codes for deciphering both the Diamond and Registration numbers can be found in most books dealing with marks as they were used for both Ceramics and Glass. Reference has to be made to the Patent Office to obtain the makers name from these two sets of marks.

It goes without saying that it is desirable whenever possible to purchase pressed glass items that carry one of the identifying marks in the same way as one would with silver or china.

Coloured glass

Coloured, slag or 'end of day', and milk white types of pressed glass are fields that already have their devotees and are outside the scope of this article. It is, however, interesting to note that these types seem to be more easily found than good examples of plain pressed glass; and more often than not they carry one of the identifying marks.

The cost of collecting

Prices are very variable, some dealers and auctioneers know that most forms of pressed glass is becoming collected, others do not; which means that a simple tumbler can vary widely from one place to another. Never neglect the boxes full of sundry glass and china made up by auctioneers who think the contents have no value, it may hurt your pride but the results can be very soothing.   P.T.

Where to buy

All country and small auctions, Junk shops and Antique markets throughout the country, but the prices are high once these dealers have recognised an item.

JOHN A. BROOKS, 2 Knights Crescent, Rothley, Leicestershire, is the only antique dealer I know who seems to be interested in pressed glass.

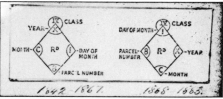

Top, left to right

Some 19th century makers trade marks. Sowerby Ellison: Greener & Co. (this mark is also found with the lion facing left without an axe): George Davidson & Co.: John Derbyshire (and Son). Unknown mark comprising 'ship's capstan with rope wound around the barrel' (not illustrated).

Above

Registration marks, left, for 1842 to 1867 and right, for 1868 to 1883.

Above, left to right

Two ½ pint, 3¾ inch (9.5 cm) high pressed tumblers with thumb print design. Left-hand example which is of quality metal carries a Davidson & Co. Trade mark.

One 3 inch (7.6 cm) high tumbler with arch design. Messrs. Sowerby Ellison listed tumblers of this design in three sizes in their design sheets of 1860-70. All about 1870.

Above

Pressed glass ale/beer cans. Left with barley and floral design, 4½ inches (10.8 cm) high. Centre and right with geometric decoration 5¼ inches (13.3 cm) high. The small half-pint can carries the trade mark of Davidson & Co., the granulated background suggests a date around 1880. Both the one-pint cans have geometric designs similar to those found in the 1860-70 pattern books of Edward Moore & Co.

Left

Four examples of pressed goblets, 5¾ to 6¼ inches (14.5-16 cm) high, from left to right: Combined thumb print and rain drop design, thumb print design with heavy knopped stem, raised arch design, Edward Moore, geometric design No. 291. About 1860-1890.

Below, left to right

Pair of cog wheel pattern pressed salt cellars 3¾ inches diameter (9.5 cm), with star base, also a pair of fiddle thread silver salt spoons by G. Adams, London, 1865. An attractive combination used by the author, about 1860.
One rectangular pressed salt 3 inches long (7.7 cm) with impressed Swan Trade mark and Registration No. 400564 for M. & J. Guggenheim Ltd, 1902.

Left

From the left, Nos. 1-3-4 are pressed beer glasses and No. 2 is a moulded type, heights 7¼ to 8 inches (18.4-20.3 cm), capacities 10 to 12 fl. ozs. The pressed glasses have a simulated thumb print design and capstan stems. The moulded glass has a diamond design and a pontil mark similar to 18th century glasses which means that it could have been made any time from about 1830 onwards whereas the pressed examples would be from 1870-90 period.

Right, left to right

Pressed geometrical design one-pint tumbler, 6 inches high (15.2 cm). Impressed mark on base PINT – 82 PINT. Probable date 1882.

Pressed half-pint tumbler, 4 inches high (10.2 cm) with INTERNAL spiral pressed design. Impressed Trade mark 'A ship's capstan with rope around'. This Trade mark not so far traced, glass also very unusual in that the design is on the inside of the glass which is the reverse of all other pressed glass found so far by the author. It is, of course, possible that it is quite modern.

Pressed granulated finish one-pint tumbler, 6⅜ inches high (16.2 cm), with Diamond Registration mark (date illegible), about 1890.

Left, left to right

Pressed milk or water jug of one pint capacity. 7 inches high (17.7 cm) with lip and geometric pattern. Probably an early example of pressed glass, about 1850-60.

Pressed milk or water jug of two pints' capacity. 5 inches high (12.7 cm) with lip, the design illustrates Burns' poem Tam o'Shanter *complete with witches, Brig o'doon, drinking scene etc., about 1880-90.*

Pressed ale/beer can, half pint, 4 inches high (10.2 cm), commemorating the 'High level bridge of Newcastle on Tyne', 'Commenced April 24 1846, Opened January 16 1850', about 1850-60.

Left, left to right

One pressed half-pint tumbler 4 inches high (10.2 cm) with all over 'rain drop' design, as illustrated Sowerby Ellison catalogue pattern No. 541. about 1870.

One thick pressed glass tumbler 3½ inches high (8.9 cm) with a form of arch design, as illustrated Sowerby Ellison catalogue pattern Nos. 534-5-6 three sizes listed, about 1870.

One pressed half-pint tumbler 4 inches high (10.2 cm) with simulated 'hob nail' design. Davidson Trade mark on bottom, about 1870-80.

Left, left to right

Pressed ice cream 'hokey pokey' cup of 19-20th century, 2⅛ inches high (5.4 cm), made from very rough glass and sometimes found with a foot and stem giving it the impression of being a deceptive glass, about 1890-1910.

Pressed bon-bon dish 2¾ inches high (7 cm) with overall hob nail design. A piece that carries the rare J. Davenport Trade mark, about 1880.

Below

A 9-inch diameter (22.9 cm), pressed dish commemorating Queen Victoria Diamond Jubilee 1897. The bust of the Queen is gilt which makes this a very decorative piece, about 1897.

Left, left to right

Pressed coffee cup (?), 2¼ inches high (5.7 cm) with 'rain drop' pattern. As illustrated Edward Moore catalogue No. 213, about 1870.

Moulded tot glass 2¼ inches high (5.7 cm), probably used for extra strong spirits, about 1890-1910.

English Ale Glasses

My interest in the drinking glasses used for ale and beer originally was confined to specimens from the 17th and 18th centuries; good examples from this period have now become scarce and expensive, so along with other collectors I have turned my attention to the 19th century, and been agreeably surprised at the result.

I assumed when starting the new venture that it would be easy to build up a collection and to obtain the necessary documentation, but was quickly disillusioned and very soon realised that there was more information available about the 17th and 18th centuries, and even more surprised when I found that there were also fewer good 19th century glasses on the market.

The drinks we call ale and beer have been in existence for some 4000 years and are consequently taken very much for granted, I find however it is useful to have some background information regarding them as they were not quite the same drink we are accustomed to today.

The difference between ale and beer has been defined by one authority as:

Ale = Malt, Yeast and Water
Beer = Malt, Yeast, Hops and Water

The hops act both as flavouring and a preservative and though used since Roman times they only became a legal addition to ale brewed for sale in England after an Act of Parliament passed in 1440.

If sufficient malt is used either ale or beer can be brewed to give a drink having an alcohol content of nearly 12 per cent, which equals that of many wines, and explains the use of a small capacity glass for drinking 'strong ale' the name usually given to the special ales and beers of the 17th and 18th centuries.

We have records of the orders passing between the London merchant John Greene and his supplier Alessio Morelli of Murano during the years 1667 to 1673 which show that many of the glasses he imported were listed for use with both 'french wine and beare', and that the capacity of these glasses varied between $3\frac{1}{2}$ and 5 Fluid Ounces. (See British Museum Sloane MSS No. 857.) We find that the same capacity of glass continued to be listed as an ale in the design books of Richardsons of Wordsley of about 1850 (in Dudley Museum and Art Gallery) and we also find that these same books contain designs of 8-10 Fluid Ounce glasses they also called ales.

The descriptions ale and beer appear to have become synonymous in England since the 17th century, though opinions about this differ, both drinks were, however, available in their 'strong' form because we find decanters of the same capacity, some engraved 'beer' and others 'ale'.

It is impossible to be definite about the strength of either drink before about the middle of the 19th century, we do however know that there were four generally recognised types called – Strong – Best – Table – and Small, the strength of any of these would vary according to the price paid and the district as would the size and type of glass used. There would probably not be so much variation in the strengths of Table and Small beers which were thirst quenchers served in silver, pewter or pottery cans according to the status of the drinker. Later in the 19th century we find that pressed cans are the cheap vessels used for drinking.

Some indication of the strength and cost can be obtained from the records of 1623 when Best ale is noted as having cost $3\frac{1}{2}$ old pence per gallon; wages for a skilled labourer were about 6 shillings per week, and small ale sold for $\frac{1}{2}$ penny (old) per gallon at this time. Again in 1680 when Parliament were discussing the prevalence of drunkenness it was stated that 'ale was being brewed so strong as to cost 16 old pence per gallon and that it burned like Sack'. (Sack was a kind of sherry.)

Readers may wonder why when some makers' design books are available we cannot be more accurate as regards dates, the reason being that the designers were very cagey and almost never put dates on their sketches.

It is not suggested that this article is a complete survey of the 19th century ale and beer glasses, it does, however, represent over two years' work and collecting.

The cost of collecting

The price of 19th century drinking glasses can only be described as 'fluid' so much depending on the quality and who is at the Auction. Collectors are, however, becoming interested, and most prices have risen appreciably – as in so many other fields – during the last five years.   P.T.

Left

Ale rummers, about 1800-1830. H 5½-6½ in. (140-165 mm). All the bowls are thin and with a capacity in excess of half a pint (10 fl. oz.). These glasses show the beginnings of the capstan stem (a feature confined almost exclusively to drinking glasses intended for ale and beer) which is combined with a collar under the bowl and a larger diameter, thicker reinforcing collar on top of the foot. The capstan stem appears to have gone out of fashion about 1860-70, various forms of round knop having been introduced by then.
Sources: Principal dealers

Left

Ale rummers, centre about 1850, others 1875-90. H 5-5¾ in. (127-146 mm). Later ale rummers are made from a crystal clear type of metal. They have a more stylised form of engraving of hops and barley (the 'strong ale' motif); this type of decoration was in use from the beginning of the 18th century. It has been suggested that glasses of this type were used for the service of best beer or of malt drinks that had been topped up with a measure of strong ale. It is curious that no manufacturer's design book illustrates glasses engraved with the strong ale motif, though other forms of floral decoration are shown. Some 19th century goblets with capstan stems and plain bowls are also found.
Sources: Principal dealers

Left

Ale tumblers. Left, made in crystal clear metal, about 1860-80, with a man hanging from a gibbet engraved into the base: all such glasses are known as 'last drop' tumblers. H 4 in. (102 mm). Centre, this has a base moulded to resemble 'star' cutting, about 1850. H 3½ in. (88.5 mm). Right, this small glass, about 1820, is the most valuable of the three with a capacity of 5 fl. oz., or half the other two. H 2¾ in. (70 mm). Tumblers of 5 fl. oz. capacity (and other forms of glasses) for use with 'French wine and beare' were ordered by the London merchant John Greene from Alessio Morelli of Murano (Venice) between 1667 and 1673, and the type continued to be used for drinking ale and beer in the 19th century. So far I have seen only one 20 fl. oz. (1 pint) 19th century tumbler engraved with the strong ale motif.
Sources: Principal dealers

Right

Ales with 'U' bowls, all plain with 'arch' moulded decoration, three knopped and one capstan stem, about 1840-50. H 5¼-7⅜ in. (133-187 mm), capacities 5-10 fl. oz. It seems possible that the 'U' bowl was intended for bottled ales. An aquatint published by C. Turner in 1821 and entitled 'Interior of the fives court, Randall and Turpin sparring' shows several 'U' bowl ales being carried on a tray; the glasses are only half full of a brown liquid (beer?) and the rest of the bowl is full of a white froth which is also seen to be bubbling over the top. The excessive froth suggests a reason for the 'U' bowl ale glasses of the period.
Sources: Provincial auction rooms

Right

Ales with conical or funnel bowls, all plain with 'arch' decoration and with capstan stems about 1800-50. H 5⅜-7⅞ in. (136-200 mm), capacities 5-10 fl. oz. This type of bowl is also confined to ale glasses and was made in as many sizes as the 'U' shapes. The small glasses are often mistaken for 18th century short ales. I have seen several 8-inch high funnel bowls engraved with the hops and barley motif: these are all modern and are traps for the inexperienced collector.
Sources: Principal dealers and auction rooms

Right

Ales with thick metal 'U' bowls, moulded wrythen and cut thumbprint decoration and knopped stems, about 1850-60. H 6⅝-7⅜ in. (168-187 mm), capacities 10-12 fl. oz. The metal used in the early 'U' bowl ales is thicker than that of 18th century glasses, but thinner than that used after the repeal of the Glass Excise in 1845 – as in these examples. Their type and decoration is similar to sketches in the design books of Richardsons (now in Dudley Museum and Art Gallery) and Sowerby Ellisons (now Sowerby's Ellison Glassworks, Gateshead).
Sources: Dealers and provincial auction rooms

Where to buy

JOHN A. BROOKS, 2 Knights Court, Rothley, Leicestershire (Rothley 2625). Mr. Brooks also deals in pressed glass.

CECIL DAVIS LTD., at Algernon Asprey Ltd., 27 Bruton Street, London w1 (01-629 2608)

W. G. T. BURNE LTD., 11 Elystan Street, London sw3 (01-589 6074)

DELOMOSNE & SON LTD., 4 Campden Hill Road, London w8 (01-937 1804)

HOWARD PHILLIPS, 11a Henrietta Place, London w1 (01-580 9844)

MAUREEN THOMPSON, 34 Kensington Church Street, London w8 (01-937 9919)

ALAN TILLMAN ANTIQUES LTD., 9 Halkin Arcade, Motcomb Street, London sw1 (01-235 8235)

Left

Pressed and moulded ales with simulated capstan stems, about 1870-90. H 7¼-8 in. (184-203 mm), capacities 10-12 fl. oz. Pressed glass was made in the United States about 1820 and is thought to have been introduced into England in 1828; as the catalogue of the 1851 Great Exhibition shows every type of glassware was available in pressed glass by then. The glass on the left is pressed and has an imitation of the earlier thumbprint decoration that was cut and polished on earlier glasses; similar pressed glasses are found in the design books of Sowerby Ellisons. The glass on the right is moulded and with a similar form of decoration; this glass could have been made any time from 1800 onwards. Sources: Provincial auction rooms

Left

Ales with 'U' bowls, cut thumbprint and arch decoration, knopped stems. About 1850-70. H 7⅛-8⅛ in. (181-206 mm), capacities 10-14 fl. oz. The metal is thicker even than that used in the facing examples though the decoration is cut and polished in the same way. Designs for these types of glass are found in the pattern books of Thomas Webb & Co. (now incorporated into the Dema Glass Co., Stourbridge). Sources: Dealers and provincial auction rooms

All the glasses illustrated are from the Author's collection. Photography by Stephanie Hobouse of Churchill, Oxfordshire

Cranberry Glass

'Cranberry glass' describes the transparent cherry-red coloured glass of the 19th century, almost exclusively made in England, and later America. The term is probably of American origin and although it has become widely accepted, many English dealers and collectors prefer other descriptive labels such as 'cherry-red glass' or 'ruby glass', the latter classification the most popular of the two but perhaps also the most inaccurate. The colour of cranberry glass is certainly variable (and can range from a pale pinkish-brown to a rich cherry-red) but it does not resemble the darker and more solid ink-red glass (the true 'ruby glass') that was made in Bohemia and elsewhere on the Continent. This deeper red colour was first devised by Johann Kunckel in Potsdam, about 1679. The process was difficult and expensive because gold chloride was employed to achieve the desired brilliance. A cheaper method was later developed in Bohemia during the 1820s by Egermann, using a copper oxide. These ruby tints were imitated in Birmingham about a century later, although coloured glass wares were also extensively imported into England from Bohemia and Czechoslovakia, and were to have considerable influence on English glass-makers.

Early 19th century developments

Not much is known about the origins of cranberry glass in England. It is thought that most of it was produced in the back-yard 'cribs' of glass-makers in the Midlands and Stourbridge areas from the early 19th century, when Victorian taste for coloured glass developed. During the years before 1845 (when all tax was removed from glass after being levied for 100 years), cranberry glass was mainly confined to simple domestic wares – wine glasses, jugs and decanters. Ornamentation was kept minimal and the use of clear glass for handles, stems and bases was more functional than decorative.

These freely-blown or mould-blown wares were made in great numbers and soon found a ready market because they were inexpensive and because the colour not only masked the rather poor quality of the glass, but also satisfied Victorian aesthetic standards.

Cranberry glass 'friggers' were also made during the first half of the 19th century. These hand-blown fanciful articles such as bells, pipes, flasks, bugles and canes were probably produced at Stourbridge, Sunderland or Warrington. They are often attributed to Bristol or Nailsea, although the question of exact provenance remains largely unresolved.

Later 19th century developments

After the glass tax was lifted, glass manufacturers regained the financial freedom to experiment with a wide variety of colours, shapes and new ways of ornamenting. The result of their efforts was displayed at the Great Exhibition of 1851, at the Crystal Palace in Hyde Park. Colourful and highly decorative 'art glass' wares soon became the rage and greatly inspired American manufacturers, who began to produce glass articles based on these mid-19th century English prototypes. The Richardson firm of Stourbridge was particularly influential and it is perhaps through this connection that cranberry glass found a popular following with American collectors.

In spite of the vast wealth of colours that appeared after 1845, the combination of clear and cranberry glass remained extensive, but now it began to take more fanciful forms – twisted, pincered, blobbed, trailed and sometimes tinted green or yellow.

Vases, jugs and decanters were decorated with clear glass shell shapes, often applied around the neck, middle or used as an extended foot. The whole body was also sometimes trailed with clear glass stems and flowers.

Handles were almost invariably composed of clear glass and remained either unadorned or revealed some form of ribbed moulding (e.g. twisted rope moulding that was especially favoured for baskets and bon-bon dishes).

The cranberry colour continued to vary; 'friggers' tend to display the most intense red shades, as do the earlier examples of the 19th century. After the mid-century, the colour became slightly paler, partly because the 'metal' was less thick. By Edwardian times, the cherry-red became more of a tawny colour.

Among the most splendid cranberry wares are the 'overlay' examples, the white

Above

Flower centrepiece, sometimes described by the French term 'épergne'. They were frequently combined with baskets hanging from twisted arms, bowls, dishes or multiple trumpet-shaped flower holders – serving a variety of purposes. Highly decorative, fanciful and colourful – these qualities accounted for its great success from the 1860s to the early 20th century. The 'épergne' today (complete with extensions) will command the highest prices. About 1880.
OLDSWINFORD ANTIQUES

Above (from left to right)

Posy vase decorated with etched floral design, clear glass faceted stem and base. Cut cranberry glass is rare. Probably made by Thomas Webb of Stourbridge. About 1880.
H 15 cm (6 in).
Carafe with faceted clear glass stopper and handle. About 1880.
H 23 cm (9 in).
Pipe with long hollow stem furnished with knop-like swellings and white enamel spiral around rim of bowl. A popular type of 'frigger', originally used as shop-signs outside tobacconists' and as tavern ornaments. About 1860.
L 30 cm (12 in).
ALL FROM MAUREEN THOMPSON

exterior cut away to reveal cranberry decorative panels beneath. Stourbridge made overlay pieces in imitation of Bohemian examples; although the latter tend to be more ornate with gilt decoration, Stourbridge wares were of cranberry and white overlay only.

During the latter part of the 19th century, shapes became more variable. Apart from the wine glasses, decanters, jugs and 'friggers' which continued to be produced, there are also many examples of patch boxes, finger bowls, scent bottles, oil lamps, toothpick holders, baskets, butter dishes, castors, gas shades, sugar bowls, knife rests, toilette sets, flower centrepieces – the list is enormous.

Hints on Collecting

Today, cranberry glass is popularly collected in America and England, in spite of its almost negligible mention in textbooks on 19th century glass.

It is also plentiful and relatively inexpensive. Most examples can be purchased for under £100 ($180) and often the simple domestic wares fetch considerably less. The 'épergnes' and overlay examples are invariably the most expensive. Cranberry glass can be purchased from bric-à-brac antique shops throughout the country (the London and Midland areas are particularly good). Glass specialists who deal in 'finer' glass wares often do not include cranberry and other 19th century types in their collections.   F.M.

Where to buy

CHRISTO ANTIQUES, High Street, Ripley, Surrey (048-643 2481)

GREEN'S ANTIQUE GALLERIES, 117 Kensington Church Street, London w8 (01-229 9618)

LEE DAVIS, Stand 46, The Antique Hypermarket, 26-40 Kensington High Street, London w8 (01-937 3670)

MERIDEN HOUSE ANTIQUES, Meriden House, 75 Market Street, Stourbridge (038 43 5384)

OLDSWINFORD ANTIQUES, 106 Hagley Road, Stourbridge (038 43 5577)

RANKIN, BEST AND GREEN LTD, The London Glass Centre, 293-5 Kingsland Road, London E8 (01-254 4901)

A. T. SILVESTER AND SONS, 2-4 High Street, Warwick (0926 42972)

MAUREEN THOMPSON, 34 Kensington Church Street, London w8 (01-937 9919)

MELVYN TRAUB ANTIQUES LTD., Grays Antique Market, 58 Davies Street, London w1 (01-629 7034)

ANNA TRIGGS SMALL ANTIQUES, Stand 49, The Antique Hypermarket, 26-40 Kensington High Street, London w8 (01-937 4871)

Where to see

BRIERLEY HILL GLASS MUSEUM AND ART GALLERY, Moor Street, Dudley

STOURBRIDGE GLASS COLLECTION, Mary Stevens Park, Stourbridge

Left
Cranberry glass toilette set with hand-painted floral decoration. About 1880-90.
W 26.5 cm (10½ in).
RANKIN, BEST AND GREEN

Below
Vase in gilt metal stand.
H 21 cm (8¼ in).
GREEN'S ANTIQUE GALLERIES

Above
Jug with ridged decoration around base portion, slight fluting up to rim and clear glass handle. Coloured glass water jugs came into vogue in England after 1845. About 1840-60.
H 15 cm (6 in)
ANNA TRIGGS

Below
Cranberry glass tumbler, the straight sides sloping slightly inwards to the base. After 1845, such drinking glasses appeared in a variety of colours, often free of surface decoration.
SILVESTER AND SONS

Above
Pale coloured cranberry bowl, possibly once belonging to a dinner service entirely composed of cranberry glass. About 1880.
D 13 cm (5 in).
ANNA TRIGGS

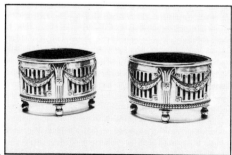

Above
Pair of salt dips composed of cranberry glass containers and Sheffield plate holders. About 1880.
W 7.5 cm (3 in)
MELVYN TRAUB

137

Left

Miniature jug and basin, the cranberry glass decorated with a gold floral design. Glass toys were made in England from the late 17th century for doll houses and for adults. Quantities were also imported from Germany and Bohemia. French examples, such as these, tend to be the most ornate. About 1880.
H (of jug) 4 cm (1.5 in) W (of bowl) 6 cm (2½ in).
MELVYN TRAUB

Left

Cranberry jug with amber coloured glass handle, applied trailing on the sides and pointed feet. The green, yellow and white enamel floral design is hand-painted – an elaborate and delicate presentation that catered for 19th century French tastes.
H 20 cm (8 in).
MELVYN TRAUB

Above
One of a pair of pale cranberry vases decorated with clear glass shell shapes.
H 10 cm (4 in).
MELVYN TRAUB

Below
Bon-bon dishes contained in silver plated stand with incised floral design around the edge.
GREEN'S ANTIQUE GALLERIES

Below

Bon-bon dish decorated with amber coloured threads around the ruffled rim, and clear glass shell shapes around middle with applied flowers and celery feet. The circular and dotted centre of each flower represents the Thomas Webb mark which also appears at the bottom underside. The fanciful decoration and orange and red colours combined, create a most striking piece.
W 13 cm (5 in).
MELVYN TRAUB

Above
Pair of dessert glasses with cranberry glass bowls and clear glass collared stems and bases.
H 10 cm (4 in).
ANNA TRIGGS

Right
Cranberry glass vase with white overlay decoration, a technique that originated in ancient Rome. It was revived on a commercial scale in Bohemia about 1815 and was much admired all over the continent. Vases, rare in Bohemia, were an English speciality – the cranberry and opaque white combination was especially popular. Cranberry overlay examples today fetch the highest prices. About 1860-70.
H 46 cm (18 in).
RANKIN, BEST AND GREEN

Left
Cranberry glass jug with clear glass handle and vaseline glass on applied floral design. The combination of two or more coloured glasses was extensive during the latter part of the 19th century. About 1870.
H 26.5 cm (10½ in).
RANKIN, BEST AND GREEN

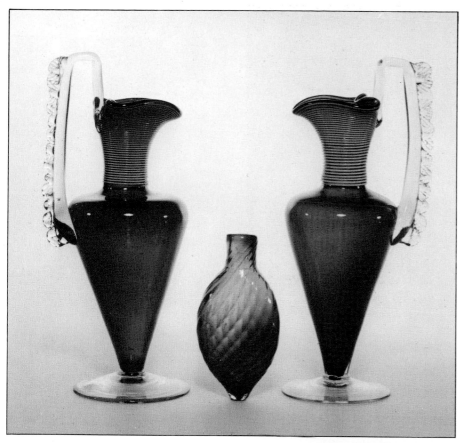

Below

Cream jug with clear glass handle and petal-shaped vein-lobed foot. The combination of cranberry and clear glass (for handles, bases or applied decoration) was most popular. After the glass tax was removed in 1845, the application of clear glass became more fanciful — twisted, blobbed and sometimes tinted green or yellow.
SILVESTER AND SONS

Above

Custard cup with cranberry coloured bowl, clear glass handle, stem and base. These were made in great numbers during the 19th century; a debased version was used in shops for selling ices.
SILVESTER AND SONS

Colour
Top left

Pair of jugs with clear glass handles decorated with shell shapes, clear glass bases and white glass applied trailing at top. About 1880.
H 25 cm (10 in).
The flask is decorated with a spiralling linear design and a subtle gradation of colour. About 1880.
H 11.5 cm (4½ in).
ALL FROM MAUREEN THOMPSON

Top right

Coloured glass bells are a popular type of 'frigger'. Victorian versions were made in various colours with clear glass decorated handles, about one foot in height. Many 'friggers' display a particularly intense cranberry colour. About 1860.
H 30.5 cm (12 in)
MELVYN TRAUB

Left

Wine glasses with cranberry coloured bowls and clear glass stems and bases. The floral and linear decoration is created by etching, where hydrofluoric acid is used to 'bite out' the design. This technique was practised in England from the 1830s and was later patented as a commercial process for use on coloured tableware by Benjamin Richardson in 1857. Made in Stourbridge, late 19th century.
MERIDEN HOUSE ANTIQUES

Glass Decanters

The first bottle decanter or serving bottle appeared in about 1623; they were blackish-green or dark brown in colour. Until George Ravenscroft, who became official glassmaker to the Glass Seller's Company in 1674, substituted an oxide of lead for a proportion of alkali, glass had been very brittle. This new formula produced glass which was heavier but as brilliant quality as Venetian glass, which had dominated the market for centuries. Leather, metals and pottery were also used as containers before glass finally established itself as the best material at the beginning of the 18th century.

History

Early decanters, which were heavy in design, had either very loose fitting stoppers or none at all. The contents were usually finished during a meal, so never stood in the decanter for more than a brief period. During the 18th century port increased in popularity; since port was improved by decanting and was preserved better in an airtight container, a close fitting stopper (which was ground into the neck of the decanter) was introduced. Whether the emergence of the decanter was purely for aesthetic reasons or due to a change in vintner's practice (perhaps by importing wine in larger casks) or purely in keeping with a more civilised and gentile approach to the dinner table, is a matter of conjecture.

Inevitably, the Government realising that the Glass Industry was booming, introduced in 1745 an Excise Tax which put a duty on the weight of materials used. Consequently, the glassmakers used less weight of glass and it can be seen that decanters immediately became more delicate.

The decanters of the mid-18th century generally were mallet shaped, so named because they were similar to a mason's tool. The necks were tall and slender, with sloping shoulders and sides either vertical or leaning slightly inwards. A spire shaped stopper was used with this type and the bodies were normally engraved with vine decoration or labelled to denote their contents.

Towards the end of the 18th century the diameter of the base increased and the neck shortened. The lip was flattened and turned outwards to prevent dribbling.

Between 2-4 rings were applied round the neck to form a hand grip. Miniature decanters of this type are found which were made by apprentices, or were used to display to potential customers as examples.

Drum shaped decanters became popular during the Regency and also the straight-sided square-based decanter, with either mushroom or bull's eye stoppers. The square-based decanter was sometimes made in sets, but it was not until the Victorian era that tantali came into vogue.

With the repeal of the Excise Act in 1845, English glass took on a new impetus. Decanters lost their Georgian elegance and became heavy and ungainly, decorated with deep cut 'Gothic' patterns. These reached their peak in the exhibits displayed at the Great Exhibition of 1851. It was not Ruskin's condemnation of all cut glass as 'barbaric' which lead to its unpopularity but the technique of pressmoulding rediscovered in America which

Left

Fine and rare pair of early facet cut decanters with matching pear shaped stoppers. About 1785. It is quite possible for pairs to be dissimilar in height or shape as they were all blown by hand.
H 29.5 cm (11½ in)
MAUREEN THOMPSON

Below

Completely plain, very popular type of decanter of about 1790, with bull's-eye stopper.
H 25 cm (9¾ in)
W. G. T. BURNE (ANTIQUE GLASS) LTD

Left

Irish club-shaped decanter decorated with part-way ribbed moulded flutes. The milled neck rings, which are like the edge of a coin, are typically Irish. The base is impressed 'Cork Glass Co'. About 1800.
H 28 cm (11 in)
EILA GRAHAME ANTIQUES

Left

Tapered decanter decorated with engraved stars and a single band. This shape was generally fitted with a pear-shaped stopper. About 1790.
H 25 cm (10 in)
ALAN TILLMAN ANTIQUES

Below

One of an elegant pair of Adam period tapered decanters decorated with wheel engraved swags and anchor shields; pear-shaped stopper. About 1790.
H 30.5 cm (12 in)
DELOMOSNE & SON LTD

Above

Pair of barrel-shaped half bottle decanters. The heavier cutting portrays the start of the more exuberant style common in the Regency. About 1810.
H 21.5 cm (8½ in)
GERALD SATTIN LTd

Left

Octagonal half bottle size decanters decorated with small facets down the sides, about 1800. Shrub was a sweet cordial generally made of blackcurrant juice, sugar and water with a spirit added, usually rum. Hollands was a more polite term for gin.
H 18 cm (7 in)
CECIL DAVIS LTD at ALGERNON ASPREY LTD

Left

Moulded spirit bottle with a spout lip. It would have been made in a two- or three-part mould. About 1790-1800.
H 19.5 cm (7¾ in)
W. G. T. Burne
(Antique Glass) Ltd

Right

Good straight sided decanter of about 1825. It is decorated in the centre with vertical panels of pillar flutes and close diamond cutting. In this example the stopper is original but many stoppers were lost or broken over the years (and have been replaced).
H 25 cm (9¾ in)
Delomosne & Son Ltd

Right

A decanter decorated with broad flutes over the entire body, known as slice cutting, star cut base and ball-shaped stopper. About 1820.
H 28 cm (11 in)
Thomas Goode
& Co Ltd

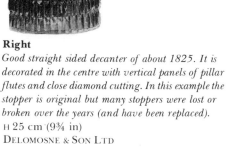

Below

Good quality pair of straight sided decanters, possibly Irish, because of the decorated band of strawberry diamond cutting. The tops of the diamonds are cut away into minute pyramids, giving the effect of the surface of a strawberry. About 1820.
H 23.5 cm (9½ in)
Cecil Davis Ltd at Algernon Asprey Ltd

Below right

Three-quarter bottle size decanter with broad and narrow flute decoration with four horizontal bands in between; mushroom stopper. About 1810.
H 25 cm (9¼ in)
Alan Tillman Antiques

Below

Magnum (2 bottle) decanter of the classical style, with four flattened neck rings and bull's-eye stopper, about 1810. Even larger decanters were made and were given Biblical names: Nebuchadnezzar, 20 bottles; Balthasar, 16 bottles; Salmanazar, 12 bottles; Methuselah, 8 bottles; Rehoboam, 6 bottles; Jeroboam, 4 bottles. H 34 cm (13½ in)
Maureen Thompson

superseded in the 1870s the art of cutting. This led to imitations of cut glass decanters decorated with stipple grounds and patterns in raised dots. Ruskin's condemnation encouraged the production of the slender more austere designs of the Art Nouveau period of the early 20th century.

Decorating

Many political and topical events in the 18th century were recorded on decanters or wine glasses (Jacobean subjects are most sought after). These were engraved with a diamond-tipped tool either by line drawing or stippling, which is a series of little dots creating a picture.

Around this time enamelling on glass became a popular decoration. The most famous work was done by a brother and sister, William and Mary Beilby of Newcastle. Generally they used white enamel and their designs included birds, butterflies, vines and landscapes of a rococo style. There exist a few signed decanters, marked 'Beilby inv. pinx.', although these are extremely rare.

Irish competition

The Excise Act in 1745 forbade glass imports from Ireland (allowing English glass to dominate the market), but in 1780 free trade was again granted between the two countries. Simultaneously excise duty was increased in England; the Irish glass factories consequently dominated the market until excise duty was increased in 1825.

The most famous Irish glass factories during this time (1780-1825) were, inter alia, Belfast, Cork, Waterford (an offshoot of the Stourbridge industry) and Dublin. The popularity of Irish glass in England developed a style of deep and heavy cutting of a very fine quality.

Decanters with moulded bases sometimes incorporated the mark of origin. Examples are: Penrose Waterford, Cork Glass Co, Waterloo Co Cork, B. Edwards Belfast, Francis Collins Dublin, C. M. Co (Charles Mulvany Dublin), Armstrong Ormond Quay and J. D. Ayckbown Dublin. These impressions were made by blowing the glass into a mould, which incised about 2 ins of vertical fluting on the side of the decanter and also the mark of origin on the base. The decanter had to be reheated to do the finishing touches, which usually resulted in the inscription becoming blurred and at times indecipherable. Modern copies exist; so beware of a very clear inscription. By 1850 the glass industry in Ireland had been almost destroyed due to heavy excise duty.

Coloured wares

The fact that opaque white glass was not included in the Excise Act until 1777 encouraged its production. Since it looked similar to porcelain it became very popular, and was often painted by the same artists who decorated porcelain. During the same period a lot of coloured glass was being made around the port of Bristol, one of the most popular colours was 'Bristol blue' obtained by the addition of zaffre

Above

Three decanters from the first half of the 19th century. On the left, a decanter and stopper with flat, line and diamond cutting, about 1820. In the centre, a Gothic design with a 'spire' stopper and flat cut, about 1840. On the right, a flat and line cut decanter with R. B. Cooper's Patent stopper: a design registered in November 1831.

A. HENNING

Right

Before being cut, this decanter would have been twice the thickness. The brilliant decoration consists of step cut shoulders and base with central pattern of strawberry diamond and small diamond cut leaves. Its slightly waisted shape suggests that this decanter may have originally had a stand. About 1820.
H 23 cm (9 in)
WARD LLOYD

Left

One of a pair of onion-shaped decanters, a favourite with the Victorians. It is decorated with heavy cut prisms; facet cut ball shaped stopper. About 1850.
H 28 cm (11 in)
W. G. T. BURNE
(ANTIQUE GLASS) LTD

(an impure oxide of cobalt). Amethyst, amber and green glass were also produced. 'The Non-Such Flint Glass Manufactory' which was started in 1805 by Lazarus and Isaac Jacobs, became well-known for gilt decoration on coloured glass. Another producer of fine gilding was James Giles, who also painted for the Chelsea porcelain factory.

Many decorative flasks and bottles were made in the 1830s near Bristol. Known as Nailsea ware, these were cheaper as they were made from bottle glass, which carried a lower excise duty. They are very distinctive, the majority being decorated either with latticinio (ribbon effect) on a clear ground or the splashing and flecking of bright colours on a dark green ground.

Cleaning

An old household method to clean wine stains from a decanter was to swill shot around it, which only results in scratching the glass. One of the best methods is to wash the decanter with warm soapy water and leave vinegar to stand in it overnight. Next day twist a piece of tissue paper around a thin curved rod and gently swivel it around the inside to wipe off the stains. Leave another piece of tissue paper in the decanter to soak up any excess moisture. A decanter should be left to dry without its stopper in, otherwise moisture will form. If a decanter is very cloudy it will have to be cleaned professionally. N.M.

Above

Rare Apsley Pellatt spirit decanter. It is decorated with alternate pillar and fine diamond cutting and has its original stopper. About 1820-30. Apsley Pellatt was famous for his invention of paste cameos and sulphides in glass. H 18.5 cm (7½ in)
DELOMOSNE & SON LTD

Below

Three bottle tantalus made in oak. Tantali could be locked to prevent the servants from helping themselves. Late 19th century. H 30.5 cm (12 in)
MAUREEN THOMPSON

Above

An extraordinary decanter with four compartments, possibly used for liqueurs. English, about 1860.
H 23 cm (9 in)
ALAN TILLMAN ANTIQUES

Where to buy

The cost of a decanter very much depends on its quality and rarity. Prices will vary enormously but buyers should be guided by their own taste and pocket. Any chips or star cracks will considerably detract from its value. If in doubt it is always safer to buy from a respectable dealer such as those listed below:
W. G. T. BURNE (Antique Glass) Ltd, 11 Elystan Street, London sw3 (01-584 6074)
CECIL DAVIS LTD at Algernon Asprey Ltd, 27 Bruton Street, London w1 (01-629 2608)
DELOMOSNE & SON LTD, 4 Campden Hill Road, London w8 (01-937 1804)
EILA GRAHAME ANTIQUES, 97a & b Kensington Church Street, London w8 (01-727 4132)
THOMAS GOODE & CO LTD, 19 South Audley Street, London w1 (01-499 2823)
A. HENNING, 48 Walton Street, Walton-on-the-Hill, Tadworth, Surrey (073781 3337)
WARD LLOYD, 11 Halkin Arcade, Motcomb Street, London sw1 (01-235 1010)
GERALD SATTIN LTD, 25 Burlington Arcade, Piccadilly, London w1 (01-493 6557)
SOTHEBY & CO (Auctioneers), 34 & 35 New Bond Street, London w1 (01-493 8080)
MAUREEN THOMPSON, 34 Kensington Church Street, London w8 (01-937 9919)
ALAN TILLMAN ANTIQUES, 9 Halkin Arcade, Motcomb Street, London sw1 (01-235 8235)

Right

Large and bulbous Stourbridge carafe decorated with leaves, having a facet cut neck. It was made without a stopper in about 1890.
H 27.5 cm (10¾ in)
ALAN TILLMAN ANTIQUES

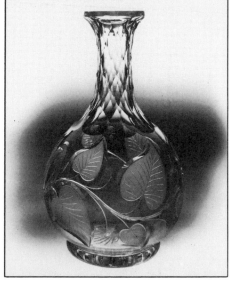

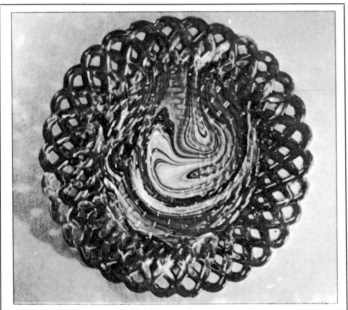
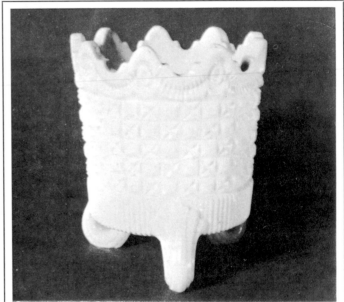

146

Slagware

Top left

Small light blue vase probably for posies, made by J. G. Sowerby, Ellison Glassworks, Gateshead, 1878. H 7.5 cm (3 in).

Marks. This piece has the Sowerby trade mark. This is a Peacock's head. Below this is the Registry Mark detailed below. This mark shows that the piece was first registered on 14 May 1878. It also shows the Class to be III i.e. Glassware.

Top right

This shows in close up the marks on the base of the posy vase shown top left.

Centre left

Pierced plate in marbled, blue and white slag glass. This piece may also be found in plain light blue. Made by J. G. Sowerby, Ellison Glassworks, Gateshead, about 1880. D 22.25 cm (8¾ in)

Marks. This piece only bears the Sowerby trade mark and has no Registry Mark.

Centre right

Small white spill-holder made by J. G. Sowerby, Ellison Glassworks, Gateshead, 1876. H 9.5 cm (3¼ in)

Marks. The Registry Mark on this piece is unusual in that it is found on the inside of the piece. It shows that the piece was first registered on 27 March 1876. It is a Class III piece, i.e. Glassware.

Bottom left

Blue and white marbled slag glass cream jug. This piece may also be found in plain, opaque light blue. Made by G. Davidson, Gateshead, 1880. H 11.5 cm (4½ in).

Marks. This is an unmarked piece.

Bottom right

Purple, blue and white marbled slag glass candle-stick. The base is surrounded by three dolphins. Made by J. G. Sowerby, Ellison Glassworks, Gateshead, about 1880. H 21 cm (8¼ in).

Marks. This piece is not marked.

Slag glass is a product of the early trend towards mass-produced imitations of high quality techniques such as hand-cutting. As such all slag ware is pressed – a mass-production technique introduced into this country from the United States by Apsley Pellatt in 1831 (see ANTIQUE COLLECTOR, June 1976).

There are almost as many names for slag as there are variations in its coloration but the name marble, or agate, glass is perhaps the most descriptive of its unique mottled appearance. As for colour this is normally either blue or mauve, and white, although many examples may be found in purple and white. Of the many explanations of the term slag only the most obvious one is correct, i.e. that the glass was made by adding slag from local steel works to the molten glass. It was because of this dependence on a local steel works that most slagware comes from the Midlands and, more especially, the Industrial North East, where Gateshead seems to have been the centre for the industry. Of the many small firms engaged in the manufacture of slagware between the years of 1840 and 1900 the Tyneside glasshouses of J. G. Sowerby and George Davidson were the most prolific.

Registration Marks

Slagware has three definite advantages for the collector: its ready availability (but it will, no doubt, increase in rarity), its relatively low price, and the fact that many pieces bear a full set of registration marks. Many designs were patented and consequently these bear registration marks which can be very useful in identifying and dating the piece. Until 1883 these marks took the form of a diamond containing day, month and year of the designs registration. This mark was surmounted by the Class number III (glassware) and the manufacturer's trade mark is often found above this. The two most common trade marks found are those of Sowerby and Davidson; that of the former being a Peacock's head while that of the latter is a Demi-Lion rampant over a crown. After 1884 the marks took the form of a patent number stamped on the base of the piece. Although a full set of marks tends to increase the value of a piece they are rather reassuring for they provide proof positive of the origin. For those wishing to consult the patent records these are now held by the Victoria and Albert Museum, London SW7.

The fascination of slagware lies not only in its myriad designs, from illustrations of 'Jack and Jill' to imitation cutting, but also in the wide range of colours available. Not only is there marble slag but also plain coloured slag in blues, whites and creams. No collection would be complete without some examples of the latter and indeed many items may be found in both marbled and plain slag. The uses of this material are also quite extensive covering almost every utility item used in the Victorian household from cream jug to candlestick.

Marks Book

Full details of Registration Marks are to be found in *19th Century British Glass* by Hugh Wakefield published in 1961 by Faber and Faber.

How and Where to Buy

In view of the widespread popularity of slagware examples are to be found throughout the country and because of its relatively low value (even first-class pieces are modestly priced) few, if any, dealers specialise in it. Examples can, however, be found in almost every dealer in the country but the collector should be rather selective in his purchases, buying only those pieces which will enhance his own collection.

It may be found advantageous to make an arrangement with your local dealers whereby they inform you when they acquire a particularly interesting piece. Most dealers are only too willing to enter into such a mutually beneficial arrangement with collectors. A third, but often less satisfactory, means of collecting is to advertise for pieces in your local paper. The disadvantage with this method being that owners of slagware often have an inflated idea of its value and one may have to pay appreciably more than the market value of a particularly desirable example.

During its heyday so much slagware was made that it is, at the moment, quite easy to build up a large collection but in time the opportunities will, no doubt, decrease as its popularity with collectors increases. A collection embodying examples of all the colours and types of slagware would indeed be extensive and truly admirable. R.A.

Roman Glass

Glass is one of man's most versatile creations – stable and durable, it is obtained by the fusion of silica (sand/quartz) with an alkali (soda) and calcium carbonate (lime), it can be coloured by the addition of metallic oxides, engraved, painted, enamelled, gilded, ground, cut and shaped. It can transmit and reflect light and radiate a sparkling brilliance. The effects are infinite and the result is a blend of both the practical and the aesthetic.

The manufacture of glass is an art based on the utilisation of fire. When and where this art began remains controversial. There is now much evidence that glass originated in Asia Minor and its early manufacture concentrated in Egypt and Mesopotamia. Beads glazed with green glass can be dated as early as 12 000 BC and the manufacture of glass became an important and stable industry in Egypt during the 18th dynasty (1570-1304).

Blow-pipe

It was not until the invention of the blow-pipe, an important discovery, that glass changed from a luxury to a common-place ware. The blow-pipe, probably invented by the Phoenicians during the first century BC, is a hollow iron tube of 4-5 feet in length, with a knob at one end which is dipped into a pot of hot, viscous glass and a mouthpiece for either blowing the glass into a mould to assume shape and decoration or for blowing a free form, controlled by the glass-maker. Earlier methods were both laborious and limited, but the blow-pipe method was simple and glass could be produced at a far quicker rate. This opened up a wealth of new shapes that were useful and inexpensive. In 14 AD a glass-makers guild was established in Rome and the specialist artisan was fully recognised, although it was not until the third century AD that mass production of glass wares had been achieved.

Impure beginnings

During the first four centuries of the Christian era, the manufacture and use of glass became widespread and flourished throughout the Roman Empire – in Egypt, Syria, Greece, Italy and the western provinces of Gaul and Brittany. During the first and second centuries AD, the quality of domestic wares was poor and the natural colour of glass was green or brownish colour due to the presence of impurities. It was not until the second and third centuries AD that the natural and paler greenish-blue colour came into being, with a greater variation in the form and design of glass wares. Translucent and brilliantly coloured glass vessels were highly admired and desirable, and the creation of deep blues, emerald greens, violets and golden browns took considerable skill, and were expensive. Usually free of decoration, such artistic wares became the object of the collector's eye. White, transparent and crystal glass could also be manufactured and precious stones of every sort could be imitated, especially for use in jewellery.

Collecting today

The collector of Roman glass today is limited because artistic glass wares that are brilliantly coloured or decorated by painting, engraving or applied glass trailing are now rare and expensive. The natural greenish-blue coloured domestic wares – the jugs, flasks, cups, plates, beakers and so on are far more common, although it should be noted that at present, the market is fairly small. It is expected that prices may increase.

Forgeries

Roman glass forgeries, recently made in Venice, Czechoslovakia and the Near East can creep into the showroom and be sold as authentic. Iridescence, the rainbow coloured flaky surface that develops on glass wares due to exposure to damp earth or humid air over long periods, is highly prized and can be faked, by glueing authentic pieces of iridescent flakes onto the glass surface or by burial of the glass ware, often in a cesspool. Glass wares can also be coated with a silver pigment and covered with particles of sand and earth; then this surface is stippled with various colours to imitate rainbow iridescence. This type of fake iridescence is easily recognised, although wares that are buried to create artificial iridescence are more difficult to detect – in general, this iridescence forms evenly over the surface, fastens firmly and is impossible to rub or wash off.

The determination of authenticity, origin and dating of Roman glass wares is *(continued on p 151)*

Left

Left: *Pale green mould blown bottle with silvery iridescence. Excavated in Lebanon. 1-3 century AD.* H 15 cm (6 in).

Right: *Pale green beaker with iridescence, decorated with 3 bands of wheelcutting. The base is heavy and is marked by an umphallus, a small protrusion that emerges on the inside, perhaps to give added weight. 4 century AD.* H 11 cm (4 in). DAVIES

Right

Rare and unusual beaker with slight iridescence and applied dots of dark blue glass arranged in groups of three. Near East, late 4 century AD. H 17 cm (7 in). MANSOUR

Left

Left: *3-handled greenish-blue beaker with dark turquoise trailing and slight iridescence. Egypt, 3 century AD.*
Far left: *copy of the above made in the early 20th century at Hebron, Jerusalem. This forgery can be detected by the clear and shiny metal and the garishly coloured turquoise trailing that is sloppily applied.* Courtesy of the ASHMOLEAN MUSEUM

Below and detail of base right

Greenish-blue mould blown square jug with wide, multi-ribbed flat handle. 1-2 century AD. Detail shows the raised pattern of circles and quadrants, possibly the maker's mark. H 23 cm (9 in). FAUSTUS

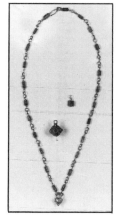

Left

Gold and green glass bead necklace. Glass was used in the imitation of precious stones, in this instance the natural crystal form of emerald (link shown at centre). Gold pendant with 2 garnets, pearl and green glass. Ancient gold is pure, about 22-24 carat, and has a tendency to soften. Necklace: 2-3 century AD. L 33 cm (13 in).
Pendant: Early Roman (about 1 century BC). L 1.5 cm (0.5 in). OGDEN AND SONS

Below

Extremely rare mould blown 4-sided jug, decorated with Christian symbols on sides – star, tree of life (shown) and the Byzantine cross. Golden-green colour with iridescence. 3-4 century. H 12 cm (5 in). SHEPPARD AND COOPER

Below

Pale green bottle with decorative winding snake trails and slight iridescence. Very rare. Syria, 2-3 century AD. H 7.1 cm (3 in). MANSOUR

149

150

Top left

Right: *aubergine coloured jug with acutely arched handle. 2 century AD.*
H 10.7 cm (4 in).
Left: *mould blown aubergine coloured jar with slight iridescence. The brown patches are surface deposits, a result of burial in an alkaline soil. 2-4 century AD.*
H 11.5 cm (4.5 in).
FAUSTUS

Top right

Multi-coloured Roman glass beads, some with iridescence. About 2 century AD.
Average diameter 1.5 (0.6 in).
OGDEN AND SONS

Centre left

2-handled beaker with dark green handles and applied trailing. 1-2 century AD. H 10 cm (4 in).
OBJECTS

Centre right

Right to left:
Mould blown aubergine coloured bottle with iridescence. Blown into a 3-piece mould. Damaged rim. Sidon, 1-2 century AD.
H 6.5 cm (2.5 in).
White, opaque coloured bottle, blown into a 3-piece mould. This mould is well-known and appears on many small bottles in a variety of colours. Sidon, 1-2 century AD.
H 8 cm (3 in).
Pinhead of Neptune. Sidon (?), 1-2 century AD.
Diameter 1.5 cm (0.6 in).
Glass counter, Phoenician, 1 century BC.
Diameter 0.5 cm (0.2 in).
Mould brown bottle with palm tree decoration and iridescence. 1-2 century AD.
H 7 cm (3 in).
Gold earrings with green glass. 1-4 century AD.
H 1 cm (0.4 in).
Theatre token with inscription. 4 century AD.
Diameter 1.5 cm (0.6 in).
Scent bottle, mould brown in 3 pieces. Decorative scenes include a couple making love and a bacchanalian revel E. Mediterranean, probably Sidon, 1-2 century AD.
H 9.5 cm (3.25 in). By courtesy.
SHEPPARD AND COOPER

Bottom left

Right to left:
Hand-painted fragment similar to those found at Pompeii. Probably Italian, 2 century AD.
H 4.5 cm (2 in).
Bottle with decorative glass applied trailing. 2-3 century AD.
H 7.5 cm (3 in).
Blue tear flask. 3 century AD.
H 3 cm (1 in).
Small amulet jug, probably worn around neck or wrist. Possibly Phoenician. 2 century AD.
H 2.5 cm (1 in).
Bottle made from the lost wax process. Rim damaged. Decoration and colour are rare. Found in Israel. 1 century AD.
H 6 cm (2 in).
Amber coloured bowl made from lost wax process, decorated with 2 wheel-cut lines. Made in Alexandria, 1 century BC-1 century AD.
Diameter 15 cm (6 in).
SHEPPARD AND COOPER

Bottom Right

Right: *mould blown head flask with 2 heads. Fine quality moulding and heavy iridescence make this rare. Near East or S Europe, 2 century AD.*
H 11.4 cm (4 in).
Left: *bowl with heavy, brilliant iridescence. Alexandrian, 1 century BC – 1 century AD.*
Diameter 8.5 cm (3 in).
MANSOUR

often problematic. Artistic styles were fairly uniform throughout the Roman Empire; artists and craftsmen migrated from the Eastern Mediterranean to England, Belgium, Gaul and the Rhineland, and spread the techniques of glass blowing and moulding and introduced a variety of shapes and colours to those lands. Glass wares that are excavated from recorded sites can indicate place of origin, but this can be deceptive because wares were commonly exported. Thus, with vast regional distribution and a uniformity in glass shapes, decoration and colours, place of origin can be difficult and requires great expertise.

Dating

Dating is generally determined on stylistic grounds and attributions exist with reference to the century, in absence of specific evidence.

The weight of ages

Authenticity can also be a tricky process. Roman glass wares are deceptively light in weight and the glass itself is generally thin and fragile. Forged pieces tend to be heavy in comparison and the walls of the glass much thicker. The decoration is also useful in identification, and strangely formed blobs, swirling handles and other decorative features can reveal a forgery to the trained eye. Colour can often be well imitated and is not the best means of detection.

Although there are no hard and fast rules, and can be no absolute certainty, it is wise for the collector to buy from the reputable dealers. A purchase is usually guaranteed. The British Museum can also help in the determination of authenticity although it does not give monetary valuations. Scientific methods for testing authenticity require the destruction of the glass ware for analysis of its composition, and are usually restricted to glass fragments.
F.M.

Where To See
Special Exhibitions

Apart from the museums that normally display examples of Roman glass, some London galleries also hold one or more exhibitions each year ... among these are CHARLES EDE and SHEPPARD AND COOPER (see addresses below). Roman glass wares that are exhibited here may also be purchased. Further information may be obtained by contacting the gallery directly.

Museums with permanent collections

ASHMOLEAN MUSEUM, Oxford
BRITISH MUSEUM, Bloomsbury, London WC1
CINZANO COMPANY, 20 Burlington Gate, London SW1
DOVER MUSEUM, Dover
FITZWILLIAM MUSEUM, Cambridge
MUSEUM OF ARCHAEOLOGY AND ETHNOLOGY, Cambridge
PILKINGTON GLASS MUSEUM, St. Helens, Lancashire
ROYAL SCOTTISH MUSEUM, Edinburgh
VICTORIA AND ALBERT MUSEUM, Exhibition Road, London SW7
YORKSHIRE MUSEUM, York

Where to buy

The Roman glass market is based in London and wares can be purchased from the following dealers and at the major auction houses. Prices may fluctuate.
CHARLES EDE, 37 Brook Street, London W1 (01-493 4944)
DAVIES ANTIQUES, Bond Street Antique Centre, Stand 37, New Bond Street, London W1 (01-493 5657)
FAUSTUS GALLERIES, 94 Jermyn Street, London W1 (01-839 3388)
MANSOUR GALLERY, 46 Davies Street, London W1 (01-491 7444)
OBJECTS, 96 Mount Street, London W1 (01-629 2986)
OGDEN AND SONS, 42 Duke Street, London W1 (01-930 3353)
SHEPPARD AND COOPER, 194 Walton Street, London SW3 (01-584 2733)

What to read

The following is a suggested reading list:
Corning Museum of Glass, Corning, New York, *Glass From The Ancient World: The Ray Winfield Smith Collection*, Corning (1957)
D. B. Harden, 'Ancient Glass II: Roman', *Archaeological Journal*, CXXVI (1969)
D. B. Harden, etc., *Masterpieces of Glass*, (British Museum), London (1968)
Charles Ede, *Collecting Antiquities: An Introductory Guide*, (1976)
Axel von Saldern, *Ancient Glass in the Museum of Fine Arts, Boston*, (1968)
George Savage, *Glass*, (1965)
Frank Davis, *Antique Glass and Glass Collecting*, (1973)
Frederic Neuburg, *Ancient Glass*, (1962)
D. A. Strong, *Roman Crafts*, 1976.

BYWAYS OF COLLECTING

Some of the most fascinating paths to follow for the collector of modest means are those that lie beyond the broad areas that have been discussed in earlier chapters. The urge to accumulate objects from the past can sometimes lead to extreme lengths of enjoyable eclecticism, as in the case of Mr Charles Wade, who began collecting in earnest around the beginning of this century; by 1951 he had filled his house, Snowshill Manor, Gloucestershire, to the brim with his vast and varied collections – Japanese lacquer cabinets, bicycles, suits of armour, spinning tools, model ships, toys, 18th century costume, Islamic saddle bags, wall clocks, Flemish tapestries, lace pillows, naval instruments, Chinese shrine cabinets, hobby horses – along with a great many other treasures.

There are not many people like Mr Wade (and those who are like him will certainly not need encouragement) but nearly everyone already has, or can develop, an affinity with, and an eye for, some nostalgic item from the past. The collection may come about in a quite haphazard way – suddenly you realise that this is the third toby jug you've bought. Or it may be that you were brought up in Brighton and have always gathered up items connected with that town. Or it may be that as a passionate gardener, you have grown to admire the antique statues that add so much charm and magnificence to even the shadiest corner of the smallest garden. Perhaps it is the intriguing implements that were used in the kitchens of the past which catch your eye. Or perhaps you feel that we are ourselves living in memorable times and that it is amusing to hold onto a handful or two of the seeds that are sown by our Western consumer society – some may only grow into tares but some will surely mature into good wheat. Often special occasions, such as the 1977 Queen's Silver Jubilee, as well as producing memorabilia of their own, bring renewed interest to connected occasions in the past.

Once you have established your penchant, that field immediately opens out with numerous possibilities. Do you collect only the best, or only the earliest, or only those of a certain colour, or a certain size? The choice, and the fun of collecting, is entirely yours. You can be certain of two things: that you will always gain a sense of achievement from collecting and that *your* collection will undoubtedly be unique.

Here we have brought together merely ten areas of collecting out of the sixty or so that we have enjoyed writing about over recent years. And for every idea that we have taken up, there are at least half a dozen others that are nonetheless ideal collector's fields. Those taken in some detail in the following pages are individually representative of wide areas of collecting.

PRICES
Patchwork quilts
Perfection of design is often imperative when collecting but happily in this field (page 154) it is not always so. Indeed small mistakes in the pattern often make the quilt more desirable. On the other hand, most of the other 'rules' of collecting do apply. So, age, rarity and, to some extent, size are factors which are always taken into account when the dealer is fixing the price. Rarity of textile (silk being more sought after than cotton) is sometimes combined with rarity of design, although the design itself can radically alter a price. The Log Cabin or Baskets designs (page 156) will cost far less than a memorial or 'family history' quilt (page 155). Prices for good designs in the fairly regular size of 130 × 140 cm (50 × 56 in) will be in the region of £120 – £170 ($216 – $306), if the item is in good condition. Outstanding examples may top the £500 ($900) mark. But it is also possible to find small sections or squares of quilting which are sometimes sold separately in the under £20 ($36) range. American quilts are much sought after by Americans interested in early settler items, while the English and Welsh examples (page 156) are more inclined to be sold to people interested in the crafts. As with many other areas of collecting, the prices are often regulated by the customer.

Playing cards
Halfway between numismatics and ephemera, playing cards (page 159) form an area of rapidly growing interest. We are just seeing the beginning of specialist auctions and these, together with more shops, are bound to proliferate. Age, and, to some extent, design are of paramount importance here. Odd cards from the 15th and 16th centuries will fetch several hundreds, while the early full packs can well cost up to £1000 ($1800). It is not until the 19th century that the prices come down. From this time you can find packs for as little as £25 – £30 ($45 – $55). For the impoverished enthusiast or novice collector, modern packs are ideal. You must be continually wary and apply strict rules of standard, then you should be able to start a worthwhile collection for a mere £2 or £3 ($4-$6).

Himalayan bronzes

One of the most notable features of Buddhist temples is often the sheer quantity of statuary packed into the hallowed space. So it is hardly surprising that quality is the all-important guideline once these statues find their way onto the Western art market. Although the most highly prized examples come from Tibet itself, the faith which caused their creation was not hemmed in by political boundaries and examples can be found from a fairly wide geographical area. As you will see, most shown on pages 162-165 are small, not to say diminutive, seldom larger than 25 cms (10 in). The early ones were often finished in gold and so fetch the highest prices, sometimes about £1000 ($1800). But later 17th and 18th century examples are usually in the £600-£800 ($1080-$1440) bracket, while £300 ($540) might be taken as a good starting point for a collection.

Scissors

This is a highly enjoyable area of collecting (page 166) which can suit everyone's pocket as there are many examples for less than £10 ($18). These are often the plainer utilitarian examples from the late 19th century or early 20th century but you may be lucky and find a charming pair of stork scissors in this price range. Scissors in their own box (as on page 167) will inevitably cost more but still under £20 ($18) for the more ordinary types. At the top of the market are the delicate French ones and the early English examples which form part of an *étui* or *châtelaine*. Here you are in the realm of a few specialist collectors so that prices will be high and unstable.

Money boxes

Money boxes (page 168) are part of the rapidly growing interest in the more amusing and light-hearted end of the 19th century. They can still be found for around £10 ($18) but it takes knowledge and expertise to recognise the rarer examples, such as the Punch and Judy, Organ Bank (page 168-9), Nigger Log Cabin or Paddy and the Pig (page 171) examples. These are now sold for around £150 ($270). This is an area where time spent on research first could save you a great deal of money later for it is vital to discover which are the sought-after styles. On the other hand there are plenty of the more usual examples around in most antique markets which sell for less than £10 ($18). These probably include the plain wooden boxes, the advertisement ones from the 1930s, the Pillar Box, straightforward animal models and the 1920s examples which have plain shapes printed with brightly coloured transfers.

Carriage Clocks

The collecting of carriage clocks (page 172) is an excellent example of an area at the top end of the market that has become not only extremely fashionable but also tax-avoiding. So it is no surprise to learn that the highest price ever paid anywhere for a clock of any kind was for a carriage clock. This is not a field of collecting for the amateur enthusiast. It is well documented and prices depend on complexity of the movement as well as the style of the case. At the bottom end, unrestored clocks with simple French movements should cost around £50 ($90), although restoration can often be lengthy and costly. Ordinary French timepieces of the turn of the century have reached the £100 ($180) mark; French clocks with alarm probably £250-£350 ($450-$630); then a jump to the strike repeat examples at around £500 ($900). From here the prices escalate rapidly; French carriage clocks with alarm and grande sonnerie, around £900-£1000 ($1620-$1800) and early English examples, around £5000 ($9000).

Rings

The range of prices of rings (page 177) can, and does, attract collectors both rich and poor. One option could be to collect charming and cheap art deco rings for about £25 ($45) each, while another might be to concentrate solely on the finest quality gems in Renaissance settings for the kind of prices that are hardly worth mentioning. If you chose to collect the gold knot rings of the 19th century, you would probably have to pay about £35 ($63) for each one, with the Arts and Crafts rings costing much about the same for the less rare examples. Much depends on the stones used, for example opals and garnets are about half the price of pearls or emeralds, while diamonds still top the list.

Early photographic postcards

The collecting of early photographic postcards (page 179) is an area for the enthusiast who likes to put his pocket money to good use: a discerning eye will find a happy treasure for a mere 50p (around $1). Your personal taste can be the guidelines to your collection, although there are certainly some kind of photographic postcards which are rarer than others. Those depicting people at work are more in demand than the stylised portraits, while those commemorating a disaster such as the Zeppelin raid (page 181), are more sought-after than those showing groups of people. Some of the prices have been affected by collectors in other areas: thus the early transport examples (as on page 180) easily cost up to £5 ($9) each for the 19th century horse and carriage pictures, or £2-£3 ($5-$6) for the early motor car shots.

Art deco cigarette cases

There's plenty of room for gradual progression in this area (page 182). Why not start your collection in the under £10 ($18) league – 1930s English metal examples – take it up through the £25-£100 ($45-$180) bracket – those with geometric decoration, the plainer French examples and the speed-orientated German types – to reach the £500 ($900) level – Van Cleefs and Arpels or smartest Cubist designs.

Early brass and copper

Collecting *early* items in brass and copper (page 184) can be an expensive business. Top prices for the rarer items, such as the plates, are often around £1000 ($1800), with top quality candlesticks, and sconces costing about £900 ($1620) for those made in England. The middle price range, £200-£900 ($360-$1620) often includes items such as kettles, cream jugs, coffee pots, plate warmers, mugs and other paraphernalia of the 18th century table. Items from the other side of the green baize door are considerably more plentiful and varied and those such as pastry jiggers and other small kitchen articles can be found for as little as £15 ($27).

GEORGINA FULLER

153

Patchwork Quilts

The story of the American patchwork is the story of the early settlers, who, although they brought the technique from Europe, were to develop a craft which assumed tremendous importance in rural parts of America. In homes all over the United States families still treasure these quilts which have been handed down through the generations and it seems appropriate with imminent 4th July festivities to celebrate an American folk tradition which is now being avidly collected on both sides of the Atlantic.

Patchwork quilting was tightly woven into the rural life of the New World. The poorly heated log cabins and cold bleak winters of the East Coast necessitated warm bedcoverings and the thrifty puritan women saved every scrap of old material, from flour bags to home spun woollens, to incorporate into their quilts. Known as 'pieced' quilts, these scraps of material were sewn together in blocks which formed part of an overall geometric design. The Log Cabin pattern (see page 157) is typical of this kind and was made mostly in the Northern States and Canada. Using a variety of different shapes and colours to explore geometrical divisions and arrangement, clever optical illusions were often created and their design theories undoubtedly had an influence on 20th c. artists such as Vasarely, Albers and Stella. If you can't afford to pay the hundreds of thousands of dollars now asked for these canvases, a 'piece quilt' costing a few hundred dollars is a very satisfying substitute. English 'piecework' differs by generally repeating one shape, e.g. hexagon, rather than combining several forms, and is often unquilted.

Throughout the 19th century patchwork quilting flourished as never before, although by the end of the century it had become a more ornamental pastime than a functional necessity. Part of the enthusiasm was the outlet it gave women to create colourful decoration which was lacking in their austere pioneer homes and part was the excuse that quilting gave for women to get together. They were not allowed to socialise without good reason in the early days and the quilting bee (parties given as communal quilting sessions) became tremendously popular. Many pictures still survive of women gathered round the quilting frame. Tradition obliged every young girl to have a dowry of twelve quilts, the thirteenth being the ceremonial Marriage Quilt, identified by the heart motifs in the quilting. Other popular quilts were the Friendship Quilts, made by the community for families moving West, and the rather macabre Memor-

Above

Dutch Pennsylvania coverlet appliquéd with a stylised Hex Signs also known as the Prince's Feather, in red and green. This pattern derived from one of the designs still to be found painted on the Pennsylvania barns which allegedly warded off the evil-eye. This particular example which is not quilted was probably used as a summer coverlet. The quilts from Dutch Pennsylvania can be generally recognised by their bold colours and stylised patterns, tulips being a popular motif. 177.8 × 213 cm (70 × 84 in)
THE JOY OF COLLECTING

Left

Child's quilt of about 1840 called the Mariner's Compass. *This is an earlier derivation of the star pattern. The changing names of the patterns with the migration west is a fascinating study in itself. 109 × 109 cm (43 × 43 in)*
THE JOY OF COLLECTING

ial Quilts, supposedly made from the clothes of the deceased and signed with the dates of their births and deaths.

As the United States grew, many areas of the country developed their own special patterns and names. In New England and the North, the 'pieced' and 'crazy' quilts with their riot of colours were the most popular; Dutch Pennsylvania and the Amish Community favoured bold stylised designs whereas the Southern States perfected highly skilled and elegant appliqued quilts in fine cottons, linens and occasionally silks. The migration West perhaps produced the most interesting patterns of all which frequently changed their names as the pioneers progressed. For example one pattern which started off as Job's Tears became the Slave Chain, then during the annexation of Texas it became Texas Tears, after the Civil War, Kansas Troubles and then finally, and not inappropriately, The Endless Chain. Others drew their names from the experience of everyday life – Indian Hatchet, Prairie Lily, Flying Geese and Wagon Wheel – just being a few. The trials, hardships, hopes and expectations of these adventurous women are sewn into these colourful designs.

Textile designs provide another fascinating study. Beginning with the hand spun, home-dyed woollens and rough and ready fabrics of the North, we then find the imported calicoes, muslins and chintzes from England, Holland and France and finally the gaudy silks and satins of the late 19th century. The same materials are often used in both English and American quilts so although they cannot be used for identification purposes they are a useful means of dating. Colours very much followed the fashion in clothes as many of the materials were dress fabrics. In the 1820s rusty browns were popular, and in the 1840s blues and purples predominated. Two particularly American colours were the indigo blue made before 1880 and the cranberry pink. The Bauhaus had a great influence on textile designs around the 1920s and certain patterns such as the Double Wedding Ring were innovated during the Depression when a great number of quilts were made.

The art of quilting has been re-established during the last few years and is another encouraging sign of the flourishing Crafts Revival. With increasing leisure time and mechanical aids such as the sewing machine, anyone can complete their own quilt with a little guidance. Joy Bergl, of The Joy of Collecting, at 73 Sloane Avenue, London SW3 (01-584 4381) has organised a series of quilting classes held

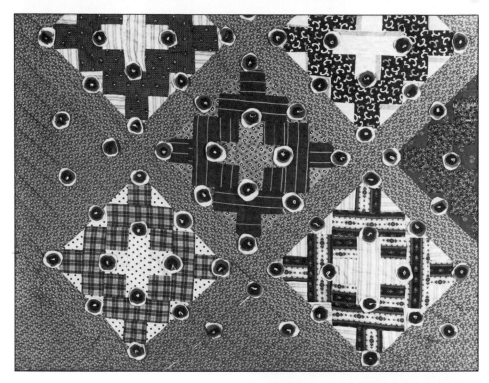

Above
'Tufted' patchwork quilt. These are quite unusual. Tufting was a method of holding the three layers of the coverlet together and pulling through and knotting the yarn or thread at spaced intervals.
198 × 220 cm (78 × 87 in)
PORTMERION ANTIQUES

from time to time which with her expert guidance should set any enthusiastic beginner well on the way. As personal, practical and colourful mementos, patchwork quilts are very much an art of the people and it is as well to remember the reminiscences of one old lady: 'It took me more than twenty years . . . my whole life was in that quilt, it scares me sometimes when I look at it. All my sorrows and all my joys are stitched into those little pieces.'

S.S.

Where to Buy
Although modern quilts are now being sold in some department stores, the shops listed below specialise in the 19th century originals. English quilts of the Victorian period can often be found in small country antique shops.
PETER ADLER, 191 Sussex Gardens, London W2 (01-262 1775)
THE JOY OF COLLECTING, 73 Sloane Avenue, London SW3 (01-584 4381)
MRS. JANE KASMIN, 20 Ifield Road, London SW10 (01-352 0746)
CONRAN SHOP, 77 Fulham Road, London SW3 (01-589 7401)
PORTMERION ANTIQUES, 5 Pont Street, London SW1 (01-235 7601)

Above, detail below
Detail of a Memorial quilt depicting the name of one of the deceased members of the family. These were usually made by one family as a method of recording their family history and were added on to by their descendants. Supposedly the material used was from the clothes of the deceased.
187.9 × 218 cm (74 × 86 in)
THE JOY OF COLLECTING

Left
*American quilt in the
popular Baskets design
carried out in an
unusual yellow ochre
and white.
Distinguished for fine
quilting.
Collection* JANE
KASMIN

Below
*English 'pieced' quilt
with very fine quilting
and interesting
combination of textiles.*
JANE KASMIN

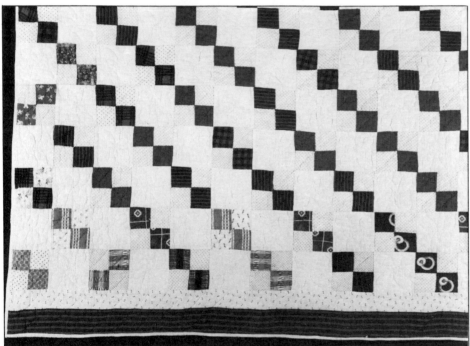

Above
*Welsh quilt of red and white with large central
medallion. It is quite easy to distinguish between
British and American quilts: American quilts tend to
have bound edges whereas the British counterpart
would have turned-in ones. British quilts generally
have a central medallion and repeat the same
geometric shape.* 203 × 218 cm (80 × 86 in)
THE JOY OF COLLECTING

Colour top left
*Piecework and Appliqué Quilt – The Star of Texas
about 1870-80. This quilt combines the 2 different
methods of quilt making – piecework, which is the
joined up pieces of material, together with the appliqué
border of green swags, appliqué being the term used
for material which is laid on. It is interesting to note
the mistake used in the centre of the star medallion
where the green and brown is irregular – this could be
intentional, echoing the belief that only the gods could
create perfection; mistakes occur in most quilts. This
idea originated from the East and always occurs in
Persian carpets but obviously appealed to the Puritan
ethic so strong in the United States during the 19th
century.*
220.9 cm × 223.5 cm (87 × 88 in)
THE JOY OF COLLECTING

Bottom right and detail
*Silk crazy quilt of about 1870 incorporating
embroidery and painting, as well as a variety of
ribbons, which were saved up in order to be inserted.
Earlier examples of silk quilts which were especially
popular in the South rarely survived as the material
rotted so easily. The painted panel is a 'Souvenir of the
World's Industrial & Cotton Centennial Exposition
New Orleans, 1884-1885'.*
129 × 142 cm (51 × 56 in)
THE JOY OF COLLECTING

Bottom left
*Patchwork quilt of the Log Cabin design. This was
one of the most popular patterns used particularly in
North America and Canada at the end of the 19th
century. It uses not only cotton but every kind of wool
and flannel material to give additional warmth. The
technique, however, is one of the most complicated, the
logs being constructed out of rectangular strips of
material built round a small central square. Colour
was used to create optical illusions as can be seen here
by the darker diamond effects.*
190.5 × 172.7 cm (75 × 68 in)
THE JOY OF COLLECTING

Top right
*English quilt which is particularly interesting for the
material stamped with Queen Victoria's Jubilee. The
tiny print designs make a fascinating study and
certain colours such as bright red, mulberry and
indigo are repeatedly used. Until 1752 English textile
printing was done on wood blocks but the drawing on
copper plate patterns enabled finer detail although
only one colour could be used at a time. Mechanical
rollers were introduced about 1815 and can be
distinguished by the repeated irregularities of a
pattern.*
248.9 cm (98 in)
PORTMERION ANTIQUES

Far left
*Dutch Pennsylvanian quilt identifiable by the bold
stylised tulip design in red, white and yellow. The
leaves which were once green have faded from
constant washing.*
180 × 238.7 cm (71 × 94 in)
JANE KASMIN

Playing Cards

The name of Oliver Cromwell has been hated or honoured through the centuries for religious and political reasons: but there is one group of people who would rather have had his head off than Charles' for entirely different reasons. They are playing card collectors, and they cordially dislike the very name of Cromwell because he despised playing cards and had them destroyed wherever he found them.

The Royalists liked their cards and were quick to use them for political propaganda. One political tract issued during the Civil War has for its title page:

> The bloody Game at Cards
> As it was played betwixt the
> KING
> of HEARTS
> and the rest of His Suite, against the residue of the packe of cards
> WHEREIN
> is discovered where faire play was plaid and where was fowle.
> Shuffled at London, Cut at Westminster, Dealt at Yorke, and Plaid in the open-field, by the City-clubs, the country Spade-men, Rich-Diamond men and Loyall Hearted Men.

The Church and Cromwell, between them, account for the great rarity of early cards. Nevertheless cards became the most popular pastime and to-day provide an insight into political and social history. Many great artists and designers have used playing cards to express their art and the game of cards remains as popular as ever.

The new collector quickly finds that playing cards have a much richer and more diversified appeal than the modern 52 card pack used universally for whist and poker. Such cards have changed little over the centuries as serious card players require standardisation to avoid distraction. But this does not prevent imaginative artists breaking with tradition and has resulted in some beautiful cards being produced, sometimes in very limited editions, which are well worth the attention of the collector.

Hearts, clubs, diamonds and spades are not the only suits, nor are the 'pip' cards necessarily plain except for the suit marks. In Italy and Spain the suit-signs are curved or short swords, clubs or batons, cups or chalices, coins or rosettes. In Germany it is hearts, bells, leaves and acorns.

East and West

Just when it all started is not known. Probably it was in China where there is evidence in the 11th century that card games were played in the middle of the T'ang dynasty and that a certain Yang Tan-ien greatly esteemed the playing of cards. However, it is likely that, as with coins, cards were developed independently in the Western world.

The evidence of cards appearing in Europe is based on negatives. Petrarch describes all the games of his time in his tract, *De remediis utriusque fortunae*, but does not mention playing cards, and as Boccaccio's famous *Decameron* fails to mention them either it is a fair assumption that they did not exist at that time.

Then, on 23 May 1376 evidence comes of a game called 'naibbe'. But even this first mention of cards is already forbidding the game! It was a decree of the city of Florence referring to the recently introduced game into that city.

Lucky is the collector who can obtain a card from the 14th or for that matter the 15th century. Most are in museums. Some are exquisitely reproduced in modern times for collectors. They can be expensive as they are usually high quality reproductions. As they represent unique packs of cards they are welcomed by collectors.

Church and Nobility

The Church did its best to crush the game altogether and as early as 1519 woodcuts exist (by Hans Schaufelein) showing the burning of cards. But early playing cards were produced almost exclusively for royalty and wealthy families who could afford to ignore the Church when it suited them. The general populace, before the introduction of wood-block printing, probably seldom saw a pack of cards. Most were hand-painted for the rich. Cards were truly a Royal game and it is no coincidence that the key figures are kings and queens.

With the introduction of wood-block printing cards swept through Europe enabling the servile populations to have some pleasant respite from their arduous lives. Some abused the game and played at all hours to the detriment of their work which was probably a major reason for the Church stepping in so strongly against the game.

Tarot

As time went on all sorts of games were introduced requiring different types of packs. The most famous of these is perhaps the Tarot pack (normally 78 cards, but variations of the game can have 54, 62, and 97). Tarots are well known to-day for their use in fortune telling. But it was once a game requiring four suits comprising, four, six or ten pip cards, court cards and 22 trump cards. They are likely to have originated in Northern Italy. The few hand-painted 15th century tarots that have survived seem to all come from Northern Italy – belonging to famous Italian families like Este, Sforza and Visconti.

Some Japanese games like the Flower game and Poems games, are played with up to 400 cards. Very large packs also come from India where circular cards are used. Korean, Persian and Arab games add to the confusion for a new collector who, however, quickly learns that a pack of cards does not necessarily have 52 cards in it!

Perhaps in an attempt to appease the Church, early cards were often educational. The plain pip cards of modern packs were often, in bygone times, decorated with educational pictures. Later these became political. Charles II is reputed to have had packs made in Europe during his exile which were against the Establishment in England. It was England where propaganda packs developed and we see *The Popish Plot, The Rump Parliament, The South Sea Bubble, All the Bubbles* and so on. Every card is pictorial. Some of these are so rare that collectors will happily settle for an odd card from a pack. Political cards have continued through the ages to modern times and at the close of last year a new political pack lampooning Giscard of France was confiscated before many collectors had a chance to get a pack. In the 1930s Russia produced a famous anti-religious pack which shows on the joker a top hatted business tycoon as God pulling strings on puppets down below.

Modern political packs which are going up in value among collectors include those connected with Nixon and Kennedy.

Rare suits

Cardmakers have tried during the history of cards, to introduce new suit marks. In England, Rowley made a famous pack using cups, pikes, facetted diamonds and trefoils, in about 1785. They did not catch on despite a wealth of publicity at the time.

Then there is the vast series of transformation cards. Again these are mainly pictorial, some were printed on cards and others were hand-drawn on normal cards. The idea was to draw pictures incorporating the suit signs into the picture, often with great humour and sometimes with great skill. Quite a few famous personalities like Thackeray are known to have engaged themselves in this pursuit.

Cards were often used as invitation cards, and in times of shortage, as money. Many cards tie up with history. A good example of this is the French Revolution where the Kings suddenly appear without their crowns – often being identical cards as before but with the crown crudely cut away on the woodblock. In some Republican packs (notably by Gayant of Paris) the kings are replaced by La Fontaine, Molière, Voltaire and Rousseau. The commune of Thiers forbade citizens to buy the old cards with the names of Kings, Dames and Valets.

There are many quite beautiful packs of the 19th century particularly the 'Costume' packs of Switzerland which show different costumes of the cantons. Some packs show reigning monarchs at the time and special packs have been made for Royal Houses using their families on the court cards.

Subjects like heraldry and astronomy feature on many early cards; even pornography has its place. Although there are to be found some very crude modern cards which lack any merit at all, there are transparent cards of the 1850s which command high prices among collectors of playing cards. Military packs are very popular and many were produced as propaganda during World War I and II.

From around 1900 another series of cards, sold as souvenir packs, was introduced showing photographic scenes. Those packs which show the Gold Rush, the early railways of Canada and USA are becoming increasingly sought after.

Dates

The new collector will find no shortage of variety in the hobby and an ample opportunity to study social and political history through cards. His main problem, which remains that of the expert, is attributing derivation to a pack, and dating it.

Many Spanish packs are actually dated but for most other packs the collector has to rely on the tax stamp. The cards themselves give some clues. Single courts, as against the present day double-ended courts, indicate an early card; square corners instead of curved also make them early though there are exceptions. The

method of printing is often an important clue.

The multitude of tax stamps are a study in themselves. Because of the variation of taxes one can often narrow the date down to within a year or two. The maker's name which appears on many packs also helps to date them.

What to buy

It is true that early cards are very hard to find and the new collector must expect to pay highly for them when they do turn up. Even so, rare early cards may be considered much less expensive than items of equivalent rarity in many other hobbies. Cards of the 19th century provide a better picking ground and when one considers the number of cards involved in a pack they can be regarded as still a good buy.

There is a lot to be said for paying more attention to playing cards of the last 50 years. Non-standard cards are usually produced in limited editions. The selective collector can do well with modern-day cards. The famous Florentine pack is an example. Beautifully produced in 1955 it could be bought at the prevailing price for a pack of cards. To-day the pack is hard to find and very much in demand.

To-days cards are tomorrows collector's items and the collector can have a lot of fun in a rapidly growing hobby.

The cost of collecting

Odd cards of the 15th and 16th centuries fetch hundreds of pounds. 17th century packs fetch between £250 and £1000 (c US $450 and $1800). Early 18th century cards are just as expensive but towards the era of the French Revolution some packs are only £100 or so (c US $180). 19th century packs are still inexpensive by comparison, and many are only £25 to £30 (c US $45 to $55) a pack despite their rarity. Modern cards which are well worth collecting average £2 or £3 (around $4 to $6) a pack. More collectors are joining the hobby and prices are rising.

Where to keep them

A good filing system is essential. Most collectors classify by countries and many just file away the packs of cards in shoe boxes marked for each country. The Playing Card Society is producing a classification system which it is hoped will be adopted by libraries and museums throughout the world. But most collectors like to display their cards and except for pictorial cards where all can be displayed, usually only the court cards are displayed. Mounted with photo-corners in loose-leaf stamp albums they can be very attractive and can be written up just like a stamp collection. The non-court cards then can be filed safely away to be looked up when required. Some collectors like to mount their choice cards on large display sheets and others use the giant postcard albums (though some care must be exercised here as certain plastic-backed cards tend to re-act to the humidity inside the pockets and transfer the colour to the holder). C.C.

a *Pack commemorating the Civil War 1861-1961. Made in Spain. Now Rare.*
9 × 6.2 cm (3½ × 2½ in)
b *Surrealist playing cards by Salvador Dali.*
9 × 5.8 cm (3½ × 2¼ in)
c *Many 15th century packs are unique but card collectors can get excellent reprints like these cards of Master PW. of the 15th century. Circular 7¼ cm (3¾ in) across, they are sold in well-made boxes complete with book of explanation.*
d *World War II pack published in 1945 in Belgium. Churchill is the King of Spades and Hitler, The Joker.*
8.8 × 5.8 cm (3½ × 2¼ in)
e *'Le Giscarte' by Eddy Munerol. 54 cards and joker depicting the French President. 1976. Confiscated in France.* 8.8 × 6.3 cm (3½ × 2½ in)

WHERE TO BUY

f *Transformation cards produced by Kinney Brothers as cigarette cards about 1890 in USA. Known as Harlequin cards to cartophilists. The pips form part of the picture.* 7 × 3.8 cm (2¾ × 1½ in)
g *The King of clubs from* The Rump Parliament *pack of the 17th century.*
h *Cards reprinted by Heimeran Verlag, Munich, of the Hofamterspiel, one of the earliest card games recorded, 15th century of which only one pack has survived. Sold in box with book.*
13.8 × 9.8 cm (5½ × 3⅞ in)
j *World Politicians. A twin pack containing 104 caricatures of political figures. Produced in Spain in 1973. Likely to be a collectors' item of tomorrow.*
88 × 57 cm (3½ × 2¼ in)

Himalayan Bronzes

Tantric Buddhism was introduced from India into Tibet in the 8th century A.D. It soon developed its own forms of art – painting (*tankas*), metalwork, woodcarving, jewellery – which were often evolved by Nepalese and Chinese craftsmen, whose workmanship the Tibetans considered superior to their own. Indeed, Tibetan art extends far beyond the confines of Tibet proper, being produced in Sikkim and Nepal to the south, and China to the East, even as far as Pekin. So even the term 'Himalayan art' is not broad enough to cover the whole area, but it does underline the fact that much art inspired by Tibetan Buddhism was made outside Tibet.

The small bronzes were generally made by the 'lost wax' method, in which the figure is modelled in wax over a clay core, and then the model is invested in a further casing of clay. The whole is heated; the molten wax escapes through vents and is replaced with molten metal. The mould is plunged into cold water, and the outer casing is broken away to reveal the casting underneath.

The metal employed is generally referred to as a bronze alloy, but in fact it was occasionally almost pure copper. The figures, which were sometimes made up of several cast parts pinned or jointed together, were either silvered, or more usually gilded. In earlier times the gold was applied over a coating of lacquer, which gave a warm effect. More recently gold leaf has been amalgamated with the bronze by means of mercury and heat. Faces were painted turquoise, black or blue (using powdered turquoise) and coral and other semi-precious stones were set in the metal to heighten the decoration.

The figures are usually supported on a hollow base, which has been made separately. This is decorated with a single or double row of lotuses, or occasionally a fringe of schematized mountains, nagas (serpents) or flames, which may help identify the demon or deity. Often the base is hinged and contains a small box for holding the dedicatory mantra (mystic formula) written on a slip of paper.

The iconography of these bronzes is often obscure, but attempts at elucidation make a fascinating study. The majority of Tibetan deities can be represented under various aspects, in which they may bear animal heads, or several heads looking different ways or piled one on top of the other, and with two, four, six or innumerable arms. (A simple but somewhat superficial explanation of the reduplication of features is that it represents the many aspects in which the god may appear.) The deity may also be accompanied by his consort, who represents his spiritual energy, and with whom he is often shown in congress, known as yab-yum ('father-mother').

Every detail of a bronze serves to identify the figure represented. The mudras are symbolic gestures closely associated with the life and teachings of Gautama, for example dhyani (meditation), hands resting in lap with palm upwards; bhumis-

Left
Maitreya (the future Buddha), seated in virasana with hands in dharmacakra (the gesture of preaching), on a double lotus base. 5 in. Bronze, Tibet, about 1600.
SPINK & SON

Left
Standing figure of Kubera (God of Wealth and Defender of the Law) trampling on a demon. 8 in. Bronze, Tibet, 18th century.
SPINK & SON

parśa (calling the Earth to witness), right hand hanging down, fingers outstretched, touching the lotus throne. The asanas are the sitting, standing or mounted positions, including riding a bull or standing on a supine woman. Many figures bear symbols in their hands or on their persons, and these include vajra (the thunderbolt sceptre), patra (the begging bowl), and damaru (a small drum made of two human skulls). The symbols, asanas and mudras tell us most about the figure's identity.

Dating. Unless a piece contains an irrefutable inscribed date, dating always must be considered tentative. It must also be realised that prices may fluctuate considerably.

What to read

There are numerous books on the art of Tibet and Nepal. Perhaps the best introduction, for it is both authoritative and a pleasure to read, is *Tibet: Land of Snows* by the greatest living Tibetan scholar in the West, Giuseppe Tucci (Elek Books, London, 1967). Two books on iconography can be recommended:
The Iconography of Tibetan Lamaism by Antoinette K. Gordon (Charles E. Tuttle, Rutland, 1967)
Iconography of the Hindus, Buddhists and Jains by K. S. Gupte (Taporevala, Bombay, 1972)

J.B.D.

Where to buy

Tibetan and Nepalese bronzes turn up fairly regularly at the London auction sales held by Christie's, 8 King Street, sw1, and Sotheby's, 34-35 New Bond Street, w1, and advance notices appear in the press.
A stock of Tibetan art is regularly held by:
GALLERY 43, 28 Davies St., London w1 (01-499 6486)
SPINK & SON LTD., 5-7 King St., London sw1 (01-930 7888)
It is always advisable to make an appointment before calling.

Left
Seated figure of Kubera holding a mongoose vomiting jewels, his foot resting on an upturned water-pot. 3½ in. Bronze, West Tibet, 14-15th century.
SPINK & SON

Right
The Bodhisattva Avalokiteśvara (the Compassionate One), his right hand in vitarka mudra (the gesture of discussion). 5½ in. Bronze gilt, Nepal, 17th century.
SPINK & SON

Left
An abbot. 6¼ in. Bronze, Tibet, about 1800.
CHRISTIE'S

Left
Sherab Seng-ge, a historical figure, member of the Ge-lugs-pa (Yellow Hat) Order. 7¼ in. Bronze, Tibet, 16th century.
CHRISTIE'S

163

Above left
Dam-can, one of the demon kings subdued by Padmasambhava. 6½ in. Bronze, Sino-Tibetan, 17-18th century.
CHRISTIE'S

Above right
Dhyani Bodhisattva, right hand in vitarka mudra, (the gesture of discussion) standing in tribhanga ('thrice bent': weight on one foot, opposite knee bent, hips and shoulders sloping in opposite directions). 6½ in. Bronze, Sino-Tibetan, 17-18th century.
CHRISTIE'S

Above
Hama, Lord and Judge of Death, with bull's head, stepping on a bull which in turn stands on a man; accompanied by his consort holding a kapala (skull cup). 6¾ in. Bronze, Nepal, 18th century.
GALLERY 43

Right
Padmapani (The Lotus Bearer), a form of Avalokiteśvara, with hands in varada mudra (the gesture of charity or bestowing gifts). 8¼ in. Bronze, Nepal, 15th century.
CHRISTIE'S

Above

*Form of Hayagriva
(Protector of Horses) in
yab-yum (in the embrace
of his female energy, or
śakti). 6¼ in. Bronze,
Nepal, 18th century.*
GALLERY 43

Left

*Seated Mamjuśri (God
of Wisdom), with
khagda (sword) in his
right hand and pustaka
(book of palm leaves
tied with string) in his
left. 4¼ in. Copper gilt,
Nepal, 15th century.*
GALLERY 43

Above

*Vajravarahi, a Dakini or minor goddess, with
karttrka (chopper) in the right hand, third eye in
the forehead, and skull in headdress, dancing on a
human figure. 6¼ in. Copper and silver, Nepal, 18th
century.*
GALLERY 43

Left

*One of the Dharmapala (The Eight Terrible Ones,
Defenders of the Law of Buddhism), in yab-yum
with his consort. 6¾ in. Copper gilt, Nepal, 18th
century.*
GALLERY 43

Scissors

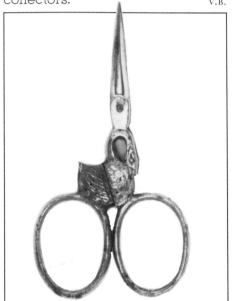

Whilst some claim that old, unusual scissors are harder than ever to find now, others insist that these needlework or manicure tools are badly neglected by collectors.

V.B.

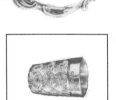

Above left and left
Pair of Victorian silver scissors and companion thimble, H. S., Birmingham 1893.
CHRISTIE'S

Left *Steel shank, with hallmarked silver Birmingham bows, decorated with lattice work design.*
BERMONDSEY MARKET

Right
Some 'industrial' scissors: **a)** *GPO official issue, about 1900.* **b)** *Chinese clipping scissors.*
JOAN SINCLAIR

Above
The rectangular gap in the blade indicates that these are buttonhole scissors, the screw being used to alter the size of the hole required. These are steel, made by Walker & Hall, Sheffield, and the mark shows a flag on a pin, flying the letters W & H. Although, like most found today, these date from the 1920s, buttonhole scissors were being made about 1816, as a pair was illustrated in Joseph Smith's Explanation or Key to the Various Manufactures of Sheffield. *(1816).*
ELIZABETH SCOTT, Richmond Antiquary

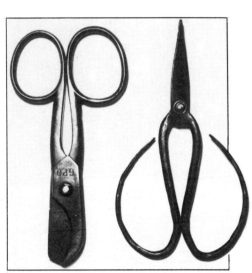

Above
A more unusual form of swan decoration, on a small and very feminine pair of scissors, with rounded blades. Marked with 'SOLID STEEL', they show traces of gilding. Possibly late Victorian.
JEANETTE WHITE, Richmond Antiquary

Where to Buy

Our scissor-hunting met with greatest success at markets like Bermondsey, London E1, on Friday mornings as early as you can manage, and of course the Portobello Road, W11, before about 9.30 am on Saturdays, and doubtless there are similar street-markets throughout the country worth exploring. Also, look at dealers specialising in small silver objects, or needlework tools, and sometimes jewellers.
CELDA ANTIQUES, 11 Queen Street, Bath, Avon (0225 22851)
JEANETTE WHITE, specialist in needlework tools, and ELIZABETH SCOTT at Richmond Antiquary, 28 Hill Rise, Richmond, Surrey (01-948 0583)
JILL LEWIS Collectors Corner, Portobello Road, London W11 (Rudgwick 2357)
JOAN SINCLAIR, South London Antiques Centre, 159 Camberwell Road, London SE5 (01-703 8089)
SHEILA SMITH ANTIQUES, 10A Queen Street, Bath (0225 60568)

Below
Examples of the well-known stork design, which was not made until the middle of the 19th century, but has been continuously produced from then until the present, both in Sheffield and in Solingen, Germany, and now in France and Spain. Notice that these Victorian storks have their tails attached to the scissor bows to make them stronger, while earlier birds are slimmer, with shorter unattached tails, and the feathers better defined. All these are steel, some partly gilt.
JOAN SINCLAIR

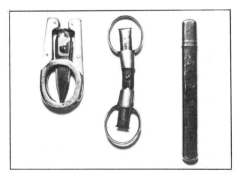

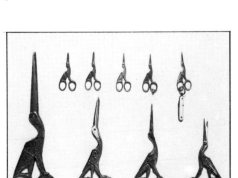

Above
a) *Three pairs of 19th century folding scissors, in brass, steel and mother of pearl. And* **b)**, *opened.*
JOAN SINCLAIR

Above

Early 19th century scissors seem very plain compared to mid and late Victorian styles, but the shapes are often neat and elegant. Here the slim pointed steel is relieved by a tiny 'frill' below the bows. At this time the central rivet was left plain, whereas later styles were nearly always decorated.
JEANETTE WHITE, Richmond Antiquary

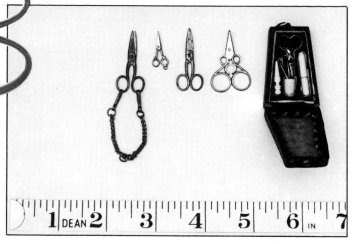

Right

A group of miniature scissors: the étui has ivory fittings, and steel scissors, 4.4 cm long (1¾ in), and the individual scissors are in steel and brass.
JILL LEWIS

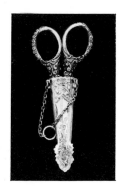

Left

Scissors found like this need checking to ensure that scissors fit case, as here they have been 'made up', scissors from one châtelaine put into a case from another. Both are silver, and look pretty enough together.
STALL 9, PORTOBELLO ROAD

Right

Unusual art deco scissors, with light and dark blue decoration, 8.9 cm long (3½ in)
Early 19th century cut steel scissors.
Both from JILL LEWIS

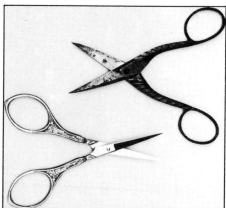

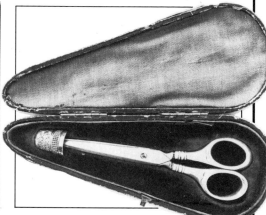

Above

Scissors boxed in this way with matching thimble are always more expensive, and sought after. This is about 1904.
BERMONDSEY MARKET

Right

Centre, early 20th century Spanish steel scissors, 20 cm long (8 in), and some 19th century English steel scissors. Some of the prettiest were made for the Great Exhibition of 1851, and were elaborately filed. They were made in this way until the First World War.
JOAN SINCLAIR

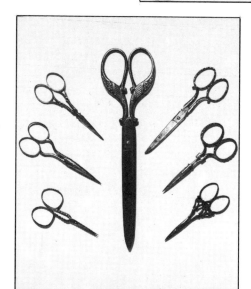

Below

Plain cut steel scissors, early to late 19th century, mostly made in Sheffield, where the scissor trade had been flourishing since the end of the 18th century, when Robert Hinchliffe first made scissors from Huntsman's crucible steel, which had a better texture and polish.
JOAN SINCLAIR

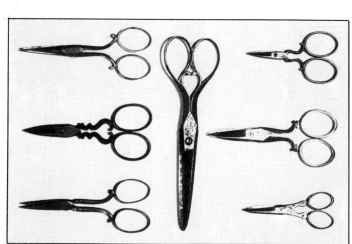

Left

The most fragile and sometimes the prettiest of embroidery scissors are French, with mother of pearl handles, made about 1800 to 1840, probably by craftsmen working around the Palais Royal in Paris. They were usually made as parts of sewing sets.
JILL LEWIS

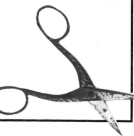

Money Boxes

If it wasn't National Savings Certificates, it was boxes. When I was a child my personal extravagance ran side by side with my ability to cheat the locks and security devices where my weekly pocket money was stored, placed there by anxious parents. Hammers, chisels, hairpins – my battery would have done justice to a cat-burglar. 'I'm sorry, Mummy, but it just fell on to the flagstones . . .'. A Post Office Account put paid to all that. And my mangled and twisted piggy banks would not fetch much on the market today in the condition in which I left them.

Money boxes come in all shapes and sizes and are made in a wide variety of materials. For obvious reasons the most uncommon are those made in frangible porcelain, pottery and glass, but those which survive are not necessarily expensive. There is a wide range of examples made in wood, cast iron, zinc and other base metals, and painted tin. The earliest examples (apart from the spectacular brass-bound and iron chests for really serious money hoarding) are of the 18th century; but these are scarce. The collector is going to find that the 19th and early 20th century are the origins of the preponderance of money boxes. Some of the more elaborate and early boxes are relatively speaking, expensive, but they are eagerly sought by an increasingly large public.

One important warning: as some money boxes are quite highly priced a collector has to take especial care, as good forgeries can be produced inexpensively, easily and on a large scale. Later examples can be 'aged'. There are many and various ways of giving a money box the look of an age greater than it has; some people bake the paints in an oven, others grind the bases, and for all we know, they may bury them as bronzes are fraudulently patinated. A keen eye can be trained to spot the fakes, but this invariably comes of experience.   G.S.

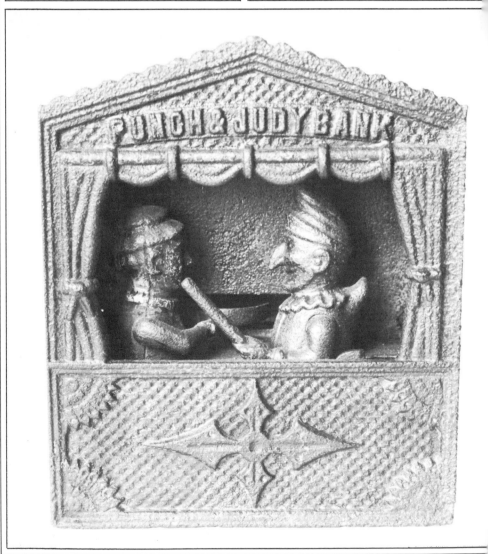

1 *Simple Victorian money box in straight grained walnut and with black lacquer beading. As a money box it is near impregnable; the slot has an angled guard inside, and the base has to be unscrewed.* H 11 cm (4½ in)
RODERICK'S

2 *This was a money box, in marquetry (satinwood and rosewood), of the Victorian period. The slot has been covered over with a brass oval plate, for no apparent reason.* H 23 cm (9 in)
RODERICK'S

3 *West Country, or Sussex, slipware money box in the form of a cottage, the base inscribed* Alice Miller 1905.
H 10 cm (4 in) HANS AND LENA SCHWARZ

4 *Pottery money box in the form of a night-capped head, with treacle glaze. This head is also found used for salt-glazed jugs of up to 1 gallon capacity. About 1840-50.* H 9.5 cm (3¾ in)
HANS AND LENA SCHWARZ

5 *Suburban half-timbered 'semi', very Betjeman, in base metal. The verse is probably not from the pen of the Laureate. 'I place my pence within these walls / For safety lest they roam, / So that when the rentman calls, / They are all found at home.'* H 15 cm (6 in)
BOB AND DAVID FINNEY

6 *Oblong money box of the late 19th century, painted on the top with dog roses and butterflies.* H 18 cm (7 in)
G. COLLINS

7 *Oxo's Coronation Treasure Chest for Edward VIII, with the unissued coinage on the lid. Safely datable to 1936.* H 10 cm (4 in)
THE COLLECTOR ON LAVENDER HILL

8 *The male equivalent of Dinah, illustrated overleaf. His method of consuming coins placed in his hand is by a helpful twist of the ear. These are much copied, the earliest being in cast iron, the later models in a base metal (of which this is an example) and the modern examples of aluminium (they could be bought in Woolworth's in the '50s).*
GERRARD ROBINSON

9 *Early Punch and Judy money bank in cast iron. These are much faked, and caution has to be exercised. Mid-19th century.*
THE COLLECTOR ON LAVENDER HILL

10 *The Coronation Chair in cast iron and with the device of the present Queen and the date 1953. The Stone of Scone serves as the bank.*
THE COLLECTOR ON LAVENDER HILL

Above
The Organ bank, apart from swallowing a coin, will play a rudimentary tune. In cast iron, of the 19th century. Rare.
THE COLLECTOR ON LAVENDER HILL

11 *Brass money box, with the injunction, 'Pass around the hat'. Late 19th century.* H 6 cm (2¼ in)
THE COLLECTOR ON LAVENDER HILL

12 *19th century organ grinder and monkey. By releasing the lever in the foreground the monkey jumps and tips any coin he is given into his master's box. These are not particularly rare, but much collected.* H 20 cm (8 in)
ARTHUR LEWIS, F.O.C. LTD

13 *This cast iron money box is known by the (nowadays) embarrassing title 'Nigger Log Cabin'. It has an unmistakable whiff of the Deep South and Mark Twain about it. 19th century.* THE COLLECTOR ON LAVENDER HILL

14 *Yet another version of the 'Nigger' money bank. In this case his eyes roll realistically as he swallows the coin. His arm movement is operated by a lever in his back.* H 15 cm (6 in)
ANDY GALE

15 *Pillar box for posting pennies, in tin. These were made until very recently. It is stuck with advertising transfers, and is almost certainly an advertising handout.* H 9 cm (3½ in)
THE COLLECTOR ON LAVENDER HILL

16 *This is a 'Piccaninny Poppet' money box, a name that has to run the gauntlet of the Race Relations Board today, so it seems best to call her by her Christian name of Dinah. She is in cast iron, and is of the 19th century. Place the coin in her hand, and she will swallow it.* H 19 cm (7½ in)
THE COLLECTOR ON LAVENDER HILL

Above
Staffordshire pottery money box in the form of a pig, holding a shamrock, with imitation treacle glaze. Continental versions are known. About 1910.
H 9.5 cm (3¾ in)
HANS AND LENA SCHWARZ

11

15

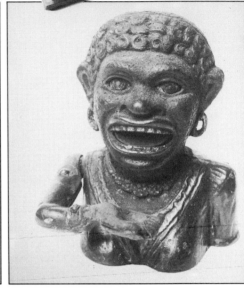

19

13

14

17

18

21

22

17 *This register bank indicates the old currency contained within, and is decorated by jubilant gnomes (not the Zürich variety). The penny illustrated bears the date 1921. These are surprisingly common.*
H 14 cm (5½ in)
THE COLLECTOR ON LAVENDER HILL

18 *West Country (?) slipware money box, beehive shape, with a bird finial. 18th century. The vertical slot is reputedly a sign of an early date.*
H 16 cm (6½ in)
HANS AND LENA SCHWARZ

19 *The Woolworth building in New York in cast iron. Made in the '20s.* H 20 cm (8 in)
THE COLLECTOR ON LAVENDER HILL

20 *This canine money box is made of painted base metal, and nods gratefully when fed through the back of the neck. Would that all parking meters would do the same. Probably late 19th century.*
H 14 cm (5½ in)
NOMAH GLATT

21 *West Country slipware money box, inscribed* John Dobson 1839, *with the slot in the base.*
H 23 cm (9 in)
HANS AND LENA SCHWARZ

22 *Paddy and the Pig, in cast iron. This is a particularly rare and desirable example of a money bank. Balance the coin on the uncomplaining pig's ears; Paddy will swallow the coin and give a very Irish wink in return.*
THE COLLECTOR ON LAVENDER HILL

WHERE TO BUY

The answer is almost anywhere; and the smaller antique shops, the antique markets and even the occasional junk stall can produce good results. There are specialist dealers, some of whom are mentioned in the list here.
THE COLLECTOR ON LAVENDER HILL, Antiquarius, Stall N12, 135 King's Road, London SW3, and
43 Lavender Hill, London SW11 (01-228 5622)
G. COLLINS, Stall 95, Chelsea Antiques Market, 243 and 253 King's Road, London SW3 (01-352 0449)
BOB AND DAVID FINNEY, Outside the Georgian Village, Camden Passage, London N1 (Weds and Sats only)
ANDY GALE, Malmesbury Antiques Market, Malmesbury, Wiltshire (Sats only)
NOMAH GLATT, Grays Antique Market, 28 Davies Street, London W1 (01-629 7034)
ARTHUR LEWIS, F.O.C. LTD, Cheltenham Antiques Market, 54 Suffolk Street, Cheltenham, Gloucestershire
GERRARD ROBINSON, Stands 672-3, Alfie's Antique Market, 13-25 Church Street, London NW8 (01-723 6066)
RODERICK'S, Stand 51, Chelsea Antique Market, 243 and 253 King's Road, London SW3 (01-352 0449)
HANS AND LENA SCHWARZ, 93 Blackheath Road, London SE10 (01-692 1652)

Carriage Clocks

Above

French carriage clock with petite sonnerie and alarm, by Le Roy & Fils, Palais Royal, about 1870. H 15 cm.

Petite sonnerie clocks strike one bell or gong on the hour : at a quarter past, they strike a double note, at half past, two double notes and at a quarter to, three double notes. This highly decorative case with supporting Atlantes is considerably rarer than those with the female equivalent, the Caryatid.

N. Bloom

Since the chronometrical achievements of the early 19th century, it has always been fashionable to own a carriage clock. They were considered an important part of the normal travelling luggage of the upper classes. Their sturdy leather or wooden travelling cases ensured their safety on the bumpy carriage journeys and erratic train rides. Today the rage has been revived but more because they are works of art than because of their practical value. A decade ago good examples were easy to find and not expensive, but this is no longer so. The world record for *any* clock sold at auction was reached in 1976 in Zurich by a carriage clock made by the famous Breguet – over £50 000 ($90 000).

Abraham Louis Breguet (1747-1823), one of France's foremost clockmakers, made his first 'pendule de voyage' about 1810. This had a highly complex mechanism showing not only calendar details but temperature levels too, and was housed in an Empire-style case decorated with pilasters. Top quality carriage clocks with extremely complicated movements were made, either for the Exhibitions or to special order, over the next hundred years.

Parallel with the production of these aristocratic clocks, an industry of semi-mass-produced carriage clocks was promoted by Paul Garnier, another Parisian clockmaker. From the 1830s on, a vast system grew up, making thousands of carriage clocks to be exported all over the world. Contrary to what might be expected, the movements were made either near Dieppe or in the Jura region of the Franche-Comte, near the Swiss border, and it was only finishing and casing that was done in Paris.

In England, carriage clocks, heavier and larger than their French counterparts, were always complex precision instruments, never intended for a large market. The English carriage clockmakers nearly always used a sophisticated and easily recognisable movement designed to ensure accurate time-keeping throughout the week.

As is to be expected, the early cases were mostly simple, well-constructed and practical – a white enamel dial, with clear Roman numerals and plain hands, was a considerable help when telling the time across a large candlelit room. Their descendants developed in keeping with the later Victorian and Edwardian eras, so that dating them is often a matter of knowledge of the current styles, but the continuous production of many of the plainer cases for some 60 years makes accurate dating less relevant. The main bulk of the carriage clock industry died out in the 1930s but there are still a few being made today in the old style, some in good faith and good quality, but there seems to be a growing number of 'French timepieces' fakes around too!

And just one word of warning. From the burglar's point of view, a carriage clock prominently displayed on a mantelpiece or opposite a window, is an open invitation. The plainer models are easy to take away, difficult to identify and very readily sold into greedy and unquestioning hands.

What to read

Carriage Clocks, Their History and Development, by Charles Allix, published by Antique Collectors' Club in 1974 is the only book devoted solely to carriage clocks and is a useful and informative guide to the field.

The cost of collecting

The price of a carriage clock has always depended more on the complexity of its movement than the case style. Twenty years ago, a basic timepiece (one that does not chime) could be bought for around £9 ($16), a striking carriage clock would have cost twice that; a repeat strike slightly more. Prices have since soared and the differentials widened, especially between the mass-produced French timepieces on one hand and the English and French carriage clocks on the other. Prices also vary from shop to shop, generally being cheaper in the specialist shops. Buying at auction is really only a game for the professional but there are certainly some bargains to be found there. The antique markets can also prove to be interesting territory for those who know what they are looking for. The cost of restoring a timepiece might well work out at more than double the purchase price and involve a two-month wait, that is if there is nothing more drastic than basic repairs to be done. It is an unsafe chance for the amateur.

Clocks with their original leather travelling cases are often imagined to be more valuable, but this is not so and a dealer will not be impressed by the usually enthusiastic 'and it's in its original case, too!'
G.F.

Where to buy

Many general clock shops carry a small stock of carriage clocks and you might also find them in jewellery and better antique shops. Below is a list of some of the more likely shops (including those larger stores which have a clock department).
ASPREY & CO. LTD., 165 New Bond Street, London W1 (01-493 6767)
AVON ANTIQUES, 26 Market Street, Bradford-on-Avon, Wilts. (Bradford-on-Avon 2052)
KEITH BANHAM, 16c Grafton Street, London W1 (01-491 2504)
N. BLOOM & SONS LTD., 40 Conduit Street, London W1 (01-629 5060)
BOBINET, Kent House, 87 Regent Street, London W1 (01-493 2404) Appointments only.
CAMERER CUSS, 54 New Oxford Street, London W1 (01-636 8968)
THE CLOCK CLINIC, 85 Lower Richmond Road, London SW15 (01-788 1407)
ANTHONY FORTESCUE, 19 Walton Street, London SW3 (01-584 7586)
GARRARD & CO. LTD., 112 Regent Street, London W1 (01-734 7020)
E. HOLLANDER, 80 Fulham Road, London SW3 (01-589 7239)
HUGGINS & HORSEY LTD., 26 Beauchamp Place, London SW3 (01-584 1685)
MEYRICK NEILSON OF TETBURY LTD., Avon House, Market Place, Tetbury, Glos. (Tetbury 52201)
STRIKE ONE LTD., 1a Camden Walk, London N1 (01-226 9709)

Left
French carriage clock with alarm, about 1920-1925. H 10 cm. The humpback, or milestone, shape of this silver-cased example is a direct descendant of some of the earliest Breguet clocks.
THE CLOCK CLINIC LTD.

Left
French strike carriage clock with alarm, signed by Le Roy & Fils, about 1845. H 13 cm. Gorge cases, such as this one, always house first-rate movements. Notice the wide Waterford crystal panels, indicative of an early date.
MEYRICK NEILSON

Left
English striking carriage clock signed BARWISE, London, No. 376, about 1845. H 22.75 cm. This clock strikes the hours on a gong but does not repeat. The case is exuberantly engraved with scrolling foliage.
ASPREY & CO. LTD.

Far left

French strike repeat carriage clock, about 1880. H 18 cm.
This case is decorated with Corinthian pilasters and the mask round the dial is silvered. Notice the Arabic numerals.
E. HOLLANDER

Left

French timepiece, about 1910. H 14 cm with handle up.
This Obis case was the standard and cheapest design with the simplest mechanism.
THE CLOCK CLINIC LTD.

Left

Miniature French timepiece, silver hallmarked for 1899. H 11.50 cm.
This charming timepiece is housed in a deep blue velvet case lined with blue satin.
THE CLOCK CLINIC LTD.

Right

English carriage clock, signed Jump, London, dated 1885, H 15 cm.
In the manner of early Breguet clocks, this case houses a striking movement which repeats the hour. On the base is a repair mark for The Earl of Altamont: the finest clocks were always made for the grandest patrons.
KEITH BANHAM

Centre right

Miniature French timepiece, signed by Le Roy & Fils, about 1880, H 7.50 cm.
This miniature Gorge case has pietra dura panels of flowers and birds.
MEYRICK NEILSON OF TETBURY LTD.

Far right

French strike repeat carriage clock with alarm, about 1860. H 11.50 cm.
This energetic rococo case and dial with Turkish numerals was part of the huge French export trade to every corner of the world.
STRIKE ONE

Right

French grande sonnerie with alarm by Drocourt, about 1880. H 17.1 cm.
This gilt brass and enamel case with its simulated bamboo pilasters was probably made for the Chinese market.
ASPREY & CO LTD.

Far right

French strike repeat carriage clock with alarm, about 1890. H 24 cm.
Cloisonné enamel on an Anglaise case. This clock was retailed by P. Kierulff, Peking.
GARRARD & CO.

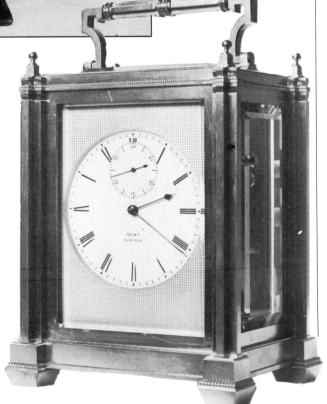

Right

English strike repeat carriage clock, signed Dent, London. H 21 cm.
This superb quality clock, housed in a beautiful Gothic-revival case, was probably made in the chronometer workshop of Dent, (the man who made Big Ben) in the 1850s. It is even fitted with a special balance to compensate for temperature changes. English clocks made by the top precision makers are extremely rare and have always been expensive.
MEYRICK NEILSON OF TETBURY LTD.

Right
Opals, often considered unlucky, were unpopular for a great part of the 19th century, but were favourite stones of Art Nouveau jewellers. The gold coils of this snake are textured to look like scales. Probably early 20th century.

Gypsy ring of high quality gold, and rubies and diamond, about 1880.
SIMEON

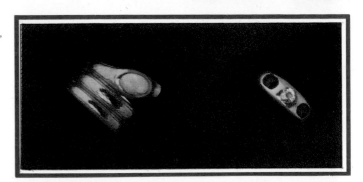

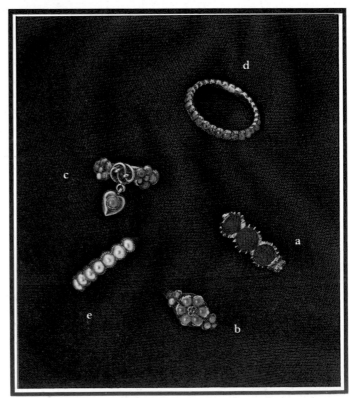

176

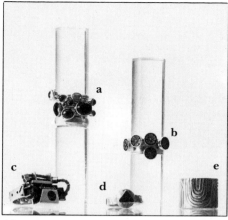

Rings
Emblems of Eternity

An expression of eternity in its very shape, the ring has remained more or less in vogue throughout the fluctuations of jewellery fashions. Although principally tokens of everlasting love, rings were often made for pure personal adornment, and for those who regard them as such and not just as frames for precious stones, this ring-casket has been chosen from the enormous display available today of Georgian and Victorian, Ancient and Art Deco finger-rings.

V.B.

Above
Rings are still an integral part of the original, modern jewellery being made by jeweller-craftsmen today.
a *and* **b** *two compound silver rings, made by Wendy Ramshaw. All the bands are separate, and can be worn alone or in any order.*
a *Set of 11 rings with smokey quartz, amethyst, garnet, moonstone and water opal.*
b *Set of 6 with carved onyx forget-me-nots.*
c *Joel Degen makes rings with radio components to give a stunning effect. Silver, gold and stainless steel screws, and blue wires.*
d *Silver triangle-decorated ring with a lapis lazuli.*
e *Wide patterned silver band.*
Both **d** *and* **e** *made by Breon O'Casey*
All from the BRITISH CRAFTS CENTRE

Colour
Centre Left
Unusual combinations of colours of stones fashionable at different periods during the years 1780-1890; shown in an embossed silver ring box.
Left to right: *Green doublets and garnets; emerald and pearls; opals with rubies, or with sapphires, or diamonds; garnets with old diamonds in an 18th century ring, and with pearls; diamonds and with pearls.*
All from LANKESTER AND STEWART

Left
Coral, turquoise, ivory were considered suitable for day wear: **a** *Georgian carved coral,* **b** *turquoise in flowers, and* **c** *in a lover's knot, the dangling heart with a locket of hair at the back, and* **d** *in an eternity ring, and* **e** *a perfectly set half hoop of pearls. All early 19th century.*
a, d, e, *from* MASSADA ANTIQUES; **b** *and* **c** *from* ARMYTAGE CLARKE

Far left
These pretty trinkets were made in vast numbers from about 1830 to 1890 with stones and settings to suit every taste and hand.
HEMING & CO

Above
Top row: *vows of everlasting love were often entwined in a strong knot of plain gold. The strap and buckle gold band can be found with infinite variations; this is a fine, heavy plain gold and very realistic buckle.*
BRIAN AND LYNN HOLMES

Bottom row: *left to right, knot of bark set with pearls, and four gold mid-Victorian rings set with pearls, turquoises, pearl and diamond, and a young girl's ring of tiny rubies and diamonds.*
JACQUELINE

Below
In the 1850s half-hoops of pearls were popular as engagement rings. Pearls may have been replaced over the years, and uniformity of colour should be checked. Often the most attractive are the original bluish-grey pearls in Georgian or early Victorian rings.
HEMING & CO

Left
18 carat gold knot with diamond centre.
THE PURPLE SHOP

Left
Arts & Crafts jewellery, often made by amateurs, used ancient designs and semi-precious stones, as in this turquoise and silver ring.
THE PURPLE SHOP

Left

Larger rings, stronger shapes and colours may appeal in preference to smaller gem-set bands, but need more careful thought when worn with other rings.
a *1920s ring, black faceted onyx and diamond.*
b *This foil-backed citrine is a deep golden in a heavy engraved shank. About 1820.*
c *Stone cameo, set in classical gold shank.*
d *Old rose-diamonds on discoloured foil in high carat gold. 18th century. Re-shanked.*
e *Foiled citrine and old bluish pearls, dated 1818.*
All from LANKESTER AND STEWART

Left

Art Nouveau rings are not easy to find now. This interpretation of the organic and natural, is a frog amongst lilies, made in silver.
THE PURPLE SHOP

Right

In the 1840s much attention was focused on the hand, and from about 1860-1890 rings were plentiful and inexpensive. Catalogues were full of the kind of rings illustrated here, bright gold set with small rubies, sapphires, amethysts. The 'sacred heart' ring is 15 carat gold decorated with blue enamel and half pearls.
SCALPAY

Above

Guardian spirit to the ancient Greeks and Romans, symbol of eternity and wisdom, the serpent has charmed its way through centuries of jewellery and appealed particularly to early Victorians, not least to Queen Victoria herself, whose betrothal ring was a gold snake set with emeralds. Single or double headed, jewelled faces or eyes, or plain gold coils.
THE PURPLE SHOP

Above

'Keeper' rings, chased gold rings without stones, were worn on the same finger as the wedding ring. They vary in design and width and several can look very effective together. A typical keeper ring is **a**, *while* **b** *and* **c** *are in pink gold, both about 1910. The gypsy ring,* **d**, *is of the 1880s in which the unusual light blue sapphires and diamonds were set into the band.*
SIMEON

Right

MIZPAH, *a word from Genesis, implying 'May the Lord watch over us while we are apart', was seen on much mid and late Victorian jewellery.*
ANNE BLOOM

Left

18 carat gold, Eastern-style betrothal and puzzle ring: a mysterious twist separates the hoops.
ANNE BLOOM

Where to buy

All jewellers sell rings, and prices are seldom as high as you imagine, except perhaps in buying precious stones, when, unless experienced, you are in the hands of the dealer in deciding whether or not the stone is good quality and worth its price. Otherwise, the choice is wide, and taste is the best guide; beware of the many reproductions of Victorian rings, and buy at first from a reputable antique jeweller.

ARMYTAGE CLARKE, 9 Blenheim Street, London W1 (01-493 8828/629 0308)

ANNE BLOOM, 4 Grosvenor Street, London W1 (01-493 0526/748 3324)

RONALD BENJAMIN ANTIQUES, 88-90 Hatton Garden, London EC1 (01-242 9105)

PETER R. BUCKIE, 31 Trinity Street, Cambridge (0223 57910)

CORNER CUPBOARD, 679 Finchley Road, London NW2 (01-435 4870)

HEMING & CO LTD, 28 Conduit Street, London W1 (01-629 4289)

LYNN AND BRIAN HOLMES, Grays Antique Market, 58 Davies Street, London W1 (01-629 7034)

INHERITANCE, 98 High Street, Islington, London N1 (01-226 8305)

JAN JAN ANTIQUES, Grays Antique Market, 58 Davies Street, London W1 (01-629 7034)

JACQUELINE, Grays Antique Market, 58 Davies Street, London W1 (01-629 7034)

LANKESTER AND STEWART, Camden Passage, London N1 (Wednesday and Saturday mornings) (01-731 4060)

MASSADA ANTIQUES, Stand 42, Bond Street Antique Centre, 124 New Bond Street, W1 (01-493 4792)

THE PURPLE SHOP, Antiquarius, 15 Flood Street, London SW3 (01-352 1127)

MADELEINE POPPER, Harris's Arcade, 163 Portobello Road, London W11 (01-727 6788)

SCALPAY LTD, Stand B2 Antiquarius, 8 Flood Street, London SW3 (01-352 8687) and at the Antique Hypermarket, 26 Kensington High Street, London W8 (01-937 9462)

SIMEON, 19 Burlington Arcade, Piccadilly, London W1 (01-493 3353)

Modern Jewellery Some very exciting modern, original rings can be found at:

THE BRITISH CRAFTS CENTRE, 43 Earlham Street, London WC2 (01-836 6993)

ARGENTA, 84 Fulham Road, London SW3 (01-584 3119)

ELECTRUM GALLERY, 21 South Molton Street, London W1 (01-629 6325)

THE CRAFTS SHOP at the Victoria and Albert Museum, South Kensington SW7.

Early Photographic Postcards

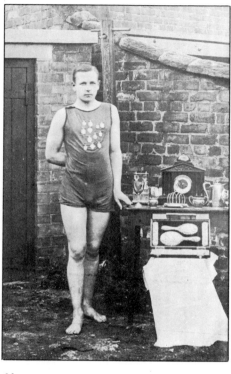

Above

Henry Freeman, Lifeboat Hero, about 1900, *the sole survivor of the 1861 Whitby Lifeboat disaster in which 12 men were drowned when their boat was capsized within only 50 or 60 yards of the pier. . . . 'Very soon Freeman, who had on a cork jacket, was seen working his way to the shore, the people rushed into his help and he was saved'* (The Whitby Gazette, 16 February, 1861).

Centre above

Bakers, about 1905.
Photograph by C. Harrison Price, Croydon. *The reverse inscribed: 'What do you think to this.'*
Photographic postcards of people at work are difficult to find, but frequently the more valuable once discovered. They include such toilers as builders and bakers, seamen and railwaymen, navigators and mill workers, in action, or briefly interrupted for the photograph to be taken.

The world's first picture postcards appeared during the very last years of the 19th century: their success was instantaneous and for the next 30 years at least picture postcards formed a familiar part of the everyday life of ordinary people.

Although the direct ancestors of picture postcards included carte-de-visite and cabinet portrait photographs, produced in their millions in the second half of the 19th century, it seems that the photographers themselves took a year or two to realise that photographic postcards – cards which were real photographs printed in the usual way on to sensitised paper which was then cut to the prescribed postcard measurements – were a natural successor to the then waning carte-de-visite and cabinet portraits; and the first picture postcards, with a picture on a part only of the available surface, were nearly all line or colour prints. Once the potentialities of photography allied to the postcard were appreciated, however, little time was lost. Photography had become much simpler during the close of

Above

Portrait card, about 1908.
The photograph, as in the case of many such cards, is almost certainly by a friend or relation, for it has been taken in the back yard of a fairly modest home.
Portrait cards, not surprisingly, are the least rare. But even here there are some that are of great interest and value – purely as photographs they can possess almost unconscious artistic and surrealistic qualities, men and their animals, prizes and prize animals especially.
An unusual type of portrait card is that in which the actual photograph forms only a small part of the picture, the greater part being taken up with graphic decoration – perhaps a sea or landscape or just flowers with Christmas and New Year greetings. A good series of this mixed medium card was started by Schofield & Co. of Burnley, some of whose photographs, measuring no more than $1\frac{1}{4}$ in. × 1 in., were set into very colourfully-printed and gilt-flower pictures.

Left

Public ox-roast at Cirencester in celebration of the coronation of King George V, 1911.
Patriotism was strong earlier this century and dated photographic postcards of community celebrations can still be found in quite good numbers.

Below

'A Good Scratch', about 1912.
Photograph by King, Bognor.

Below

The Flamboro' Carrier, about 1908.
Photograph by W. R. Readhead, Flainburg.
Good action cards of horse-drawn working vehicles, or hand-propelled delivery carts, etc., are comparatively rare. Condition, as with all cards, is of great importance and very faded examples are best turned down.

Above

Prize rabbit and attendants/owners, about 1905.

Photograph by an unknown studio photographer.
The reverse inscribed: 'Compliments of Lady Cornforth, Winner of 17 Firsts, 12 specials, twice Best in Show. Yours J. C. Nelson.'

Right

A UNIC motor car and chauffeur, about 1910.
Cards involving trams and trains, motor cars and bicycles, offering as they do accurate visual records, are already in demand by collectors who specialise in the subjects concerned.

Photograph by Whitfield, Cosser & Co., Colchester, Salisbury, Ipswich and Bath.

Above
The result of a Zeppelin raid on Bury
St. Edmunds, 30 April, 1915.
*The fascination with disasters and death – not
solely a Victorian characteristic – led to many
postcards of a grim, but nevertheless interesting,
nature. And the demand for disaster cards has
slightly increased their price.*

Below
Mr. Freeman and his Berkshire Bees.
Postmarked for July 1910 (Walsall).
*The reverse inscribed (in part) : 'Thought you
you would like a PC of Mr. Freeman and his
Berkshire Bees, this is awfully good of
him. . . .'*

main attraction in this case, nor is it the names of the photographers themselves – in fact the majority of photographic postcards are anonymous. Above all it is the subject matter that renders these cards so interesting and valuable as social documents.

Essentially the picture postcard is a popular phenomenon and it is the photographs of the popular activities – the pageants, processions, community celebrations, groups, teams, people at work, people in transport, people around transport – that are now among the most interesting, and a well-balanced collection of early photographic postcards can provide a good picture of life in the first quarter of the 20th century.

Most of the photographic cards still existing are unique, for only a very few of each would have been printed in the first place and the chances of more than one copy remaining in satisfactory condition are slender. On the other hand, so many different cards were produced that there are today enough excellent examples to engage companies of collectors for several years yet.

the 19th century with the introduction of the Dry Plate process (in the early 1870s), celluloid film (in the late 1880s), and all the innumerable improved camera and shutter mechanisms, and the taking and making of photographs precisely conforming to the postcard format presented little difficulty.

Many of the earliest examples were topographical, turned out by such well-known firms as Frith & Co. of Reigate, G. W. Wilson of Aberdeen, and the perfectionist Fred Judge of Hastings for sale on a large scale. While some of the names previously associated with cartes-de-visite are also found on the first photographic postcards: Boxell & Co. of Scarborough, Hughes & Mullins of Ryde, and J. White of Littlehampton, along with those two firms who, possessed of numerous branches in England and America, had both claimed at some stage of the 19th century to be 'The Largest Photographers in the World' – Brown, Barnes & Bell, and A. & G. Taylor. But it is not the topographical cards published by the famous firms which are the

The cost of collecting

When first produced photographic postcards, if taken by a studio photographer, cost the customer/subject around 1s. or 1s. 6d. a time. Today, among the stock of postcard dealers (where they are sometimes in a special photographic section, but it is none the less wise to scan all sections) prices are usually least costly for ordinary portrait cards, and progress steadily upwards for good documentary cards, groups, and some transport (most bicycles and horse-drawn vehicles), rising again for unusual documentary and motor cars, and reaching a peak with the more advanced forms of transport, aeroplanes, their successes and disasters.

Where to buy

Among good postcard dealers in the London area are HANS & LENA SCHWARZ (93 Blackheath Road, SE10) and PLEASURES OF PAST TIMES (11 Cecil Court, Charing Cross Road, WC2); and in the King's Road there are stalls in the CHELSEA ANTIQUES MARKET, the BEAUFORT ANTIQUE CENTRE, and ANTIQUARIUS. While outside the capital, a fruitful source of supply can be all the small antiques fairs which are currently appearing up and down the country.

O.M.

Art Deco Cigarette Cases

Art Deco, a jazzy phrase coined after the 1925 Exhibition of Decorative and Industrial Art held in Paris, describes a variety of international and decorative styles of the 1920s and 30s. This was a new epoch that took delight in the exotic and bizarre.

F.M.

Above

These scurrying rabbits, like the prancing horse and the greyhound which commonly appear as decorative motifs, emphasise the 1920s fascination for accelerated motion. Silver case with red leather pouch, probably German.
7.5 × 8 cm (3 × 3 in)
DEMAS

Where to buy

A variety of Art Deco cigarette cases can easily be found, although good lacquer and enamel examples tend to be rare and expensive. Cartier, Boucheron and Van Cleef and Arpels' cases are extremely rare and will be the most costly.

ANTIQUARIUS MARKET, 135 King's Road, Chelsea, London SW3:
    ACUSHLA HICKS, Stand P10 (01-352 8882)
    VICKI, Stand J1 (01-352 7989)
    BARRY ROSE, Stand N5 (01-352 2203)
    URSULA, Stand P16 (01-352 2203)
    COCHRANE, Stand P12 (01-352 2203)
    BELLAMY, Stand N11 (01-352 3334)
BUTLER AND WILSON, 189 Fulham Road, London SW3 (01-351 0375)
JOAN KOMLOSY, Stand 238, Antique Supermarket, Barrett Street, London W1 (02-935 0389)
GRAUS ANTIQUES, 125 New Bond Street, London W1 (01-629 6680)
NONESUCH ANTIQUES, Stand 4, Bond Street Antique Centre, 124 New Bond Street, London

Above

Interesting concave shaped silver cigarette case with incised geometric decoration on front and back. Made in England, 1932.
7 × 8.5 cm (2.75 × 3 in)
URSULA

Below

Gold and black enamel cigarette case with diamond monogram in the centre, made by Cartier in 1934. Precious jewellery of this sort tended to be more conservative and classic in design.
5.5 × 8 cm (2 × 3 in)
VIEYRA AND CO

Right

'La Minaudière' was a new fashion accessory invented and made by Van Cleef and Arpels in 1935. As an efficient evening bag, it had compartments for cigarettes, lighter, lipstick, compact and money purse. Composed of lightweight metal and decorated with gold, rubies and diamonds. Sold exclusively in England by Asprey's.
5 × 12 cm (2 × 5 in)
GRAUS

Opposite

a *Cigarette case of marcasites and amazonite, a semi-precious green but opaque stone, highly favoured in ancient Egypt. The discovery of Tutankhamen's tomb in 1922 led to a revival of Egyptian tastes. Probably English, 1920s.*
6.5 × 9 cm (2.5 × 3.5 in)
NONESUCH ANTIQUES

b *French black enamel cigarette case with silver borders and green enamel and marcasite geometric design at the side. About 1923.*
6 × 8 cm (2 × 3 in)
BUTLER AND WILSON

c *A most unusual cigarette case made of yellow transparent bakelite with a Swiss watch fixed at the centre. Bakelite is a plastic, named after its inventor, L. H. Baekeland in 1913, and was frequently used for jewellery and fashion accessories during the 1920s and 30s.* 7 × 12.5 cm (2.75 × 5 in)
JOAN KOMLOSY

d *Chinese motifs frequently appear on 1920s cigarette cases and compacts. This unusual cigarette case and lighter combined, features a Chinese dragon amidst stylized clouds (also on reverse) of cloisonné enamel in orange, green, black and silver. Made by Dunhill, probably late 1920s.* 6 × 10 cm (2 × 4 in)
ACUSHLA HICKS

e *English silver cigarette case with sunburst design on front and back, dated 1925.* 7 × 8.5 cm (2.75 × 3 in)
URSULA

f *English cigarette case with green coloured shagreen on the exterior. Dated 1932.* 8 × 8.5 cm (3 × 3 in)
COCHRANE

g *This cigarette case, match box and compact of green and black enamel was made for Harrods. Finely incised lines create a surface pattern while the brilliant sheen mimics the sunburst motif.* 6 × 8 cm and 4.5 × 6 cm (1.75 × 3 in) and (2 × 2 in)
BARRY ROSE

h *This English metal cigarette case with yellow, red and white paint reveals some deterioration of the chrome surface, an outcome of the cheap materials used in mass production and everyday usage. An interesting feature is the flip-up top.* 7.5 × 8.5 cm (2.75 × 3 in)
DEMAS

j *French cigarette case with black lacquer exterior. The two rectangular stripes are composed of crushed eggshell, delicately sprinkled onto the adhesive surface and polished. This technique was often used by the French Art Deco designer, Jean Dunand.* 7.5 × 8.5 cm (3 × 3 in)
BELLAMY

k *The streamlined streak design of this German metal cigarette case and compact, spray painted in blue, black and grey, recalls the Art Deco craze for speed.* 5 × 11.5 cm (2 × 4.5 in)
COCHRANE

l *1930s gentleman's cigarette case of metal composition with geometric surface design in grey, yellow and black paint with chrome strips. These cheap materials were used in England and America.* 8 × 17.5 cm (3 × 7 in)
VICKI

m *Art Deco Modernist design, an offshoot of Cubism and Futurism, emphasised a precise handling of geometric forms, as illustrated on the cover of this French cigarette case of red and blue lacquer with crushed eggshell on a black base.*
8 × 10 cm (3 × 4 in)
ACUSHLA HICKS

n *This unusual surface design is composed of layers of orange, blue and black lacquer, a technique that originated in the Orient, applied onto a silver base.* 8 × 12 cm (3 × 5 in)
ACUSHLA HICKS

p *1930s English cigarette metal case with chrome strips and spray painted sections in red and black.* 7.5 × 9 cm (3 × 3.5 in)
VICKI

Early Brass and Copper

It is said that the Industrial Revolution had as its most undesirable feature the tendency to mass produce. Mass production is not of itself undesirable where the finished product is as 'good' as the hand-made equivalent. This point is not often taken, with the result that examples of good design are, like the baby in the bath water, thrown out. But, having made this caveat, the author proposes to concentrate on the period that precedes the age of mass production, where fine examples of brass and copper are to be found. It should be noted at the outset, that copper is a metal principally used for domestic utensils.

Silver is a rich man's metal, and is a common way by which the owner estimates his own importance in the world, and publishes the fact. Charles James Fox, on leaving Eton, immediately caused to be made a set of silver spoons for his own use. The middle classes preferred brass, a metal which combined economy and practicality, and required a developed skill in production. But the design of brass followed (usually some years after) the patterns for silver until patternbooks were printed for brass alone. (This makes brass rather more difficult to date.)

Copper is an element that occurs in nature in such a way as to make its production a simple process. Brass, on the other hand, is the result of a complex procedure, and it is thought unlikely that it was produced in England before the 16th century. It is an amalgamation of copper and zinc, in differing proportions (and therefore can possess different characteristics). Usually brass is constituted of those metals with zinc taking a proportion between 15% and 30%. Further, there are other alloys that are so similar as properly to be treated under the same heading. (For example, paktong and bell-metal.)

History

Before the 16th century brass was imported, but Elizabeth I encouraged an indigenous industry using materials readily available. Zinc was obtained from lapis calaminaris, copper from English mines. The technique of manufacture was complicated and the skill was known only to European brassmakers who were induced to come to England. In 1568 two companies were formed, The Company of the Mines Royall, and the Mineral and Battery Works, best described as a mixture of Royal and noble patronage. The need in those times was for brass for cannon, but in subsequent times of peace the production was switched to more domesticated articles. Unfortunately the Civil War, in its need for ordnance, melted down these smaller products, so the collector can only expect to begin his collection with pieces made after 1660. As usual the unrest on the Continent resulted in Dutch and North German workers (the Allemanes) giving impetus to the recovering produc-

Above
This skirt base coffee pot is a good-looking example, but the base also has the practical aspect of trapping the grounds when pouring. About 1780.
H 23 cm (9 in)
RUPERT GENTLE ANTIQUES

tion and the creation of articles stylistically indistinguishable from those they had been making abroad. The 18th century marks the real development of English style in brassware (as in so many other aspects of the decorative arts) and the technical advances of that period are of lesser importance except in terms of greater facility in manufacture. What is interesting in the 18th century is the increase in the total weight of brass made, and the widening geographical location of the factories. In 1783 Henry Cort used steam power in rolling mills, the indirect result of which was to enable large quantities of brass to be fashioned without the intervention of man – mass production. In the 19th century the sense of design almost totally degenerated, and the appeal of articles made at that time must be looked for elsewhere.

Paktong, bell metal, etc.

Paktong is the best of metals based on brass, and contains a considerable percentage (apparently somewhat variable) of nickel. It was originally imported from China and there seems to be no evidence of any manufacture in England, but the quantities used seem to suggest some source other than the East. Robert Adam used it for magnificent fire grates in his grandest houses, Osterley, Syon, Nostell and Saltram, between 1760-80. These are of extreme rarity, but the collector can still find the alloy in the form of candlesticks, and small articles. Its especial quality is that it does not tarnish. Its use ceased with the arrival of Sheffield plate and German silver.

Bell metal, as the name suggests, is used primarily for bells, and is usually composed of copper and tin. It is common particularly with candlesticks, but is usually cast, being a brittle alloy, like bronze.

Copper

There has been copper production in England since before the Romans. It is very easily worked, and its prime use was for domestic cooking utensils. It is dangerous to heat copper (poisonous salts are given off) unless the inside is coated with tin. Fine pieces of copper were produced for its decorative qualities but it is always advisable to examine the edges closely: the article may be Sheffield plate with the silver worn off.

Many people will have decided that brass and copper are not the subject for them to collect having seen so many late pieces, and will be aware that copper in particular has been much faked. They might well be advised to reconsider in the light of recent studies, most important of which is *English Domestic Brass, 1680-1810* by Rupert Gentle and Rachel Feild, published by Paul Elek. 1975.   G.S.

Above

Copper 4-gallon haystack jug made sometime between 1790 and 1810. These jugs also come in smaller capacities and a set is particularly desirable.
H 50 cm (20 in)
STAIR AND COMPANY

Right

One of a pair of candlesticks, dated 1660 and a variation of the trumpet design. There is lathe-turned decoration on the stem and base, and the foot is pronounced.
H 15 cm (6 in)
RUPERT GENTLE ANTIQUES

Below

Pair of bell metal pricket candlesticks dated about 1680. These would have originally been cast in about 5 pieces and then brazed together. H 31 cm (12 in)
STAIR AND COMPANY

Above

This snuff or tobacco box bears the date 1890, but is thought to have been made about 1840. The stamped engraving is frequently a later addition. This example was probably a workman's.
L 8 cm (3 in)   TROLL

Far left

Late 18th century brass tipstaff with an oak shaft. This would be used by the beadle in execution of the Poor Laws in a parish. This tipstaff bears the date 1794. H 60 cm (24 in)
JELLINEK AND SAMPSON

Above

Fine fire grate in the style of Robert Adam pierced with acanthus and 'S' decoration, and engraved with scrolling flowers and oval and diamond shaped lozenges. There are four classical finials. About 1775.
CROWTHER OF SYON LODGE

Below and detail

It is not usual to find a plate in brass and most unusual to find engraved on it a coat of arms. There are no traces of silvering on this example. First half of the 18th century. D 25 cm (10 in)
JELLINEK AND SAMPSON

Left

Typical copper kettle and jelly mould of about 1800-1820. Both these articles are tinned inside.
J. & J. BAKER

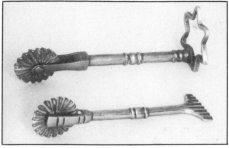

Above

Two brass pastry jiggers and prickers. These are fairly common, presumably because they can still be used. Large numbers are thought to have been made. About 1750-1800.
L 10 cm (4 in)
RUPERT GENTLE ANTIQUES

Above

Copper barber's bowl with tinned rim and bowl of about 1750-70. This was made in either England or Holland.
D 26.5 cm (10⅞ in)
RUPERT GENTLE ANTIQUES

Above

17th century 4-light wall sconce made in Scandinavia; such an early example is rare. The polished reflector is surrounded with repoussé decoration and some engraving. It is very large.
H 76 cm (30 in)
TROLL

Right

This copper jardinière was made about 1800 and is very boldly decorated. It is thought to have been made in England or Scotland.
H 40 cm (16 in)
TROLL

Right

Early tinder pistol or 'strike-a-light' in brass and iron. This example was probably made in Scandinavia. The flint when struck against the iron caused a spark to ignite tinder in the small compartment, in its turn used to ignite a small candle attached.
L 12.5 cm (5 in)
PETER PLACE

Above

Simple brass cream jug of the mid-18th century, with an attractive scrolling handle.
H 10 cm (4 in)
RUPERT GENTLE ANTIQUES

Left

Large copper coffee kettle made about 1770. In Scandinavia it is the custom to keep coffee simmering on the stove all day long, hence the lid on the spout to prevent evaporation. Surprisingly, very good coffee is the result. The inside is tinned. H 36 cm (14 in)
TROLL

Right

One of a pair of Italian brass altar candlesticks with pricket top. First half of the 17th century.
H 74 cm (29 in)
STAIR AND COMPANY

Far right

One of a pair of Italian altar candlesticks of ornate Baroque design of about 1680. They are made of paktong, or a similar metal, and are an early use of this alloy. The metal is beaten to the design and then laid on to the structure of the candlestick. H 87 cm (26½ in)
T. G. BAYNE

Left

Small Queen Anne wall sconce, pierced and engraved. About 1714.
H 16.5 cm (6½ in)
STAIR AND COMPANY

Right

This pocket inkpot and penholder is thought to have been made by John Madin, of Sheffield, and is dated 1656. The decoration is engraved and punched. The inscription reads
'I was in sheffield made and any can Witnes: I was not made by any man'.
L 10 cm (4 in)
TOBIAS JELLINEK

Left

Pair of mid-18th century Rococo candlesticks in brass. They have been cast in several pieces, and afterwards chiselled to heighten the detail.
H 20 cm (8 in)
RUPERT GENTLE ANTIQUES

Below

This domestic brass taper jack dates from the last quarter of the 18th century and bears traces of gilding.
H 14 cm (5½ in)
RUPERT GENTLE ANTIQUES

Left

This is a tally or goffering iron of brass with paktong legs. A hot iron is introduced into the horizonal hollow bar and the frills and flounces of 17th and 18th century England were ironed with a greater delicacy than with a flat iron. This example is late 18th century and has pretty acorn finials.
H 52.5 cm (20¾ in)
RUPERT GENTLE ANTIQUES

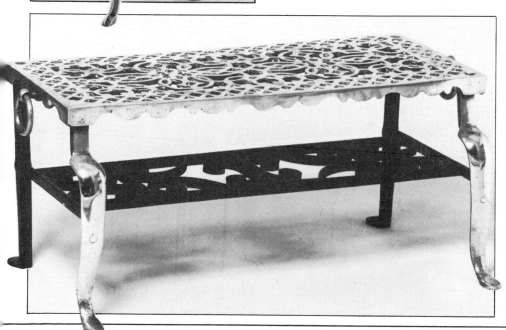

Left

Late 18th century plate warmer in brass and wrought iron. The top in this example is cast brass.
H 30.5 cm (12 in) L 61 cm (24 in) D 28 cm (11 in)
STAIR AND COMPANY

Where to buy

Almost every shop in England will sell copper or brass; few specialise in early or good pieces. As will be seen the good pieces are by no means inexpensive, but they are rare and collected enthusiastically by the cognoscenti. The following list includes the main dealers, who are extremely helpful in explaining the finer points.

J. AND J. BAKER, 12-14 Water Street, Lavenham, Suffolk (078724-610)

T. G. BAYNE, 98 Crawford Street, London W1 (01-723 6466)

CROWTHER OF SYON LODGE, Isleworth, Middlesex (01-560 7978)

ARTHUR DAVIDSON, 78-9 Jermyn Street, London SW1 (01-930 6687)

RUPERT GENTLE ANTIQUES, The Manor House, Milton Lilbourne, Pewsey, Wiltshire (067 26-3344)

TOBIAS JELLINEK, 66c Kensington Church Street, London W8 (01-727 5980)

JELLINEK AND SAMPSON, 156 Brompton Road, London SW3 (01-589 5272)

PETER PLACE, 156 Walton Street, London SW3 (01-589 2568)

STAIR AND COMPANY, 120 Mount Street, London W1 (01-499 1784)

TROLL, 27 Beauchamp Place, London SW3 (01-589 5870)

Right and detail below

One of a pair of remarkable brass lanterns designed for carrying, although for display it is mounted on a modern wrought iron tripod. This type may have been used outdoors or in draughty conditions, perhaps in a church, but the heart and cupids (see detail) suggest that this was not the function of this particular article. 17th century and English. It is glazed.
H 165 cm (66 in)
PETER PLACE

Above and left

The pair of Queen Anne candlesticks are of a pleasing simplicity and have the unusual feature of a maker's mark on the base (see detail). The chocolate pot has a sturdy elegance and shows the turning marks well. The brass lock, with its original key was made towards the end of the 18th century, and the bold engraving is very much of the period.
PETER PLACE

Above

One of a pair of Paktong candlesticks, dated about 1760, bearing characteristics found in pattern books of the period. They are almost indistinguishable from silver. H 28 cm (11 in)
RUPERT GENTLE ANTIQUES

Left

Three early 19th century 2-handled loving cups in copper. These are of exceptional quality and show how copper has been used in a role unconnected with the kitchen. H 20.5 and 16 cm (8⅛ and 6¼ in)
RUPERT GENTLE ANTIQUES

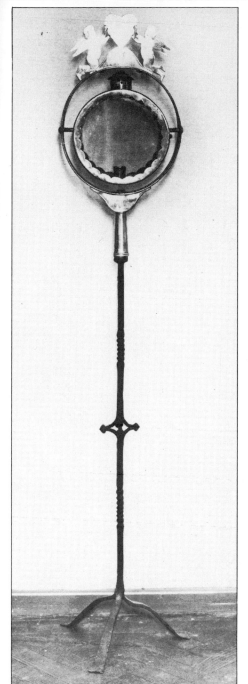

Right
This dog collar with the owner's name inscribed was made in the latter part of the 18th century and very probably for an extremely vicious dog.
PETER PLACE

Below
Six-light chandelier in brass. Behind each candle bracket is a highly polished pair of small reflectors. About 1800.
H 45 cm (18 in)
TROLL

Above
This three-light wall bracket bears the date 1713 and was made in Denmark. The drip pans are very broad and there are attractive obelisk finials between the brackets.
TROLL

Left
Mid-18th century chamberstick with pierced and engraved decoration. The box beneath is probably for tinder.
L 19 cm (7½ in)

STAIR AND
COMPANY

189

Further Reading

Furniture

ASLIN, Elizabeth: *Nineteenth Century English Furniture,* Faber, 1962

COLERIDGE, Anthony: *Chippendale Furniture*, Faber, 1968

EDWARDS, Ralph: *The Shorter Dictionary of English* Furniture, Hamlyn, 1964

FASTNEDGE, Ralph: *Sheraton Furniture*, Faber, 1962

FILBEE, Marjorie: *Dictionary of Country Furniture*, The Connoisseur, 1977

GLOAG, John: *A Short Dictionary of Furniture*, Allen and Unwin, 1969

HAYWARD, Charles H: *English Period Furniture*, Evans, 1977

HAYWARD, Helena (Editor): *World Furniture*, Hamlyn, 1975

JOURDAIN, Margaret: *Regency Furniture*, Country Life, 1949

MACQUOID, Percy and EDWARDS, Ralph: *The Dictionary of English Furniture*, Country Life, 1954

PEVSNER, Nikolaus: *Pioneers of Modern Design*, Penguin, 1960

SPARKES, Ivan: *The English Country Chair*, Spurbooks, 1973

WOLSEY, S. W. and LUFF, R. W. P: *Furniture in England*, Barker, 1968

Pictures

CLARK, Kenneth: *Civilisation*, J. Murray, 1971

GAUNT, William: *Marine Painting, an historical Survey*, Martin Secker and Warburg, 1975.

GERHARD, H. P: *The World of Icons*, J. Murray, 1971

GOMBRICH, E. H: *The Story of Art*, Phaidon Press, 1972

HARDIE, Martin: Watercolour Painting in Britain (3 vols), Batsford, 1974

JOHNSON, J. and GREUTZNER, A: *The Dictionary of British Artists*, Antique Collectors' Club, 1976

LEVEY, Michael: *Concise History of Painting: From Giotto to Cezanne*, Thames and Hudson, 1962

The Illustrated Catalogue of the National Gallery of London, Publications Department, National Gallery, London, 1973

The Illustrated Catalogue of the National Gallery of Washington

VASARI, Giorgio: *Lives of the Artists*, Penguin, 1970

Silver

ASH, D. (Editor): *Dictionary of British Antique Silver*, Pelham Books, 1975

BANISTER, Judith: *English Silver*, Hamlyn, 1969
Late Georgian and Regency Silver, Country Life, 1971
Collecting Antique Silver, Ward Lock, 1972

BENNETT, D: *Irish Georgian Silver*, Cassell, 1973

BRUNNER, H: *Old Table Silver: Handbook for Collectors and Amateurs*, Faber, 1967

EDWARDS, Ralph and RAMSEY, L. G. G.(Editors): *The Connoisseur Period Guides*, The Connoisseur, 1956-8

Grimwade, A: Rococo Silver 1727-1765, Faber, 1974

HAYWARD, J. F: *Huguenot Silver in England 1688-1727*, Faber, 1959

HUGHES, G. Bernard: *Antique Sheffield Plate*, Batsford, 1970

OMAN, C: *English Domestic Silver*, Black, 1968

WILKINSON, Wynyard: *History of Hallmarks*, Queen Anne, 1975

Pottery and Porcelain

BARNARD, J: *Victorian Ceramic Tiles*, Studio Vista, 1972

CHAFFERS, Wm: *Marks and Monograms on European and Oriental Pottery and Porcelain*, 14th Revised Edition, William Reeves, 1946

CHARLESTON, Robert J: *World Ceramics, An Illustrated History*, Hamlyn, 1975

COYSH, A. W: *British Art Pottery, 1870-1940*, David and Charles, 1976

GODDEN, Geoffrey A: *Victorian Porcelain*, Herbert Jenkins, 1961
An Illustrated Encyclopaedia of British Pottery and Porcelain, Herbert Jenkins, 1966

HAGGAR, Reginald G: *The Concise Encyclopaedia of Continental Pottery and Porcelain*, Andre Deutsch, 1960

HONEY, W. B: *English Pottery and Porcelain*, A. &. C. Black, 1933
The Ceramic Art of China and Other Countries of the Far East, Faber, 1945

HUGHES, G. Bernard: *The Country Life Collector's Pocket Book of China*, Revised Edition, Country Life, 1977

SAVAGE, George: *Porcelain Through the Ages*, Pelican, 1954
Pottery Through the Ages, Pelican, 1959

SAVAGE, George and NEWMAN, Harold: *An Illustrated Dictionary of Ceramics*, Thames and Hudson, 1974

SHINN, Charles and Dorrie: *The Illustrated Guide to Parian China*, Barrie and Jenkins, 1971

WAKEFIELD, Hugh: *Victorian Pottery*, Herbert Jenkins, 1962

Glass

CROMPTON, Sidney (Editor): *English Glass*, Ward Lock & Co., 1967

DAVIS, Derek C. and MIDDLEMAS, Keith: *Coloured Glass*, Herbert Jenkins, 1968

DAVIS, Frank: *The Country Life Book of Glass*, Country Life, 1971

Antique Glass and Glass Collecting, Hamlyn, 1973

ELVILLE, E. M: *The Collector's Dictionary of Glass*, Country Life, 1967

GARDNER, Sylvia Coppen-: *A Background for Glass Collectors*, Pelham Books, 1975

NORMAN, Barbara: *Engraving and Decorating Glass*, David and Charles, 1972

PAYTON, Mary and Geoffrey: *The Observer's Book of Glass*, Frederick Warne & Co., 1976

POLAK, Ada: *Glass, Its Makers and its public*, Weidenfeld & Nicolson, 1975

SAVAGE, George: *Glass*, Weidenfeld and Nicolson, 1965

WAKEFIELD, Hugh: *Nineteenth Century British Glass*, Faber, 1961

WILLS, Geoffrey: *Victorian Glass*, G. Bell and Sons, 1977

Byways of Collecting

ALLIX, Charles: *Carriage Clocks: Their History and Development*, Antique Collectors' Club, 1974

ANDERSON BLACK, J: *A History of Jewels*, Orbis Publishing, 1974

BAILLIE, G. H: *Watchmakers and Clockmakers of the World – Vol 1*, N.A.G. Press, 1976 (see also Loomes)

EDE, Charles: *Collecting Antiquities: an introductory guide*, J. M. Dent, 1976

Encyclopaedia of Antiques, Collins, 1973

GENTLE, Rupert and FEILD, Raphael: *English Domestic Brass 1680-1810 and the History of its Origins*, Paul Elek, 1975

ISAACSON, Philip M: *The American Eagle*, New York Graphic Society, 1975

LOOMES, Brian: *Watchmakers and Clockmakers of the World – Vol 2*, N.A.G. Press, 1976

MACKAY, James: *An Encyclopaedia of Small Antiques*, Ward Lock, 1975

Nursery Antiques, Ward Lock, 1976

MARSHALL, Jo: *Kitchenware*, Pitman, 1976

MOUNTFIELD, David (Editor): *The Antique Collectors' Illustrated Dictionary*, Hamlyn, 1975

Musical Instruments of the World: An Illustrated Encyclopaedia, Paddington Press, 1976

OSBORNE, Harold (Editor): *The Oxford Companion to the Decorative Arts*, Oxford University Press, 1975

RAMSEY, L. G. G. (Editor): *The Connoisseur Complete Encyclopaedia of Antiques*, The Connoisseur, 1975

RANDIER, Jean: *Nautical Antiques*, Barrie & Jenkins, 1976

The Collector's Encyclopaedia: Victoriana to Art Deco, Collins, 1974

WHITE, Gwen: *Toys, Dolls, Automata: Marks and Labels*, Batsford, 1975

WILKINSON, Frederick: *Military Antiques*, Ward Lock, 1976